There is no God like Thee . . .
which keepest covenant.

The Eternal Covenant Of Peace

STANLEY W. PAHER

LAS VEGAS
NEVADA PUBLICATIONS
1996

The front cover depicts artist Roy Purcell's rendition of "walking through the pieces," the ancient covenantal ceremony described on pages 20–21. When tribal representatives walked among the pieces of dead animals they committed themselves to one another. To initiate God's everlasting covenant with man, He alone in the form of a torch passed between mounds of flesh, taking man's place in the ceremony as well (Genesis 15:7-18).

Published by Nevada Publications
Box 15444, Las Vegas, Nevada 89114
   702-747-0800

Proudly printed in the United States of America

Table of Contents

Introduction

F ROM THE TIME of Genesis, until the present and to the day of eternity, God has interacted with man within a single framework, the eternal (everlasting) covenant of peace. He initiated this saving commitment with man to reveal His mind and will, His gracious plan, so that He could dispense blessings and salvation to imperfect creatures. By the eternal peace compact, and through Israel of old, God would ultimately bless all peoples and nations as the eternal covenant reached a messianic climax of development in the life and death of Jesus of Nazareth.

By means of the eternal covenant God formally relates himself to every good-hearted, moral person in any era who actively wishes to display solidarity with the Creator of heaven and earth. All God-fearers who seek goodness and righteousness embrace all of God's revelation they can find, and do not reject it, whether disclosed through nature, Moses and the Jewish prophets, or Jesus and His apostles.

God first extended the formal covenant (Gen. 15-17), described as "everlasting" (17:7), to Abraham, unconditionally granting spiritual promises to his seed forever. From this inception, God unfolded his virtually unbreakable, eternal bond with His people throughout the ages as He continued to interact intimately with man (Psalm 105:8-10). To Israel, the nation of His own choosing, God renewed the covenant made with Abraham amid many promises (I Chron. 16:15-17f).

By the time of David (c. 1000 B.C.), God extended and enlarged the everlasting covenant through specific revelation that the anointed descendant, Christ (Psa. 2:2, I Chron. 17:11-27) would come through David's family. Three centuries later, Isaiah reviewed the ancient agreement made with Abraham, the everlasting covenant (54:10, 55:3), before the people (41:8, 51:2, 63:16).

During the turbulent years before the fall of Jerusalem in 586 B.C., the prophet Jeremiah reiterated the Abrahamic covenant (33:26; see also Ezek. 33:24), setting forth in 31:31-34 its unchangeable terms: (1) the promise of a new heart; (2) the law written in the heart; (3) God and man interdwelling in a purposeful relationship; (4) the promise of a new spirit; and (5) the remission of sins.

Ezekiel restated the covenantal terms in 36:25-28, showing that God would sprinkle clean water upon His covenanted ones, cleansing them from all impurities and giving them a new heart and a new spirit, as they returned from Babylonian exile (see Chapter Ten). These comforting words to lovers of God reside within the everlasting covenant (Jer. 32:40, Ezek. 37:6). Ezra, Haggai, Zechariah, and non-canonical writers explained how the covenant began to be renewed in the late Jewish period by the people's repentance and intent to serve God.

In the first century, God manifested his absolute, unfailing coventantal commitment in the consummately obedient life, sacrificial death, and mighty resurrection of

Jesus of Nazareth. In the covenant victim (see Chapter Three), all believers' hope and trust in God is perfected. Even in Jesus' infancy, Zechariah proclaimed God's glorious holy oath and display of mercy, which dated from the time of Abraham (Luke 1:54-55, 71-73). Though springing from a Jewish fountain, covenantal blessings ultimately would flow to all Gentile peoples.

Jesus thus fulfilled the longstanding hope and expectation of generations of covenant Jews by being crowned King over a spiritual kingdom embracing people from all nations, simultaneously assuming the headship of the *ekklesia,* or the called-out ones of God – the church. His reign would extend over the house of Jacob forever, and this kingdom, like the everlasting covenant, would have no end (Luke 1:32-33). Verily, all of the holy men of old, from ancient times and into the apostolic era, disclose the glorious unfolding of God's plan of redemption and bestowal of blessings from His grace in the eternal covenant and royal rule (kingship) of Christ.

In opposition to the single everlasting covenant concept, various teachers see an old one of Moses and a new Christian one, differing in word and content and diverse in purpose and intent, together with contrasting laws – of Moses (Rom. 3:19) and of Christ (see Gal. 6:2). The time before the cross was allegedly the age of law leading toward death, while the Christian covenant bathes in the era of grace and life.

In this manner two-covenant advocates often minimize the degree of faith which numerous Old Testament worthies possessed. Christian are supposedly the only ones who "sit in heavenly places" (Eph. 2:6) enjoying the spiritual gifts and the powers of the world to come, uniquely experiencing Ezekiel's promise of new hearts and spirits.

The Christian covenant is said to point to a "new way" of gaining access to God. The old covenant is believed to be merely a temporary contract between God and the people, while the superior new covenant is a permanent arrangement. Similar misconceptions of the nature of covenant, especially as unapplicable to faithful Jews of old, are outlined on pages 237–239, and 274–277.

Incredibly, two-covenanters say that the Mosaic arrangement was a "covenant of the law that brought death," a pitiful misrepresentation not only of God's intimate relationship with the ancient Jewish faithful but also of the text of II Corinthians itself (see pp. 218–220, 255–258). A scriptural covenant of death is described in Isaiah 28.

For all good hearts before the cross, God always provided the "way" of gaining access to Him (see p. 233). The Psalms and the prophets amply display the robustness of the covenant remnant in Old Testament times and their authentic, intimate life with God. Scripture uses various figures and images to portray these people transcending all constructed covenantal distinctions (Chapter Six). The quality of faith and commitment to covenant of these ancient worthies is not one whit less than that of Christians (Rom. 4). They did, as we can, lean upon God and live attentive to His precepts, which brought spiritual vitality through the everlasting covenant.

In their walk with God, unwavering saints of old who trusted in the Lord (Psa. 26:1, 28:7) were supremely comforted and showered with innumerable blessings (Psa. 13:6, 23:1-6, etc.). Israel's poets did not hesitate to speak of the One who was involved in all of life's spiritual and everyday matters, happily acknowledging this Source of their full life strength. These believers did not divide their religious life into "God's part" and "man's part," but wholly sought divine strength to ease every burden.

Christians can learn much about authentic, heartfelt worship by contemplating how saints of old strove to please the God of heaven. They knew that outward circumcision, or any other rite or ordinance, had no value without inward renewal (Lev. 26:41; Deut. 10:16, 30:6). Jeremiah rebuked prideful, ritualistic worshipers routinely performing specific acts as "uncircumcised in heart" – people who were no better off than evildoers.

Similarly, Paul taught that true circumcision was an inward heart process (Rom. 2:25; see also Phil. 3:2-6, Col. 2:11-15). On either side of the cross, a person's heart must first be right with God, and *only* then might external expressions of worship be acceptable – a principle which amply displays a doctrinal continuity (Psa. 51:10-19; Isa. 1:10-17; Hos. 6:4-6; Mic. 6:6-8; Rom. 6:17, 10:10; Eph. 5:19, etc.).

The first century Christians employed the Old Testament writings as scripture. The reading of Genesis and the law, and the psalms and the prophets, enriched their worship and led to salvation by faith and equipped believers for every good work (II Tim. 3:15-16). In these scriptures they learned of the Creator's mighty works and promises, and how in every place God continually sustained his faithful, giving them strength and protection throughout their lives. The appropriate response for all covenanters, then, is heartfelt thanksgiving to the great God upon high who is above all and in all, the King over all creation.

Since the vital truths believed and practiced by the earliest Christians were rooted in the law and the prophets, the first century church assemblies taught nothing new. Though the flower of messianic fulfillment was but recently bloomed, its root and stem had existed for centuries (see Chapter Eight). In fact, the everlasting (eternal) covenant bonded all faithful God-fearers, perfecting them in one body through Christ (see Chapter Five). But the two-covenant doctrine often leads to spiritual elitism, wherein the "new" covenant they enjoy (together with a new church and kingdom) is perceived to be a superior arrangement over God's interaction with His holy ones before the cross.

The dispensational two-covenant view, by freely speaking of Patriarchal, Mosaic, and Christian historical segments — artificial compartments not found in scripture — stresses discontinuity between Old and New Testament people. On the other hand, one-covenant theology positions *all* people of faith in a common spiritual house, and properly focuses upon the principal doctrines of the nature and person of God and how mere man can have a relationship with Him through the eternal covenant. Such continuity directly addresses God's promises and their fulfillment for the benfit of *all* of His children.

Thus, the writings of the apostles do not tell a *different* story from the recorded in the Old Testament, but supply its final chapter, topping off God's special revelations to man. Indeed, the continuity of divine purpose and intent, from Genesis through Revelation, discloses the vital nature of covenant, and shows that throughout the ages the God of grace and truth has always called to Himself a moral community of believers who sought fellowship with their God (see Chapter Six).

Unfortunately, for far too long Christians have compartmentalized various Bible statements and teachings into contrasting notions of old and new, Jew and Gentile, physical and spiritual, and so on. Such dichotomies very often lead to confusion, and stand as serious roadblocks to a full understanding of God's will, His mind, and His plan for man. Such notions actually militate against biblical ones, as expressed in Ephesians 4:3-5 (see pp. 100–101, 275–276), and the continuity of various time-honored doctrines through the ages, especially Heaven's instruction about the everlasting covenant.

—*Stanley W. Paher*

Chapter One

The Covenant
People of God

T HE ETERNAL COVENANT denotes a secure, loving relationship between God and His people in any era.
A scriptural covenant is God's ordinance expressing rights and
responsibilities to a specific people set apart from all others on
the earth. They are uniquely joined to God in a gracious,
saving commitment underscored by continuous forgiveness, a
blessing embodied in the Hebrew word for steadfast love, *chesed*.
Though forgiveness is not the meaning of that word, it is
certainly implied, for it is the ultimate extension of mercy. In
a covenant relationship God continuously keeps intact a people
of His own possession, a devoted family of faithful which extends from the time of Genesis to the day of eternity.

Chesed, translated "mercy" in the King James Version, is
also frequently rendered "lovingkindness." In every biblical
occurrence it assumes that a covenant has been made between
God and man. More than a mere concept, *chesed* is an action
word demonstrating God's continual service in man's behalf
through a relationship. It is His steadfast loyalty to the cov-

enant, through a love as tenacious as a mother's dutiful care and concern for her offspring, protecting them even unto death. Thus, *chesed* is essentially an "abbreviation" for all covenant ritual, and God's loving deeds done in absolute faithfulness to a relationship, and not because of what man is doing, day by day.

The Greek word for covenant, *diatheke*, signifies a coming together, an agreement, a mutual undertaking, such as between God and Israel in Deuteronomy 28-30. In Luke 1:72-73 , the covenant is the *oath* sworn to father Abraham wherein God showed mercy. Displaying *mercy* also defines the nature of the covenantal relationship. When God told Israel to possess Canaan, He said to "make no treaty [covenant] with them, and show them no mercy" (Deut. 7:2). But the faithful Covenant Maker continually displayed mercy to all of Israel "to those who love Him and keep His commandments" (v.9).

Paul told the Galatians that the covenant is a *promise*, something apart from but not contrary to law (3:15-16, 17-18; see also I Chron. 16:16). This promise given to Abraham looked to Christ to establish an inheritance, and to perfect the believer's undeniable right standing before God. As W. E. Vine succinctly states: "God enjoined upon Abraham the rite of circumcision, but His promise to Abraham, here called a covenant, was not conditional upon the observance of circumcision, though a penalty was attached to its non-observance" (*Dictionary of New Testament Words*, p. 253).

In earthly covenantal arrangements, two parties come to a mutual understanding; some bargaining goes on in negotiating the treaty. Fearing destruction, a weaker tribe would seek to "cut the covenant" with stronger tribes, so that it might be preserved. In time the details were finalized and its contents written down, signed, sealed and read publicly. Since the covenant involved the ceremonial shedding of blood, it was called a blood covenant (see Chapter Three). Similar arrangements were also followed after warfare, as the conqueror brought the defeated into permanent submission.

In contrast, as God offers His eternal covenant to man, there is no negotiation, and man never takes any initiative to dictate its terms. Instead, the God who cannot lie descends to the level of man in lovingkindness, making available the covenant relationship. Throughout the ages man has either refused the offer of grace and *agape* love or accepted the covenant by faith, knowing that the King and Sustainer of righteousness would meet every need and fulfill all promises extended.

History of Covenant

Genesis 12:1-3, 7, introduces the greatest of all such treaties, God's everlasting covenant with man (Gen. 17:13). God swore to Abraham that He would enter into a spiritual agreement with man, in order to bestow blessings and favors upon His created. Acts 7:1-8 relates how the God of glory appeared to the ancient Patriarch, revealing Himself in promise (see also Gal. 3:6, 4:30, especially 3:19; 4:23, 28).

God told Abraham to separate himself from the godless moon worshipers in idolatrous Ur and relocate to another land, where by and by he would conceive a son, through whom a multitude of people would form the nation Israel and ultimately secure a homeland. Beyond this, Abraham would also father a spiritual family that eventually would be as multitudinous as seashore sand and nighttime stars. Thus, Abraham would be great, with his name undeniably honored in man's history, for through his seed "all nations of the earth would be blessed" (Gen. 12:3). This spiritual nation would bring salvation through Jesus Christ.

The prophets of Israel and Judah and various apostolic writers often elaborated upon this twofold promise. Blessings would come first to the company of Israel, and ultimately by way of a particular Descendant through whom all families of the earth would spiritually benefit. The cursed earth (Gen. 3:14-19) would share a common blessing and be made supremely happy in a purposeful spiritual walk with the Creator Himself, wherein

His purpose and glory would be upheld. More than Israel would be affected; innumerable others would be called into a gracious covenant relationship with people from every nation and tribe and tongue (see Rev. 5:9).

Discussion of Heaven's arrangements with man through Abraham continued into Genesis 13:14-18 and Chapter 15, wherein God promised that He would be Abraham's shield. With God's reaffirmation that a son would be forthcoming, Abraham surrendered totally to God, giving himself wholly to the Creator. Abraham understood God's promises, "and he believed . . . and it was counted to him for righteousness" (Gen. 15:6). This quality of dependent faith and unqualified commitment was the standard of later Jewish prophets and New Testament writers, for it underlies all of God's blessings which culminate in spiritual deliverance through Jesus Christ.

God embodied these twin promises to Abraham in a covenant oath, swearing by Himself, in His own name and on His own initiative, just as He had in Genesis 12:1-7. As related in Genesis 15:7-18, God ordered Abraham to kill a heifer, a goat, and a ram, and to cut each animal down the middle and separate the resulting halves. (Two birds also were sacrificed.) At sunset, in a trance-like vision, Abraham saw a smoking fire pot and a flaming torch distinctly passing between the bloody piles. In this act God had become the covenant representative on behalf of both himself and Abraham. Obviously, such favor did not come because of anything Abraham did, i.e., his works, but *wholly* because of what God was continually doing for him and promising to him.

Abraham's circumcision constituted a seal of the covenant (Gen. 17:11, 26; Acts 7:8); it also resulted in a changing of his name from Abram, and his wife's name from Sarai to Sarah. The treaty with God became fully operative after He shared a covenant meal with Abraham (Gen. 18:8). Now, more than an exalted father among fellow patriarchs, Abraham would be the "father of a multitude" (v. 17:5). The Almighty One (*El Shaddai* – 17:1) promised him that all of his descendants would be included in the same everlasting (eternal) covenant, sworn by Himself, by the word of the covenant oath. It was passed on to Isaac, then confirmed to Jacob (who was renamed Israel), whose sons would head up the historical twelve tribes.

Over a period of at least four centuries, the covenant people developed as Abraham's descendants evolved from a nomadic family tribe into a kingdom under God among the neighboring heathens. Through 460 years of Egyptian bondage and exodus to its establishment as a nation in the land of Canaan, covenant Israel perceived God as working in and through them, creating a people for His own possession. The God of heaven was the Lord of Israel, and Israel was the people of God.

Egyptian deliverance was perhaps Israel's most significant historical event, for it showed that God was mightier than Pharaoh or any god of the surrounding nations. The drying up of the Red Sea, certainly no freak act of nature but a true wonder, was still another sign of God's covenantal activity in and among Israel. As He summoned the forces of nature to serve Him, the gracious Father showed pity on oppressed people.

God delivered His blood covenant people from their enemies, pestilence, and diseases. "I am the Lord that healeth thee," declared God after the people had marched out of Egypt unscathed (Ex. 15:26). During the forty years of wandering in the Sinai desert, the Provider furnished the Israelites food from heaven and water from springs and rocks. The covenant Protector brought forth a cloud to shield them from the fierce sun, and a pillar of fire for light and heat during the chilly nights.

Once in the promised land, the tiny nation sought to understand God's purpose and meaning. Moses' writings demonstrated that Israel's election was grounded in inexplicable steadfast love — *chesed*, as stated in Deuteronomy 7:7-8: "It was not because you were more numerous than any other people that the Lord set His love upon you and chose you, for you were the fewest of all peoples . . . but it was because the Lord loved you, and kept the oath which he swore to your fathers . . . " (see also Luke 1:68, 72-73).

As a Help of the helpless, God had set them free. These gospel stories were oft repeated among the Israelites in family situations and later in synagogue assemblies. In common preaching the prophets rehearsed these events concerning Egypt; they showed that God had established covenant relationships with the people, saving and comforting them. This is the "story" aspect of the law, or Torah, pointing to a gracious God who was on Israel's side and always keeping His promises to the faithful.

A written expression of the covenant came with the revelation at Mount Sinai of the Ten Commandments to Moses in about 1450 B.C., during the wilderness journey after deliverance from Egyptian oppression. All of these events are inseparable. Moses succinctly defined God's enduring covenant relationship with each of His elect: "Now therefore if you will obey my voice and keep my covenant, you shall be my own possession among all peoples, for all the earth is mine, and you shall be to me a kingdom of priests and a holy nation" (Ex. 19:5-6; see also I Pet. 2:9).

Faithful obedience to God's Ten Commandments did not redeem Israel; rather, adherence to them was the *result* of redemption (Ex. 20:2). Nothing said by Moses and the prophets pointed to God ever imposing a covenant of works upon Old Testament faithful. Yahweh's graceful deliverance of the children of Israel from Egyptian oppression actually preceded the formal revelation of the written moral standard, the Ten Commandments. God's purpose in issuing them was to guide the lives of people who were *already* redeemed, showing how through loving acts of devotion they could express gratitude to God for their salvation.

Through the period of the Judges, the united kingdom under Saul, David and Solomon, and the division of the twelve tribes into Israel and Judah, the covenant people were more or less faithful to God. When they adhered to God's ways, the people enjoyed all blessings of the covenant: spiritual strength, good health, prowess in war, abundant crops in irrigated fields and valleys, and multiplication of their herds and flocks. To the Jews, there was no city like Jerusalem with Solomon's magnificent stone edifice brilliantly displayed atop the Temple Mount.

Because of disobedience and idolatry, The God of covenant allowed the ten tribes of Israel to be carried away into Assyrian captivity in 721 B.C. Similarly, He stirred up the Babylonians to subdue rebellious Judah in 586 B.C., when Jerusalem was captured and its revered temple and stone buildings were reduced to rubble and ashes. Though the nation had broken its contract with God (Jer. 11:9-13), and covenant curses had been unleashed upon them (Babylonian captivity), God raised up Jeremiah, Ezekiel, and other prophets who brought the faithful remnant great comfort and hope through preaching about the ultimate renewal of the ancient agreement, as a reinstatement of God's commitment to them (see Chapter Ten).

Suzerain Treaty

Common between nations contemporary with Moses was a special type of relationship formed as result of political covenants or treaties. It involved a "suzerain" king and a vassal. It was not a parity treaty. More than just a conqueror, a suzerain was a sovereign over many rulers. The big, powerful conqueror graciously sought the vassal's submission with gratitude, and not out of mere legal compulsion. The suzerain promised protection and blessings to the conquered, expecting faithful obedience in return, concluding the peace treaty with blessings and cursings.

The suzerain treaty is precisely what is demonstrated in God's giving of the Ten Commandments. He told Israel to serve Him exclusively and He would bless them. Mutual oaths were exchanged, sealing the treaty relationship. But even in the structure of the "harsh" Ten Commandments, He included a statement of grace (*chesed*), great favor. The last part of the second commandment states that "God is a jealous God, visiting iniquity on the [people] and showing lovingkindness (*chesed*) to them that love Him and keep His commandments" (Ex. 20:5-6).

As the two parties entered into a treaty arrangement, they became functionally one; a preamble to the treaty defined the relationship. They exchanged gifts and opened themselves to one another by reading the terms of the covenant. In such a treaty one primitive chieftain might hand over his best spear or a prize animal to another. Representatives for each side might cut their wrists, while swearing to the covenantal terms. They thus became blood brothers because, as they clasped their hands and wrists, their blood intermingled. Assets of one party would be made available to the other, solidifying the sealing of the covenant in the flesh.

Symbolically binding the parties together was the covenant sacrifice, the splitting of a calf or some other animal down the center, resulting in two bloody piles of carcasses. Each side's representative would walk between the two halves of dark red meat, perhaps in an elongated figure eight symbolizing infinity. This "walking through the pieces" signified infinite commitment, a mutual giving of each other, with each party to the covenant vowing to supply mutual needs and to defend each other even to the death (see Jer. 34:18-19).

Significantly, in the Abrahamic covenant, God *alone* passed between the mounds of flesh, taking Abraham's place in the ceremony as well (Gen. 15:7-18). Therefore the covenant with Abraham depended upon him in no sense, for he slept through it all, doing no works. In this ceremony God solidified His promises, swearing by Himself, that Abraham would be blessed materially and spiritually.

A treaty also involved a name change, as from Abram to Abraham (Gen. 17:5, 15), and a covenant meal usually consisting of a peaceful partaking of bread and wine, as did Abraham and Melchizedek (Gen. 14:18). As reported in Genesis 18:1-8, Abraham communed with God (who came in the form of a man) by eating flour cakes, veal, and drinking milk together.

Thereafter the parties were forever bound in love and kindness – lovingkindness! Here was covenant loyalty in a purposeful, chosen bond, the ultimate in commitment. Throughout time God's covenant with man has been perpetual, indissoluble, so sacred that even children to the third and fourth generations revered it and kept it.

Early British colonists and North American Indians understood well the seriousness of entering and keeping such a treaty. William Penn initiated peaceful relations with the red man by promising them that their hunting grounds would remain intact and that there would not be any trade abuses. Each party promised never to injure or defraud the another, "as long as the river shall run, as long as the sun shall shine" – a permanent, sacred commitment.

So it is with the agreement God extends toward man. The everlasting covenant bound Him to Abraham and his descendants in such a way that it could not be annulled. It served as the structure for defining the relationship God had in the future with the nation Israel and ultimately with the people of God in the era of Christ and into infinity. In heading up a covenanted people, Abraham thus became the father of the faithful, who were as numerous as the stars of heaven (Gen. 22:16-17). Swearing by Himself, God has sustained and protected the saints throughout the ages.

In ancient earthly treaties two copies of the agreement were written, and each king stored his copy in his sacred place. But in the God-Israel relationship *both* tables of stone (each containing the entire treaty, i.e., all Ten Commandments) were retained in the ark of the covenant; the atoning blood placed on the mercy seat above the ark declared that there would be no other testimony to God except through blood. In the peace treaty or covenant with God there was only one depository, indicating that the Suzerain was always with His vassal, Israel. It is a gracious, saving relationship.

God wrote upon the two tables the words of the covenant (Ex. 34:28). The faithful of Israel never perceived it as a legal, codified rule system wherein any transgression invalidated the treaty. Rather, while the people of Israel were exclusively committed to God and doing His will to the best of their ability, they remained *continually* allied with Him, despite falling short and committing sin. This is always the nature of covenant relationship with God, for He relates to us through mercy (the mercy seat). God's tabernacle is ever with men (Rev. 21:3; see also 11:19), indicating that He is steadfastly faithful to the covenantal agreement.

This comforting treaty relationship forcefully demonstrates the tender interaction between God and His people. The covenant adequately points to a relationship of utter dependence in which we have constant discourse with God, who continually forgives us. It does not give us license to act as we please, but rather calls us into constant service, prompting mature, responsible behavior. We continue in love for God, which makes possible love for neighbor.

A Loving Relationship

The principal term for describing the covenant relationship, *chesed*, corresponds somewhat to *agape* of the New Testament. It means covenant faithfulness or steadfast love, necessarily requiring God's forgiveness. It is characterized by divine mercy. It is impossible to extend mercy to sinless people. Jeremiah realized that Israel's very existence depended on this quality of relationship: "I have loved you with an everlasting love; therefore I have continued my faithfulness to you" (31:3). Thus, covenant rests on God's gracious, saving acts and not on our imperfect response to various commandments and scripture statements.

Covenant benefits and blessings always come because of a relationship with God which results in remission of sin. It never depended upon adhering to structured forms, or even serving God acceptably in every instance, because all blessings are inherent in the covenant relationship. Moreover, this status was never meant to be institutionalized, so Jeremiah, Amos, and other prophets constantly warned people who would consider the presence of the temple as a guarantee of Israel's invulnerability. "Woe to those who are at ease in Zion . . . " (Amos 6:1) echoes Jeremiah 7:4 which warns, "Do not trust in these deceptive words, this is the temple of the Lord, the temple of the Lord, the temple of the Lord . . . " The latter corresponds to Jesus' statement to unfaithful people: "Why do you call me Lord, Lord . . . " (Luke 6:46; see also Matt. 7:21).

With the destruction of the temple in 586 B.C., symbolic of God's displeasure, the covenant people entered into Babylonian captivity. Soon, however, preoccupation with externals and concern about leadership further perverted religious life; religious practice tended to focus on lawkeeping and lawmaking, rather than on the Author-Giver. After the time of Ezra, righteousness became defined in terms of obeying static rules, priestly deductions, and interpretations of prophetic writings. Structured law, eventually a mixture of God's guidance and man's traditions and rules, distracted the people from full moral responsibility, in time reducing God's standard of righteous living to the stunted spiritual size of the institutional priests and the scribes.

In contrast, God's prophets continually warned against any kind of law dependency, noted the vanity of sacrifices, the reciting and copying of the law, and decried the perversion of weekly and yearly sacrifices. Micah succinctly described authentic covenant service: "[God] has shown you, O' man, what is good; and what does the Lord require of you but to do justice, and to love kindness and to walk humbly with your God" (6:8; see also Jeremiah 9:23-24). Amos put it this way: "Seek good and not evil, that you may live; and so Yahweh, the God of hosts, will be with you . . . establish justice in the gate . . . " (5:14-15). Our covenant brother, Hosea, recognized the same principle by saying, "For I desire goodness [kindness] and not sacrifice; and the knowledge of God more than burnt offerings" (6:6).

Throughout the latter part of the Jewish period, God had a special messianic mission. The very foundation of God's dealing with man is that all nations would be blessed through the promise made to Abraham. This precious covenant passed through his seed to Isaac, Jacob (Israel), and his twelve sons. Israel laid his hands on his son, Judah, saying, "He who is worthy shall come." By 1000 B.C. an excited King David learned that through his family would come the anointed One (Psa. 2:2). This Christ would preside as King over an everlasting kingdom in lovingkindness (Psa. 89:1-4, 27ff), fulfilling all covenantal promises God had uttered to Abraham and to subsequent generations.

As if peering down through the centuries, God's faithful prophets in the kingdoms of Israel and Judah preached and wrote about Someone coming. Isaiah mentioned Immanuel, "God with us," born of a virgin (Matt. 1:23), whose name would be called Wonderful Counselor, Prince of Peace, the mighty God (9:6-7). Micah foretold that the One would be born in tiny Bethlehem of Judea. Other men of God said that He would be a Prophet, Priest, and King.

The prophet Daniel saw Him taking the crown and being made king over all peoples. Every nation would flow to His presence (Isa. 2:2-5), so that all might be taught the Lord's ways. Swords and spears would be beaten into plowshares and pruning hooks (Micah 4:3), and spiritual peace was depicted as coming when the lion would lie down with the lamb (Isa. 11:6f). Blessings would now replace the cursings of Genesis in a victorious reversal of man's original fall. Joyous people would enter a renewed covenant relationship with God under Christ, resulting in comfort, consolation, and peace.

Isaiah 35:10 describes multitudes of confident covenanters singing, shouting, and dancing, experiencing unspeakable joy because of what God would be doing for them. Malachi saw this Seed of Abraham rising as the morning sun, casting healing beams across the sin-filled world and touching free people who would come to God as excited calves gamboling in their stalls

(4:2). Thus, over many centuries before Christ, holy men of God portrayed a hopeful picture of what covenant life with God would be like when the Anointed one spoken of by David would dwell among men. All earthy people would be blessed!

Matthew 1 and Luke 3 contain the genealogies of the Seed of Abraham, and "this seed was Christ" (Gal. 3:16). The child that resided in Mary is the one about whom God spoke to Abraham – the seed of covenant (in remembrance of God's mercy). Zechariah, the father of John the Baptist, said that his son would prepare the way for Jesus. John's mission would transpire so that Judah would recognize that the oath given to Abraham was now coming to pass. The God of Israel would be "mindful of his holy covenant, of the oath that he swore to Abraham . . . " (Luke 1:72-73). Indeed, Jesus said that when Abraham saw "[His] day" he was glad. Jesus truly made Abraham happy (John 8:56).

And so, throughout the time of the judges, the kings, and the prophets up to John the Baptist, God was not setting up through the faithful of Israel a *contrast* with something that was going to happen, the coming of Jesus the Messiah early in the first century, but rather He was preparing covenant people for a way of life which would be fully in harmony with and in continuity with the way He had always dealt with Israel since the time of Abraham and Egyptian captivity. Historical development lived out in the lives of God's Old Testament faithful naturally led to the expanded new (renewed) covenant under Christ. All of these people of God ultimately found their promises fulfilled in Jesus Christ and the renewed Israel, which also included a worldwide salvation focus involving the Gentiles, as prophesied.

The manner in which faithful covenantal Jews perceived their responsibilities helped prepare the first century saints' understanding of their obligations before God. As Chapter Five shows, all people of God in every era are in one perfected body, all saved by grace through faith. All are in the same eternal covenant (Heb. 13:20), with the perfect sacrifice made by the eternal Christ guaranteeing an eternal inheritance for the faithful of God in all ages (Heb. 9:15), all bonded together by love for God as well as for each other.

Covenant and Law

Though the word "covenant" properly describes a legal relationship between God and man, in no sense does it involve a works system wherein man employs scripture as the well-spring of what is perceived as "the law" with structured commands and statements obeyed in view of a "man's part" and a "God's part" in the salvation process. This man-devised approach toward serving God, adhered to by various ancient Jewish parties, is historically developed in Chapter Four.

How God's people in any era perceive law and doctrine has always been crucial. Ezekiel, Isaiah and many other covenant faithful were certainly not legalists, for they were aware of the basic meaning of Torah (law) as "pointing the way." The writings of Moses and other prophets showed faithful Jews how to achieve life and vitality before God and properly behave among their fellow men. Paul, Luke, Mark, and others amplified these noble designs and purposes for saints after the cross.

For a person enjoying a relationship with God, responding to laws and commandments has never been an end in itself, "to bring one closer to the Lord." Authentic life for covenant people was never determined by searching through available scripture to compile laws to follow – a "find the commandments" game (see John 5:39). Rather, for God's faithful in any era, a relationship with Him who makes the covenant has been paramount.

Heaven's love-rooted system means that we actively show concern for our neighbor through unselfish service without unseemly concern over who our neighbor is. In Jesus' Good Samaritan story, it was a despised Samaritan, who upheld the principles of covenant by continually caring for the injured traveler, who showed how to love and help another. He, not the smug, ceremonially clean Levite priest, correctly responded to God's second great command to love neighbor as self.

Covenant and Grace

In bold contrast to all rigid, self-centered, legal systems, a grace-based approach toward religion resting squarely upon the righteousness of God has always been in place among covenant people (Rom. 3:21-29). Instead of a concept of patterned do's and dont's, its address is to the inward man's intents, motivation, and disposition, pointing to non-codified moral precepts which center on loving God and neighbor. This law of the mind and heart places the responsibility for transgression directly upon the thoughts and attitudes of the inner self, where all sin arises: "The things that proceed out of the heart of man are those that defile the man" (Mark 7:15).

This non-legalistic moral law in the heart transcends time and all so-called "dispensations" from Genesis to the day of eternity, yet future. Its positive and negative guidance is always true, for it is rooted in the very character of God. The faithful mentioned in Genesis heeded it, Moses and the prophets embodied it in scripture, and it continues as the "law of Christ" (Gal. 6:2) of the present era.

Thus, Abraham and other patriarchs never had to systematize available commandments into a structured Torah, nor did the faithful at the time of the prophets codify the writings of Jeremiah, Isaiah, etc. into patterns of synagogue worship. If the covenant faithful had heard of such concepts, they would not have understood at all. So it was with the apostles. Are the New Testament scriptures clusters of systematized rules and regulations, or are these writings the revelation of God's grace, showing covenant people how to respond to His favor while *already* keeping commandments and enjoying a gracious, saving relationship?

To all in covenant with God, law is certainly never a burden but a tool to allow saints to function acceptably in the creation. This understanding preserves God's grace system of salvation. Authentic service to God has always been characterized by zest for life, vivaciousness, unselfish respect for others, and emotional flesh-and-blood relationships in which brethren are treated graciously as warm, loving friends sharing a covenant with God, rather than objects to be manipulated and dominated.

Covenant and the Gospel

As with the faithful of God among Israel, the people of Christ were first recipients of the gospel and various blessings before coming into contact with the apostles' teaching. The gospel centers around the life and work of the Son of God, Jesus Christ, who, in the covenant relationship, represents man in Heaven's arrangement with the created. Flawlessly, He faced temptation in His earthly life, and at the cross lifted forever the sin-curse brought by Adam.

This could be accomplished only by one who was simultaneously man in the flesh and God's Anointed, His representative, having been fathered by the Spirit and deposited into the womb of a young virgin. Jesus stood in behalf of all mankind to bring all faithful God-lovers into a gracious, saving union with the Father, so that they might enjoy a covenant relationship with their Creator.

True to the suzerain treaty concept, the God of heaven provided the ultimate sacrifice, so that His promises of covenantal blessings and salvation might be realized. His Son, Jesus, willingly entered into death, for God has made Him to be sin for us (see II Cor. 5:21). Christ stood in place of wayward mankind, so that the divine covenant might be perfected. The Seed of Abraham went to the cross as sin bearer and conquered death when God raised Him (Acts 2:24-32, 10:40, 13:30-37;

Col. 2:12). In response to this gospel, we gratefully reply, "Thank you Lord!"

Today's spiritual family, Israel, consists of all who have come to the Seed. The marvelous Abrahamic and Davidic promises are fulfilled in Christ (Gal. 3:1f); all we have to do is embrace this precious gospel which God has graciously provided. This is indeed good news! The people of Christ who thus respond are now Heaven's true seed, and can rightfully shout, "Thou art my God!"

In such a comforting covenant relationship, God neither demands nor expects day-in and day-out flawless performance, because continuous forgiveness of our shortcomings resides in the covenant with God. Away with despair, worry, and any concern about our standing of salvation with God, day by day, hour by hour! In this abundance of grace (II Cor. 4:15) we are at peace with our Maker and Creator. The Lord never rejects those who truly love Him, and are pure in heart, though from time to time they might fall short of God's standard. Assuredly, He does not count transgressions as some sort of heavenly auditor (Psa. 130:2-3, but see also Rom. 4:1-5).

Instead, God knows that even the most careful among His covenant faithful will fall short of the divine arrangement, sinning in thought, word, or action. A repentant one's response upon learning about transgression is "to go and sin no more," humbly approaching the Lord with the attitude "God be merciful to me, the sinner" (Luke 18:13). These are the proper responses of a presently saved person (Matt. 10:32, I Cor. 1:18).

Such prayerful repentance and outward confession does not blot out transgressions and bring us back to a right standing before God, for in the covenant relationship itself He is *already* merciful and constantly forgiving and gracious toward His children's shortcomings. Man's continual response to such marvelous heavenly favor can only be godly behavior and holiness appropriate to the covenantal community.

BANKS OF RIVER JORDAN

Chapter Two

❦

The Scope of the Covenant of Peace

A S THE COVENANT PEOPLE Israel left the Red Sea and the Egyptian host drowning in it, Moses sang a song of redemption, praising the mighty name and lovingkindness of God (Ex. 15:1-18). In verse 11, he asked rhetorically, "Who is like unto thee, O Yahweh, among the Gods?," for none other could match His righteousness and holiness. In the covenantal relationship, God had spared His children from a devastating oppressor, saving and comforting them. God was evidently mindful of His covenant (Psa. 111:5).

Moses' question needed no answer, but later Solomon prayed, "There is no God like thee, in heaven or on earth, who keepest covenant and lovingkindness with thy servants that walk before thee with all their heart . . ." (II Chron. 6:14; see also I Kgs. 8:22). In this gracious relationship with God, all of the faithful throughout time may be fully assured that He is always conscious of the covenant, for He is the God who cannot lie. Having given His pledge, it is inconceivable that He should depart from it. Instead, He continually blesses good-hearted, properly motivated individuals as a people of His own possession. Here is the genius of the eternal covenant.

On one occasion the sweet psalmist, David, earnestly asked of God, "What is man, that thou art mindful of him? And the son of man, that thou visitest him?" (Psa. 8:4). The fact that God should make man in His image and be gracious to him is wonderful enough. But that He would touch hands – "cut" a covenant – with His creation, and place before it His own veracity and good name, majesty, and unbreakable promises, is indeed marvelous!

God entering into a covenant with mere mortals is indeed exceedingly good news. Do not apologize for your excitement. To William Tyndale, such "good, merry, glad and joyful tidings makes a man's heart glad, makes him sing, dance, and leap for joy!" The heart of the gospel is God's covenant with man – the announcement that Heaven has revealed the divine mind and will to the created, who can either accept or reject the offer of a relationship with Him. The choice is like the difference between abiding in the stark cool shadows of twilight over the comfort of the early morning wintertime sun.

God in the Everlasting Covenant

Far above the circle of the earth and the habitations of mortal man dwells the incomparable Creator-God who "makes the clouds His chariot and rides on the wings of the wind. He makes winds His messengers, and flames of fire His servants . . . ." (Psa. 104:3-4). As the King of Glory, He constantly intervenes in world events, and is desirous of drawing from all nations and tribes right-hearted people into the eternal covenant, authored and perfected by Himself. The salvation compact is therefore wholly His work.

Yet, two-covenant advocates staunchly insist that in this relationship and a present rightstanding before heaven, there is somehow a "God's part" and a "man's part." But as Chapter

One explains, God not only initiates but also fully sustains the covenant. Otherwise, if the covenant depended even fractionally on mere man for its maintenance, the covenantal arrangement could never be secure. Because the covenant is wholly God's work, the faithful are presently saved and supremely blessed, for God *will* fulfill all of His promises. How infinitely superior is this arrangement over anything that man devises to reach up to God, such as a meritorious works system!

In the eternal covenant of grace, God has given us life in Christ Jesus, now and forevermore. He is the heir of all things, and God has made us joint heirs with Him. Through the covenant, God Himself becomes the believer's own portion and inheritance, a very special blessing, indeed. All of that and much more is meant by the word God. This Creator, Guardian, Preserver of life, Judge, the Source of all goodness is the covenanter's own property, for He said, "I will be their God."

In such a comforting phrase, God exercises His sovereignty by grace and grace only. He makes His children vessels of mercy who shall be to His honor forever and heirs to everlasting life. In contrast, all who continue in sin will experience the wrath of His punitive vengeance. For the covenanter God only grasps the chastening rod, but the wicked experience the sharp sword of His rulership.

God as Judge has universal power over all of His creatures. For the faithful in covenant, the condemnation sentence will never come, only acquittal, because of the righteousness of Christ. Believers have passed from death unto life (John 5:24, I John 3:14), standing blameless before Him in love. We are in the Lamb's book of life, registered as citizens in the heavenly family. Outside of God's presence are willful sinners and immoral persons – murderers, idolaters, liars, etc. (Rev. 22:15) – who will experience a certain terrifying expectation of judgment and the consuming fire (Heb. 10:26-27).

For the man of covenant, Yahweh is the God of our election, choosing us before the foundation of the world (Eph. 1:4). He has been constantly providing for us, even as Psalm

81:10 promises: "Open your mouth wide and I will fill it." Covenanters are thus to be as a nest of baby birds, wholly dependent upon the Sustainer for all good things, and continual protection and guidance, with the expectancy based on God's lovingkindness.

Standing presently justified, holy, and blameless before the Creator in love, the covenanter can say, "O, God, thou art *my* God." *My* personalizes the comforting reality that we are in the fold of the Continual Provider. The sinners can only say, "Oh, God!" picturing Him as an angry, offended deity. At peace with God, the righteous one can always draw near to *his* God, as a comforter and friend. Best of all, we are His friend also, and we are His children by adoption. It is a holy relationship in which we can address Him as "*Our* Father." In contrast, sinners run from God, for they have no special claim to Him. They hide in the medieval forest, but just men can live in the castle of the Great King.

Having God as our own far exceeds the riches of yellow harvests stretching from stately mansions filled with expensive treasures. The praise of a 21-gun salute and the longest standing ovation pale without God in our lives. The sweetest music is simply, "*my* God." We can say with David, "My cup runneth over" (Psa. 23:5), knowing that we have more than our hearts can wish. We can dance with joy in our hearts, knowing with certainty that He is *our* God, and that we are in a healthy spiritual state with Him. The realization that God is mine, and I am His, is an exceedingly comforting thought, and we may know confidently that we will be with Him in heaven in due time.

This promise is absolutely certain to all covenanters, for the prophets positively assure us that "I will be their God and they will be my people." In that statement there is no equivocation or "perhaps," but "*will be.*" How reassuring to know with certainty that we are in union with the One from whom all blessings flow. Therefore, "let us draw near with confidence to His throne of grace, so that we may receive mercy and grace to help in time of need" (Heb. 4:16; see also 10:19-24 and Eph. 3:21).

Christ in the Everlasting Covenant

As the mediator of the covenant, Jesus of Nazareth descended from heaven to take the form of a bond servant, and announced to man that abundant grace is promised in a relationship with God, and then humbled Himself by experiencing pain and death on the cross as a thief (see Phil. 2:7-8). Though sinless, He was tempted in all points as we are.

He is the Surety of the covenant, who on our behalf paid all debts of sin through the shedding of His blood. In this way, we can be presented unblemished, complete, and beyond reproach before the Father in love (see Col. 1:22). Indeed, Christ is the apex, the sum and substance of the everlasting covenant.

In this longstanding agreement, Jesus is the personal property of all believers and God-fearers. In one life He has the attributes of both God and of a perfect man. Best of all, everything Christ did belongs to us. His love, grace, firm faithfulness, His power and love — all are ours. He is our Prophet and Priest, *our* King. As a complete man who stood before the Father "full of grace and truth," He is totally ours.

The perfect righteousness which Jesus experienced, when through an earthly sinless life He had dominion over the creation, makes it possible for all covenant believers to maintain continual access to the Father and be constantly bathed with His blessings and favor. By keeping the law of God in all respects, He was qualified to do God's will, which was to atone for our sins. From the foundation of the world, Christ came to fulfill God's eternal plan, and doing the Father's will in a pleasing sacrifice was His delight (see Heb. 10:9).

By His enabling sacrifice, the blessings of grace are freely given to the sons of men. Especially, our sins are not counted against us (Psa. 32:1, Rom. 4:6-8). And so, through His sacrifice, righteousness is imparted to every covenanter, not as some sort of nebulous "experience" but as a legal fact, in that God has forgiven us of our sins as a blessing of living in the eternal covenant. In bearing the sins of many (Isa. 53:11), Christ shouldered our transgressions for us. Declaring us righteous, God makes us like Himself.

By the covenant death of Christ, many are justified (Isa. 53:11) – made sinless before God (see Rom. 5:19). Since we are in Christ, we are saved because He suffered for us (Heb. 5:8-9). In the covenant of grace, we are part and parcel of the "seed" to whom the promise was made (Gen. 15:1-6). We can rightfully sing, "Clothed in His righteousness alone, faultless to stand before the throne." Altering this metaphor, we are acquitted, just as if Christ were on trial, instead of us, and the verdict related to Him. Thus, we are undeservedly forgiven and reconciled, as a gift which was nothing less than God's own self.

As God looks on the faithful among His created, He sees our imperfect life of good and bad deeds, our sins, through the blood of the victorious Christ, even as God saw the faithful Israelites through the mercy seat (Lev. 16:1f). So it has been for the righteous in every era of covenantal history. Righteousness was credited to Abraham as soon as he believed in God. Other saints of old, such as Moses and David, continued in obedience as a proof of faith; but works did not make them better persons, for righteousness was *already* credited to them through the covenantal relationship. Many good-standing Jews during the time of the Assyrian and Babylonian ascendancies had faith in their hearts, and trusted in God's faithfulness, as expressed by Habakkuk in the famous covenant-bridging passage, "The righteous shall live by faith" (2:4).

Quoted twice by the apostle Paul, as he discussed the covenantal relationship with God, this phrase of Habakkuk is even more significantly referenced by the author of Hebrews, in a context discussing authentic faith (10:38). While doing so, the writer naturally assumed that the Israel of old and his Christian audience are covenantally one, emphatically declaring that God's faithful during the time of the prophets are not perfect without the people of Christ (Heb. 11:40). Thus, the same essence which made perfect the Jews is the very means by which Christians are also justified, an obvious continuity. Both were made complete in the covenant death of Christ, as expressed in Hebrews 9:15-28 (see Chapter Three).

Indeed, we are sons of God through the very faith which Christ uniquely brought to earth (Gal. 3:26). In Galatians 3:23-25 Christ is personified as "faith" three times (compare with v. 19). And so, the source of our salvation is not only our faith but also the faith embodied *in* Christ Jesus (II Tim. 3:15), for He is its Pioneer and Perfecter (Heb. 12:2), the One who provides for and sustains us.

The good news given by God is plain. The faithful suffering of Christ even unto death is put to man's account, because of His steadfastness to the Father's eternal covenantal plan. By himself, man could never be righteous, despite all of his good efforts and compliance to law (Gal. 2:21). Nevertheless, covenanters are counted righteous because of Christ's faithfulness and their faith in Christ, and all the more as they rely upon Him, hide in Him, pray through Him, and live for Him. In this godly walk, the blood of Jesus constantly cleanses our sins (I John 1:7), and righteousness is credited to us in precisely the same manner that God does not count our sins against us. Rather, they are placed upon Christ (I Cor. 1:30, II Cor. 5:21, Phil. 3:9).

It is as if Paul told both the Romans and the Galatians that they had not put the law in its proper place. Justification is not of works (Eph. 2:8-9). Instead, God's grace reigns through the righteousness of His Son, and salvation is extended in a comforting relationship with God Himself, sealed by the blood of the everlasting covenant.

Jesus Christ in the covenant thus offers comfort to all who receive the gospel by faith. He promises rest and mercy to the unworthy (Matt. 11:28), reassuring any doubting saint who fails to see that perfection is found only in God. He sympathizes with our weaknesses (Heb. 4:15) and His blood-filled fountain washes away all sin. Man must seek salvation and strip himself of his own righteousness, by allowing Christ to cover him with the robes of His righteousness (Isa. 61:10). Then we are surely Christ's indeed, in a mercy- and grace-tempered covenant relationship.

The Seal of the Everlasting Covenant

After an extended discourse on the nature of covenant in Hebrews 8:7-10:18, the writer concludes with a covenant prayer: "Now the God of peace, that brought again from the dead our Lord Jesus, that Great Shepherd of the sheep, through the blood of the everlasting covenant, makes you perfect in every good work to His will, working with you that which is well pleasing in His sight, through Jesus Christ . . ." (13:20).

To represent the everlasting One, the author called the Father the "God of peace." As He made a "covenant of peace" with man (Ezek. 37:26), God satisfied all that the ancient prophets promised in regard to the coming of the covenant Messiah. Jesus, as the "Great Shepherd of the sheep," stood by God through His life, even to the obedience of the cross, and the shedding of blood for the sheep, covenanters throughout history. To them, God has given full pardon, acceptance, adoption, and eternal life. All who enter this longstanding covenant by faith are in absolute union with a just and loving God. Now at peace, they live for His glory and He promises never to forsake or deny them.

As Christ shed His blood, He confirmed and fulfilled the everlasting covenant. The Good Shepherd died as the unique covenant victim, perfecting the heavenly arrangement with man (see Chapter Three). His blood makes it so binding that the world itself would first pass away before even part of the covenant would fail, for it stands firm upon the sure word of the faithful and true God, whose nature requires that He keep

His promises. The author calls this perfected covenant "eternal" because the effect of Christ's blood covers the sins of all righteous people backward from the cross to Genesis and forward to the day of eternity (II Pet. 3:18).

Christ kept the law in His life. On our behalf everything is fulfilled in the gospel. He suffered for our sins, yielding up Himself on the cross, and was taken to the grave. But as a part of man's redemption, God saw that Christ's flesh would not see corruption (Acts 2:31). On the third morning the promised time came. He arose! Christ on His cross represents all who believe on Him, for in baptism we are crucified with Him (Rom. 6:2f). The entombed Jesus also represents us, for in water we are buried with Him. Similarly, in His resurrection we arise with Him. What a Saviour!

After the stone guarding Christ's tomb was rolled away, various angels witnessed His liberation. In the garden He spoke to several disciples and during the next forty days many friends saw Him (I Cor. 15:4-8). From the Mount of Olives He ascended beyond a cloud to be welcomed into heaven, where He now sits at the Father's right hand (Matt. 26:64, Acts 2:33), highly exalted as King of kings and possessing a name above all others.

Jesus Christ now reigns in glory, because as High Priest he has carried His blood into the most holy place, heaven itself (Heb. 9:27-28), and presented it as the vital component of the everlasting covenant. Now in heaven He serves as our advocate, the Shepherd of the flock of covenant believers, who live because the Shepherd lives. He perfects us, even as He is perfect. In the same manner that the God of peace glorified His son, so also He will gather the chosen gloriously to participate in eternal life with Him.

Standing with Christ, as a covenant blessing God will make us perfect in every good work to do His will (see Col. 4:12). In a relationship with Him, God gives us power to serve Him. It is not an indefinite conditional promise, but a bold covenantal one: "I will and you shall . . . ," because the covenant is a finished agreement that does not require us to perform a list of deeds to maintain it. Though God summons us to do good works (Eph. 2:9), the covenant itself does not rely on them, but solely upon the great promise that God will continually sanctify and cleanse us, to be suitable to serve Him. For these reasons, the covenant is not a "last will and testament" (see Chapter Three).

In the doxology, "To whom be the glory forever and ever..," all covenanters honor a God who has entered into a solemn compact with Christ on our behalf, to save us presently and completely keeping us to the end and making us perfect. If there is anything that would make man praise God, it is the reassuring thought that he has covenanted with the Creator, who is ever mindful of man, keeping and saving those that are His own.

Man in the Everlasting Covenant

The true covenanter has made the greatest discovery of all time – he has found the one Creator-God. He resolves to be on active terms with Him now and forevermore, always wishing to see more, ever more, of Him. He is determined to stay at peace with God and in league with Him. As he hungers and thirsts for this living God, the ennobled covenanter rises above the perishing state of sinners; he is born from above.

The man of covenant desires the will of God. With pure intent, he wishes to please God from the heart, not just ritualistically obey scripture commandments. He loves God's eternal plan, delighting in the law of the Lord (Psa. 1:2). His passion is day-in, day-out holiness, consenting to do only the good. He constantly seeks to strengthen his divine life with God, reflecting upon the Divine One from above. The intimate fellowship with God is a vital and complete union, impelling the man of faith to live a consecrated life.

Anyone who has entered into the covenant is a subject of

God's special call, who has said to him, "I have called thee by thy name, and thou art mine" (Isa. 43:1). Such a reception has the force and certainty of Abraham's call (Gen. 12-15-17). The man of covenant has been brought out of darkness into God's marvelous light (I Pet. 2:9b). The gospel of Christ is His power, and God's all-pervading grace arouses his soul. He continually seeks God's face, to whom he is bound eternally in covenant.

Now united with Christ Jesus, he reigns coextensively with Him in righteousness. He is functionally part of an elect race, a royal priesthood, and a holy nation (I Pet. 2:9a). He bears the very stamp of his Lord Jesus, who is the sum, surety, and seal of the eternal agreement. The man of Christ is altogether enamored with grace and is repelled by the very idea that acceptance before God is conditioned upon human merit and personal righteousness.

He has a high regard for the life and triumph of faith, causing him to grow in grace. All things are done through faith. He holds to each of God's gracious promises, whose dealings with His people are in righteousness. Through the ages, God's family has resolved to preserve this gospel of the covenant in its purity, and deliver it intact to the next generation. In short, this means exalting Jesus of Nazareth as the Christ of God and loving the right and hating evil, ever seeking the maximum good for all men.

What bliss it is to have embarked upon the spiritual life and to be in covenant with the living God! In holiness we have solidarity with God, built upon a sure foundation of the eternal Rock. In a life consecrated to God by covenant, the more we uncover the riches of heavenly mercy and grace, the more we are certain of dwelling with the Son in righteousness in a spiritual land "flowing with milk and honey." Believing and living in a link with God is indeed the supreme reality, for whosoever believeth in Christ Jesus has everlasting life (see John 3:16).

Surely this is the blessing of the eternal covenant, for in mercy God said that He would make an agreement of peace with His people, further promising to tabernacle in the midst of us forevermore (Ezek. 37:26-28). In this covenant, all participants are His priests, servants, children, and friends. They dwell in His presence, serving Him day and night in His temple. All of these promises are made to those with good hearts who are willing to receive the covenant, and surrender self-righteousness and the rubbish of their own works.

Therefore, strong men should not boast in their might. Rich men should not flaunt their money and property. Wise men must not revel in wisdom. Any boast, says the Lord, should be that the Lord knows and understands me. "I am a God of righteousness, and of justice and of lovingkindness on earth . . . In these things I take pleasure, declares the Lord" (Jer. 9:23-24).

Blessings of the Covenant

Chapter Ten explains in detail how Jeremiah's new covenant statement (31:31-34) was directed toward the Jews returning from Babylonian captivity, then also renewed in Christ for this era, as presented in Hebrews 8:6-10:16. The sure application of this famous prophetic announcement to God's saints living both before and after the cross shows covenantal continuity and consistency for all ages. Indeed, all share in precisely the same blessings, all of which are bound up in various terms of the new covenant reviewed below.

(1) Promise of a New Heart. Ezekiel emphasizes the fact that all covenant people will receive a new heart, thus enabling them to keep the law of God through spiritual renewal: "A new heart also will I give you, and a new spirit will I put within you, and I will take away the stony heart out of your flesh, and I will give you a heart of flesh . . ." (36:26). The prophet did not say that God would help us to renew our spirit, but that He *will* do it. Further, Ezekiel did not conclude that God "will help us to make ourselves a new heart," but

plainly says that "I *will give* you a new heart." How reassuring!

After having been cleansed and functioning in the covenant, man left to himself will soon go afoul, especially if he is ensnared in a works-oriented system. But the God of covenant and grace promises that He will help His chosen ones through continuous heart renewal, a process which strikes at the very center of man's nature. In forgiving all iniquity, God takes away a stony heart of flesh by replacing it with a new heart of love.

Further, God also promises His chosen that "I will give them one heart and one way, so that they may fear me forever . . ." (Jer. 32:39). Evidently, godly fear is part of true righteousness, and the Father says that He will give this to His children. Thus he bestows upon His covenant ones that veneration of His sacred name which is the foundation of all godliness. Man must be willing to receive this gift from Jesus Himself, for it is one of the covenant blessings.

No one can ever make an impression upon a petrified heart, save God who is able to change it and renew it, even as a polluted spring once cleansed can again furnish sweet water. Similarly, according to promise, believers receive the covenantal assurance of a new heart, for their names stand in the eternal record. The prophet's vital words of comfort adequately show the completion (fullness) that all men can find in a peace relationship with God. Such was the prophet's plea to ancient Jews, and these words of reassurance equally inspire every man of God today, seeking life through a re-creation of his heart.

(2) The Law Written in the Heart. Writing laws *on* the heart is admittedly a difficult task, but only a loving, caring God can inscribe His plan and purpose in the hearts of men. This is precisely what He promised through Jeremiah when the prophet announced, "I will write my law in their hearts . . ." (31:33). Such a great promise means far more than mere awareness of law, for God said He would engrave His very mind and will in the minds of men, as a guide for His people, then and now, throughout their lifetimes.

No longer would God's chosen put darkness for light or substitute the bitter for the sweet. Their trained consciences would tell them the right and the wrong, discerning speedily between good and evil. The God of covenant promises His own that, instead of writing a law upon scrolls, or on the pages of books and letters, Heaven's ways would be engraved upon the tablets of their hearts. Instead of coming as crushing obligations, God's commandments would be placed within covenant people as objects of love and delight. What a privilege this is!

Beyond this, the covenanter loves the law. He does not tamper with it or rationalize away any of its duties. Thus, if the law accuses, he bows and confesses the wrong. Along with the ancient Psalmists, he cries, "Lord, turn unto me, have mercy upon me . . . incline my heart to perform your statutes" (Psa. 86:16, 119:112). God makes man love His will and delight in truth, righteousness, and holiness. A relationship with God assuredly cannot rest on a legal basis, and the law is never a burden, for God put it in the heart.

(3) God and Man Bound Together in Love. The oft-stated promise of covenant, "I will be their God, and they shall be my people," expresses an intimate, comforting relationship in which man has been fully reconciled with his Creator. All offenses are set aside as God blesses, honors, and provides for His people, for He is their portion. As with Abraham, God is their shield and exceedingly great reward (see Gen. 15:1). He is everything!

Through Jesus Christ, the God of heaven is a loving, tender Father, a watchful Guardian of the flock, a Friend that sticks closer than a brother. God is our rock, a refuge, a fortress of defense, and our dwelling place. All of this is encompassed in the simple statement, "I will be their God . . ." What assurance! He is the One who provides for the cattle on a thousand hills, offering comfort and consolation through all of life's trials, and giving guidance through His infinite wisdom and His great plan for man. Heavenly support comes through His eternal power, the same which guards the mountains and valleys, the plants and animals, and everything else over which God has given dominion to man.

The equally comforting statement, "and they shall be my people . . ." means that even the vilest of sinners – worshipers of Baal, offerers of children to Molech, ancient and modern idolaters, murderers, adulterers, etc. – can come to the living God through faith, and be in a vital union with Christ in which there is complete pardon. The past no longer counts, for it is forgotten. Even wayward covenanters who may have pro-voked God to anger can return to Him in sincere repentance, and it is still said of them, "They shall be my people."

As the covenant-making God says to the faithful that they are "my people," all spiritual blessings are their possession. They have everything that the angels claim and more – all that heaven is, and the fullness of God. It all belongs to the people of the covenant, through Christ. How rich and blessed, how august and noble are those in confederation with heaven! Best of all, this God shall rule over those He calls "my people" not only today and tomorrow, but forevermore.

(4) The Promise of a New Spirit. In the eternal covenant of grace, God promised through Ezekiel that He "will put a new spirit within you . . . [He will] cause you to walk in my statutes, and ye shall keep my judgments and do them . . ." (36:26-27). Prompted by new and proper desires, the old heart of sin would yield to a new heart of love. In holy conversation and intimacy, God's very personality is identified with all cov-enanters, whether they are the Jews whom Ezekiel promised would return from Babylon, or God's people today. All would have a new spirit, assigned to each covenanter by God Him-self. It is reflected in new attitudes and righteous dispositions.

As God deals with man in this gracious manner, He not only calls them to holiness, but he also imputes that holiness to them. He commands that His people walk in His way; in fact, He assists in the walk, not by compulsion or force, but by the constraints of love. As a man's heart is changed internally through His Spirit, this visible life is transformed to walk in newness of life. Such a turning of men from darkness to light, from Satan's domain to God's, is surely the standing wonder of the gospel of Jesus Christ. Thus sprinkled clean by God, His people are kept clean through the blood of Christ.

A life given security by the everlasting peace pact means that the child of God is continually green with life as a fruitful branch on salvation's olive tree (see Chapter Six). The very Spirit of God is the nourishment that continually flows through what would otherwise be poor dry branches. In this way, all people of covenant bring forth fruit unto God. Jesus Himself said that it is the Spirit that quickeneth (John 6:63); thus, man is dead and unprofitable until He breathes upon us.

Therefore, whatever God has ordained us to do in this life, we are certain to have the assistance of His Spirit. God's great promise, "I will put my Spirit within you," means that Christ's blood is constantly applied to us as acts of mercy and grace, so that we can enjoy complete pardon today in the covenant relationship, and eventually be seated in heaven.

With the promise of the Spirit as a guide in our daily walk, there is the absolute certainty of salvation for every believer. Sinners distance themselves from God by their wicked deeds, and they will not come to God for life; but all who are born from above (John 3:5) live by God's promise that He will put His Spirit within them. He impels such men to abide with Him. Now in relationship with God, the covenant one is no longer judged by man's standard, wherein one transgression brings a reversal of blessings and instant damnation. Rather, when God blesses the faithful with His Spirit, He will comfort such ones and spare them the judgment. How absolutely certain, then, is the salvation of every elect soul!

(5) Remission of Sins. In the covenantal term, "they shall be forgiven of their iniquities and I will remember their sins no more," God makes a clean sweep of sins, forgiving and forgetting them. Transgressions are blotted out, never to be reviewed

and mentioned again. In God's covenant of grace, there are no "if's" or "but's" in the promise of forgiveness. Instead, the focus is directly upon the certainties of "I will" and "they shall," for our charter with Heaven rests securely upon God's very word of covenant.

But there is more! Through Ezekiel God promised that upon all covenanted ones He "will sprinkle clean water upon your hearts, and you shall be clean; from all filthiness, and from all your idols, will I cleanse you . . ." (36:25). In the covenant, God demands nothing of the faithful, asks no price, insists upon no payment. Rather, He sets forth promise after promise, all freely made according to His liberality, conditioned only upon faithfulness.

This cleansing may be related to Paul's "washing of water through the word" (Eph. 5:26). Though polluted inside and out, a virtual spiritual leper, the sinner has God's promise that He will sprinkle him with clean water and make him whiter than snow (Isa. 1:18). As every fleshly lust and filthy act is forgiven, man experiences the greatest of all blessings found in the eternal covenant of grace.

The smug perfectionists, claiming near sinless lives, have little need for God's gift of free pardon. To them, God's great promise of forgetting sins is just another tenet in a structured doctrinal system. When Mary sang, "He hath filled the hungry with good things, and the rich he hath sent empty away," she was contrasting these two kinds of people (Luke 1:53). The complacent rich "spiritually superior" one declares that he is virtually sinless, while the hungry ones, ever conscious of sin, confess their transgressions.

Admitting to sin is always man's proper course before God. Burdened by sin, the faithful jump for joy over the words, "I will cleanse you . . . I will remember their sin no more" (Ezek. 36:33; Jer. 31:34), as great promises of a merciful God, who continually extends pardon to His children, freeing them from their transgressions. In contrast, the "deadpan" works mindset regards Ezekiel's comforting words as nothing more than God's part of a recurring pattern: i.e., man commits sin, man prays for forgiveness, thus obligating God to pardon strictly on a legal basis, bound to law.

While blotting out all transgressions, God treats the covenanter as if he had never offended Him. Though such a one may be guilty by earthly standards, God promises that He will not impute iniquity, but will forgive. The Great Judge wears white gloves, not the black hat. Because of the perfection of Christ, we exhibit no dust of dirt, but are clean. Various accusers might plead against the covenanter in the heavenly court by saying, "Lord, he did this or that," but hear only, "I do not remember it." Because Christ paid the penalty, the transgression is forever gone.

For the covenanter, there are only blank pages (and not logged in lists of sins) in the great Book of Remembrance. Thus, he will appear before God whiter than snow (Isa. 1:18), enjoying complete pardon for sin – each "covered" (Psa. 32:1), "cast behind His back" (Isa. 38:17), removed "as far as the east is from the west" (Psa. 103:12). "I will remember their sin no more" is therefore an exceedingly comforting statement. O' blessed covenant! O' sovereign grace and mercy!

Respecting the Covenant

The great spiritual force of the eternal covenant with man is the veracity of God, who is absolutely trustworthy and reliable. His very word and will is secure in sacred jealousy for His honor. This rock-solid agreement with man is solemnly bound by the very Word that created the heavens and the earth. Once initiated with Abraham and confirmed by an oath, and then renewed with Moses, David, and the saints of the prophetic era, the eternal covenant of grace was ultimately sealed with the blood of Jesus. Throughout the ages, God has delighted in the covenant.

Having made the agreement with man, God is ever mindful

to His promises, because He cannot lie. If God says He will do something, it will indeed be accomplished. The covenant of grace provides for the blotting out of sin, and God's people constantly stand pure before Him. Believers in Christ now enjoy salvation because of this positive covenantal relationship. They have drunk of the water given by Christ, and it springs up into everlasting life (John 4:14).

Man's duty, then, is to constantly respect the heavenly agreement (Psa. 74:20). The covenanter does not allow it to lapse, for he is pleased to keep it. He understands the terms of covenant, and actively honors its Maker, allowing nothing to frustrate the divine purposes and diminish Heaven's covenantal promises.

God's people joyfully live the covenant, eagerly joining the psalmist David in saying, "although my house be not so with God, yet he hath made with me an everlasting covenant" (II Sam. 23:5). They believe in it, for the covenant stands sure. They gratefully give thanks to the Originator of the covenant, who condescended to man to enter into this gracious, saving agreement (see Chapter One).

Especially, the man of God jealously respects the covenant, allowing nothing resembling a law-centered works system to be intertwined with it. Never! He disregards any teaching which does not discriminate between God's covenant of grace and a soul-crippling, law-works system. A clear line must always separate the two, for it is far better to bask in God's favor in holiness than to be shaped and molded by law-minded taskmasters.

Covenant people under grace are conscious of their sins in grateful self-loathing, as expressed by Ezekiel: "Then shall you remember your evil ways, and your doings that were not good, and shall loath yourself in your own sight for your iniquities and for your abominations" (36:31-32). God's gracious favor makes good men detest each bad action. While reflecting upon how much God has done for us, and how often even the strongest man of covenant has disappointed Him, the pure in heart can still arise from sin with a repentant attitude, respecting the God who has furnished the everlasting covenant to man.

This process involves needful chastisement, for the Father has placed a correcting rod in the covenant, administering discipline in love. The Psalmist said of God, "If His sons forsake my law . . . I will punish their sin with the rod, and their iniquity with stripes; but I will not take my lovingkindness from him, nor betray my faithfulness" (89:30-33; see also II Sam. 7:14). In the superlative, God will always be "gracious to whom He would be gracious and have compassion on whom He would have compassion" (Ex. 33:19). In this way, God calls upon us to respect the covenant.

Pleading the Covenant

In response to such a display of heavenly favor and concern, the man of God pleads the covenant throughout his highs and lows of life. If he should drift away from holiness, the covenanter can find comfort in God's famous promise: "I will put my law in their inward parts, and write it in their hearts" (Jer. 31:33). He acknowledges that he has neglected the holy commandments and broken them, therefore prays that they may be written on the fleshly tablets of his heart, that he again may serve the God of salvation properly.

If there arise various temptations to return to former ways of sin, and the covenanter wishes that God might uphold him against strong temptation, he is again reminded by God, "I will put my fear in their hearts, that they shall not depart from me . . ." (Jer. 32:40). The man of covenant can plead to the Lord, knowing that His word is his solace, and prays that God puts respect in his heart to fulfill the ancient promises, that the covenant will not leave him. Surely here is the way of perseverance.

When a distressed covenanter needs reassurance in a difficult time, he can reflect upon the longstanding promise, "As a mother comforteth her children, even so I will comfort thee . . . for Yahweh has comforted Zion . . ." (Isa. 66:13, 51:3). Regardless of the degree of trouble, the gates of hell shall not bar the implementation of God's covenantal blessings (see Matt. 16:18). The man of God, while pleading the covenant, prays that God's strength would stand between him and trouble, so that he might be strengthened and spared harm. Though dark places and cold alleys harbor cruelty and evil, the covenanter knows that God's glory covers the entire earth, and all flesh can benefit by union with God and find salvation. What a great thought!

Especially, the man of Christ pleads the everlasting covenant with a real consciousness of sin, when he feels the guilt of transgression of the divine standard. Astonishingly, some religionists insist that, under such a circumstance, all who strive to please the Lord despite good intent, are out of favor with God and immediately lost, cut off from all blessings and the heavenly reward until such time as they specifically repent and confess each and every sin.

Nothing in scripture sustains such an impersonal view of forgiveness. Instead, they reveal a wonderful God in infinite, boundless mercy, who has entered into an everlasting agreement with man in a forgiving relationship, based upon the state of the heart. The God of covenant gracefully promises that, by being joined to Him, sins are wiped out. For the pure in heart, Jeremiah's great truths, "I will show mercies unto you . . . Their sin will I remember no more" (42:12, 31:34) means that the transgression is not charged against him. Instead, God forgives and cleanses him. He acknowledges the sin – that, in fact, he did it – confidently knowing that his transgressions are continually covered while always continuing to depend upon the living God. Such a faith consistently leads to life, and can always be pled before God.

Summary

In His mercy and steadfast (*chesed*) lovingkindness, the God of selfless *agape* love has allowed man to strike a covenant with Him, to touch fingers with the very Creator of the universe in a committed relationship which abounds in blessings and favor. It is not a casual liaison, wherein man is in and out of favor with God day by day, depending on the commission of sin. Rather, God considers us already clean by virtue of having made peace with Him in the covenant, as revealed through His Son, whose very blood sealed the everlasting agreement. In this gracious covenant, God presently saves man, and accepts him despite imperfections, not casting him off because of transgressions.

As God through His Son calls people into the covenantal partnership, there is no room for spiritual self-reliance upon a human-devised works system. Rather, we are comforted in knowing that God continually interacts with us in specific, discernible ways, always for our own good, so that we can live with and for Him out of sheer gratitude for His magnificent salvation.

Through the covenant, the God of grace steadfastly and enthusiastically promises every person that his sins are remembered no more, and he has a new spirit and a new heart. In fact, the law is written in the heart. He is numbered among other faithful people, past and present, and God constantly dwells in him. God's ordinances are kept with no other motive than to please Him. He is always for us (Rom. 8:35-39) for He is compassionate and gracious, slow to anger, ever abounding in love and faithfulness (Ex. 34:6).

All who understand the nature of God's gracious covenant have found the marrow of theology; ignorance of it results in a superficial faith which focuses upon human achievement in "doing things for God." Such man-centered religious systems mean that all of God's blessings are uncertain and merely possible, filled with negative "if's" and "buts". Salvation on the basis of reward for doing has been tried for centuries, and ultimately breaks down, because in part it depends on man. Most mistakes made concerning biblical doctrines occur because of fundamental misunderstandings about the nature and scope of the eternal covenant.

Chapter Three

Christ the Covenant Victim – Not a Testator

A S PART OF THE POPULAR THEOLOGY of the establishment of a new-in-kind covenant after the death of Christ, there is often an appeal to Hebrews 9:15-18 to set forth the notion that, in God's plan for man's redemption, He established a "last will and testament" as part of a proper understanding of the nature of law. Five times this key passage contains the significant Greek word *diatheke*, which has been translated both "covenant" and "testament."

The two-covenant advocates insist that *diatheke* be translated "testament," to allow a new law given by Christ to be instituted alongside a new covenant, just as the law of Moses was the legal auxiliary to an old covenant. The King James Version of Hebrews 9:15-18 encourages the testamental view: "And for this cause, He is the mediator of the new testament . . . For where a testament is, there must also of necessity be the death of a testator. For a testament is of force after men are dead . . . (In that same passage the words "first testament" also appear twice.)

Since in classical Greek *diatheke* can carry the idea of "testament," a disposition of property by will at the death of its maker, advocates of two covenants insist upon that rendering in Hebrews 9:15-18, rather than covenant. Significantly, the corresponding word in Hebrew, *berith*, never means "testament," but always "covenant," and the great Septuagint translation of Hebrew into Greek, the LXX, uniformly translates *berith* as *diatheke* – "covenant."

William Lane has analyzed the use of the word *diatheke* in the apostolic era, in respect to its use with various forms of Hellenistic, Egyptian, and Roman practice. He notes that wills and testaments were not valid *only* when the testator died. Instead, "a will became operative as soon as it was properly drafted, witnessed and notarized. Moreover, inheritance did not occur only after the death of a testator, since it was a common legal practice for an inheritance, as parental distribution . . . among the survivors, to take place before death" [emphasis supplied] (*Commentary on Hebrews*, p. 231). Recall that, in the parable of the Prodigal Son, the father gave to his younger son his portion of property upon request (Luke 15:11-12).

Since the Septuagint and other Jewish religious sources (including the Dead Sea Scrolls) unanimously favor the meaning of *diatheke* as covenant in the Old Testament sense of *berith*, O. Palmer Robertson concludes that "presumption strongly favors the rendering covenant' [in Hebrews 9:15-18], especially in view of the unity of the usage of the term throughout Hebrews, which is due mainly to its dependence on the term as it appears in the Septuagint" (*The Wilderness Tradition in Israelite Thought*, PhD dissertation, p. 43). According to Robertson, the problem is permanently avoided by understanding that the primary thesis in Hebrews is the relationship of death and *diatheke*, and rendering that word consistently as "covenant" throughout Hebrews 9. The term "testament" utterly fails to explain this relationship.

To allow the introduction of the word "testament" in 9:15-18, it must be assumed that, in employment of the term *diatheke*, the author of Hebrews has shifted from a covenant usage in 8:6 – 9:14 to "testament" in 9:15-18, and then back to covenant from 9:19 through the remainder of the book. In view of the context, a predisposition to see a "last will and testament" in 9:15-18 is an unwarranted change of the treatment of the word *diatheke* as used throughout the remainder of Hebrews, wherein *diatheke* in most translations is consistently rendered covenant.

The "last will and testament" application to Hebrews 9:15-18 has gained acceptance because of the King James Version's rendering of *diatheke* as "testament," not only there but in several other places (Matt. 26:28, Mark 14:24, Luke 22:20, I Cor. 11:25, II Cor. 3:6-14, Heb. 7:22, Rev. 11:19). In each instance, "testament" should be "covenant," a word that far better describes God's disposition and arrangement in a divine agreement with man, a *diatheke*.

The natural and most defensible conclusion is that, within the structure of Hebrews, the same Greek word should be translated the same throughout a given context, normally the safest course with *any* foreign word. The vital section on covenant begins with 8:8-12 and ends with 10:16-17. These two passages, each a quotation of Jeremiah 31:31-34, function as scripture "bookends," wherein every occurrence of *diatheke* should be translated the same. Nobody doubts that both the first and last part of Hebrews 8:8 – 10:17 discuss God's covenant with man. But an insistence that the mid-passage 9:15-18 refers to a testament and a will, wherein the meaning of *diatheke* radically changes from covenant to "testament," and then back to covenant, seriously interrupts if not destroys the continuity of the entire section.

Therefore, *diatheke* in 9:15-18 should be rendered "covenant." The "testament" rendering specially pleads to maintain an agenda, namely that, along with the inauguration of a new covenant after the cross, there was also a new law established. The "testament" concept accommodates a theory which otherwise has absolutely no biblical support.

Read naturally, the entire section 8:6 – 10:18 is evidently a

Christian commentary on Jeremiah 31:31–34 and the ancient prophet's explanation of covenant, not a "last will and testament." Elsewhere, the author of Hebrews engages in extended discussions of common Jewish concepts (compare Psalm 95 with chapters 3-4; Psalm 2 with chapters 1 and 5:1–10; and Psalm 110 with chapters 5-7). Now, in chapters 8-10, the author of Hebrews similarly analyzes at length related Old Testament material, which centers upon an analysis and interpretation of the longstanding *diatheke* and *berith*, God's covenant with man.

The Historical Context of Hebrews 9:15-18

When two-covenant proponents make Christ a testator instead of a covenant victim, they ignore the historical background of Hebrews 8-10, wherein the recipients, chiefly messianic Jews, would not at all contemplate a "last will and testament" in 9:15-18. Such a concept would be totally foreign to their culture.

Instead, first-century Jewish Christians, all with some knowledge of covenant procedures, would be recalling the use of sacrificial victims, wherein blood was shed to enact an agreement, to bring it into force (9:17). In historical context, then, the Hebrew letter should be read as the death related to a *diatheke*, not as a will.

Indeed, the entire Hebrew epistle constantly draws from Moses and other prophets for its vocabulary – the priesthood, the tabernacle, covenant, the ceremonial practices of blood sacrifices and cleansings, and various types and shadows. It is a world far removed from classical Greek, wherein *diatheke* may alternatively carry the idea of testament or a will.

The connection of covenant with a death, particularly with the shedding of blood in sacrifice, is found throughout Hebrew history. For example, when God confirmed the everlasting covenant with Abraham, there were animal sacrifices (Gen.

15:9-17). When national Israel became God's covenanted ones (Ex. 20:1f), the event was dedicated with the blood of young bulls (24:4-8) and a covenant meal (v. 11).

Therefore, the language of Hebrews 9:15-18 would not conjure up, in the minds of Hebrew Christians, the idea of a testator making a will. The thrust of the argument in Hebrews 9 shows an intimate relationship between *diatheke* and the blood of a victim. As aptly stated by M. A. Hatch, "There can be little doubt that the word [*diatheke*] must be invariably taken in the sense of covenant' in the New Testament, and especially in a book . . . so impregnated with the language of the Septuagint as the Epistle to the Hebrews (*Essays in Biblical Greek*, p. 48). Such Christians, then, would view the passage as the death of a victim to implement a covenant, or to give it substance. *Diatheke's* meaning in Hebrews 9:15-18 should be precisely the same as in all other instances throughout the letter to the Hebrews and the 26 other New Testament books, initially written mostly to messianic Jews in various localities.

Further, Jewish people well knew that if they violated a covenant, they were worthy of death. A curse provision is inherent in all covenantal systems, and such knowledge was natural for people saturated with the teaching of the prophets from synagogue school to adulthood. Since all men have sinned (Rom. 3:23), they have broken the covenant and warrant punishment. Divine justice demands their death to satisfy the sin debt; otherwise the covenant would lack force and meaning.

The death could have been satisfied either with (1) Jesus dying in our stead, or (2) faithful people experiencing eternal destruction, a choice rejected by God as against His desire to show mercy and save man. Because Christ endured the cross, the people could now circumvent that deserved death through personal repentance and covenant renewal.

The Literary Context of Hebrews 9:15-18

Hebrews chapter 9 discusses at length the relationship of Christ to Moses' Levitical priesthood. The superiority of Christ's sacrificial offering to animal sacrifices and the shedding of His blood to purify consciences, is explained (v. 13). In verses 15-18 the author specifically returns to the word *diatheke*, the subject of the entire eighth chapter and also the middle of chapter 10. The debatable question is, does *diatheke*, rendered everywhere else in the book of Hebrews as covenant, in 9:15-18 carry the idea of a last will and testament? In other words, is Christ a covenant mediator or a testator?

The renowned Adam Clarke concluded that *diatheke* refers to God's arrangement in a covenant and not to a testament. "Covenant is undoubtedly the meaning of this passage [9:15-18], and we should endeavor to forget that testament and testator were ever introduced; for they totally change the apostle's meaning" (*Commentary*, Vol. 6, pp. 747-748).

W. E. Vine also rejects the rendering of Hebrews 9:15-18 in the King James and the Authorized Versions, stating that "the rendering the 'death of a testator' would make Christ a testator, which he is not . . . . The idea of making a will destroys the argument of verse 18" (*Expository Dictionary of New Testament Words*, p. 1142). M. R. Vincent (*Word Studies in the New Testament*, pp. 1140-1141) and Robertson Nicholl, the author of *The Expositor's Greek Testament*, concur.

Christ is a mediator because He fulfilled his stated purpose in the eternal covenant for man, and His death, as the supreme sacrifice, enabled the pardoning of all transgression, so that the called seed of Abraham might receive the promised eternal inheritance (Gal. 3:15-29). Jesus is fittingly the covenant intercessor, in precisely the same sense that God's oath, in Hebrews 6:17, mediated (confirmed) His promise to Abraham of many descendants. Christ the covenant victim ratified His Father's everlasting agreement through blood. As the superior non-

Levitical High Priest "after the order of Melchizedek, without beginning or ending," Jesus offered Himself as the once-for-all covenant sacrifice, obedient to the cross to do God's will (Heb. 5:8-9). Now from heaven He dispenses blessings to all in the covenantal community.

In Hebrews 9, the author developed a time line, arguing that Jesus died to provide the blood of the covenant, redeeming and paying in full for the sins of people then living, and for the transgressions of the Jews of old. Christ's blood clearly intertwines with all phases of the eternal covenant (see page 270). Assuredly, God did not remit the sins of covenanters before and after the cross in different ways.

The person of Jesus Christ supremely realizes the meaning of the longstanding covenant, namely, that God is merciful to His people. Christ is the *means* by which that benefit is conferred, for He, as the Mercy seat, paid the price which the animal sacrifices and offerings on the ancient mercy seat in the tabernacle could only foreshadow (Heb. 9:1-5, 10:5-6). By His death, Christ renewed and perfected the covenant relationship with man, paying for all sins as the mediator of a fully implemented eternal covenant, whose author is God.

Is Jesus Christ a Testator?

Despite the strong evidence that Christ is a covenant mediator, advocates of two-covenants insist that He is instead a testator of a will, a new law which would take effect at His death when an alleged new covenant superseded the first (Mosaic) covenant (Heb. 9:15). Here, then, is a distinct departure from the development of covenant advanced in Hebrews 8 to the idea of a will. This radical shift in the author's discussion fails to harmonize with the historical context of 9:15-18 (see above), and also brings problems to the text itself.

For instance, if a will confers a valuable consideration to another, who may either accept it or reject it, whose death enacted the old testament? Was it God or Moses? Did either of them have to die to render the will effective? The King James Version says that a will is in force only when somebody has died, when the testator is dead (9:17b). So if Christ allegedly came to enact a new testament, dying to validate it, and then on the third day came forth alive from the grave, would not His resurrection invalidate the testament? If not, why not?

Designating Christ as testator of a will in Hebrews 9:15-18 brings further confusion, when that doctrine confronts the established truth that Christ is the mediator of the covenant. These two terms said to describe Christ are assuredly neither synonymous nor interchangeable. When did a mediator ever need a will? Can one be the testator of a *covenant*? When was it ever necessary that a testator of a new testament should have to die to redeem the transgressions of a *former* testament (9:18, KJV)?

Other concepts besides covenant in Hebrews 9 are altogether foreign to the testament doctrine: the sprinkling of legatees with blood, the ratification of an agreement by animal sacrifices, mixing calf blood with water, scarlet wool and hyssop branches, the sprinkling of a scroll and other ceremony, and the death of a victim as a sacrifice for sin. On the other hand, if Christ is the mediator of a covenant, then all of this language is used properly.

Hebrews 9:16 explains the covenantal significance of Jesus, who had to die to ratify His Father's covenant, to confirm the agreement. As in Genesis 15-18, a covenant is established over the exhibition of dead things; it is not of force while that which established the covenant is alive. In verse 17 these assertions are amplified, explaining *how* a covenant is ratified: "A covenant is firm over dead sacrifices [when somebody has died], seeing it never has force while the appointed sacrifice lives" (New Translation by Macknight).

The King James Version, as well as the NASV, renders verse 17 as "For a testament is of force after men are dead . . ." Unfortunately, such a translation only bring confusion, for "men" is not in *any* of the oldest Greek manuscripts. Assuredly, the text does not mean that "men" die to ratify a testament or will. Rather, a *covenant* is of force only after there has been a death (see Gen. 15:18a).

In verse 17, the author of Hebrews conveys the idea that, according to the practice of both God and man, a covenant is made firm over dead sacrifices, seeing that it never avails while the victim (bull, calf, or other animal) appointed as the sacrifice or ratification of the covenant lives. A covenant is confirmed over dead victims, the appointed animal sacrifices, which must be brought in (see v. 16).

In the case of God's eternal covenant with man, it was necessary to show the propriety of the death of Christ to ratify the covenant. When confirmed by sacrifice, the covenant was made legally secure; it had full legitimacy after Christ endured the cross. The *Emphatic Diaglott* has it: "For where a covenant exists, the death of that which has ratified it is necessary to be produced; because a covenant is firm over dead victims, since it was never valid when that which ratifies it lives." Christ as the covenant victim had to be brought in, or appointed, as in Luke 22:29, where the Lord appointed His disciples a kingdom. The sacrifice needed to be produced, as if it were evidence in a law court. In this way, the eternal covenant was made firm over dead sacrifices (v. 17a).

Constantly, the author of Hebrews built his argument on the readers' assumed familiarity with centuries-old covenantal procedure and items of worship. Any agreement was tentative until the death of the covenant victim, and only after that time was the covenant legally confirmed. In ancient treaties among the nations, animals were cut in two and the parties making the agreement "walked between the pieces" of flesh, as explained in Chapter One. In the case of God's eternal covenant with man, ratification was made at Calvary.

Therefore, Christ had to die in order to become the priestly mediator of the covenant. His sacrificial blood, shed as He endured the cross, made legally valid the two millennia oath and promise. This deeply imbedded covenantal practice is vividly explained by Jeremiah (34:17-20), who told the people that, as they walked through the pieces of dead animals, they agreed to be committed to God. When they broke the covenant, God sent them into Babylonian captivity.

Verse 9:18 rounds out the thought. From the beginning God ratified His covenant to man by sacrifices, as with Abraham and in the Mosaic system, so as to preserve among His people the expectation of the ultimate sacrifice of the Lamb of God, Jesus. In this way, the ancient covenant was dedicated with blood. Since a "last will and testament" is not so dedicated (for it can become operative when the testator is still alive), it cannot be under consideration in Hebrews 9:15-18.

This validation of the covenant literally means "renewed," signifying that the agreement at the time of Moses was an extension of the one given to Abraham. Covenant advances came at the time of David and in the era of the prophets. As Christ offered Himself as the anticipated sacrifice, the longstanding agreement saw its ultimate renewal to enable all saints throughout the ages to enter the sanctuary (i.e. heaven) which only He Himself could open (dedicate) for us through the curtain – His flesh (Heb. 10:20). Now Abraham's family, together with the faithful at the time of Moses, David and the prophets, could access heaven, a truth that demonstrates covenantal continuity. Jesus' pleasing sacrifice (Heb. 10:9) opened the way to heaven for every faithful one from the time of Genesis to the day of eternity (II Pet. 3:18).

The Social Context of Hebrews 9:15-18

Besides historical and literary considerations of Hebrews 9, the social context must be considered as well. At the time of the writing of Hebrews, probably about AD 64-67, its recipients were experiencing persecution. Hebrew Christians particularly needed to be warned of the danger of falling away from a relationship with God. Many of them were wrestling with a particular problem: if Jesus Christ is our heaven-sent protector, why did He die? What value is He to us? Perhaps some among the messianic Jews were looking for a more powerful God, one who did not undergo death.

But the author of Hebrews shows that Jesus' experience on the cross was not enacted out of weakness, but of strength and love for His people, through a commitment to maintain the covenant. Thus, as Christ died as the covenant victim, all saints might be assured that during distressing times, as described in Hebrews 2:1-4, 6:1-6, 10:26-39, and 12:1-11, God would protect the faithful and allow them to endure and stay together.

Further, the author wished to build among the persecuted full confidence in Jesus as the heavenly High Priest who continually dispensed blessings (Heb. 4:14-5:10, 7:1-8:4). But the fainthearted saw Christ as weak, since He died on the cross and became invisible by His ascension. Others might have thought, in view of the suffering, that it would be unwise to abandon Jewish ceremonial law as proscribed by Moses. They reasoned that perhaps the Pharisees and the Jerusalem temple cult were right after all, for they appeared to thrive despite trouble.

The author of Hebrews assured wavering readers that God had made a commitment to be faithful to them, and its quality is reflected in His Son dying the death that we, as covenant breakers, should have died to enforce the covenant. Christ's passing from this life as High Priest was not a defeat, for it demonstrated the very essence of the commitment of the Divine Warrior to be the covenant victim, dying in our stead as an act of faithfulness and trustworthiness. Therefore, the author admonished his readers to be faithful to Jesus, not by shrinking back into sin, but instead by maintaining the faith unto the saving of the soul (Heb. 10:39). Since He died and was resurrected, then, if believers should perish in the persecution, they would also be raised in glory.

Hebrews 9:19-28

The material that follows the pivotal verses Hebrews 9:15-18, commented upon extensively above, likewise sustains the ancient covenantal ceremony. As explained in verses 19-21, blood was sprinkled on the vessels used in the worship to God, as well as upon the people who stood around the altar and the book of the law which represented God. This entire act prefigured the sacrifice of Christ. Evidently, there is an intimate relationship between covenant and sacrificial blood, as stated in verse 22: "Without the shedding of blood [to satisfy the covenant], there is no remission of sin."

But *better* is the cleansing sacrifice of Christ Jesus on the cross than the offerings of bulls and goats which were mere deliberately inadequate antecedents (v. 23) which were never intended to serve as a permanent arrangement. Even the original covenant sacrifice of Abraham's vision, executed on the very day God extended the eternal agreement to man in Genesis 15:9-17, similarly could not take away sin (Heb. 10:4). As our High Priest, Christ did not enter into the holy place where man went once a year, but into the *most* holy place, heaven itself, just one time for Abraham, Moses, David, other faithful Jews, as well as saints in Christ – everyone who has ever entered the eternal covenant by trusting in God.

Evidently, Christ did not have to make offerings in the heavenly holy place (v. 25), in the way which the earthly high priest annually had to display the blood of animals. He killed a lamb on an altar and brought the blood into the most holy place, an act foreshadowing Jesus' appearance in the presence of God, when He offered His blood (Himself) for the sins of all mankind. Thus, He offered Himself *just once* at the cross, actualizing and validating the eternal covenant, bringing it to its full expression. In fact, Christ came to abolish the provisional Levitical sin offerings by the sacrifice of Himself (v. 26b) to put away sin (Dan. 9:24).

Verses 27-28 pictures the high priest disappearing into the holy place and then emerging, "appearing unto salvation . . . to those who eagerly wait for him," as the Jews under Moses awaited the reappearance of the high priest after the day of atonement. This illustration offers an interesting parallel. As man dies once and then comes judgment, Christ as our High Priest offered Himself once to atone for the sins of many.

God then raised Him from the dead, and certified that this sacrifice was sufficient to bring all believers safely past the bar of divine judgment. The victorious Christ will appear a second time, not again as a sacrificial death, but to bestow upon His covenanted ones the eagerly anticipated salvation. These comforting truths brought consolation to persecuted Hebrew Christians. Therefore, the blood of the covenant was poured out for the remission of sins, and not to initiate a new–in–kind covenant or a new will and testament.

Sacrificial Blood and the Covenantal Curse

The principal thrust of Hebrews 9:11-28 is the intimate relationship between the eternal covenant and sacrificial blood. In Jewish times the covenant was ratified by the sacrifices of slain animals (vv. 19-20; see Ex. 24:8). But Christ has obtained eternal redemption through the putting away of sin by the offering of Himself (vv. 12-14), becoming the ultimate covenant ratifier. The blood of Christ (as in verse 14) is in fact a synonym for His death as a one-time sacrificial offering.

At Calvary, then, Christ redeemed all transgressors throughout time by taking upon Himself the covenantal curse, invoked by God when the agreement was broken or ignored. He died a representative death as the cursed one, standing in place for the real violators, all people throughout the ages. The importance of shedding blood to satisfy the demand of a broken covenant is stressed repeatedly throughout Hebrews 9.

While animal blood sufficed for the provisional service in

the earthly Jewish temple, there had to be the ultimate sacrifice of the One who was presented in the heavenly tabernacle for man's sins. Both were offered with regard to the eternal covenant. As the better sacrifice (Heb. 9:23-25), only the blood of the sinless Son of God would satisfy. Therefore, Christ had to enter the heavenly sanctuary through His own blood (v. 12).

The blood of Christ is the sign of the eternal covenant (Heb. 13:20), the basis of peace with God (Col. 1:20). Through that blood we have redemption (Eph. 1:7), because He bore our sins on the tree (I Pet. 2:24). Though knowing no sin, He thus became a curse for us at Calvary, for "cursed is every man that hangeth upon a tree" (Gal. 3:10, Deut. 21:23). Through this declaration of His righteousness, we are made nigh to Christ (Eph. 2:13); it is a propitiation through faith in His blood (Rom. 3:25).

As a consequence of Christ's atoning work, covenantal blessings are freely given to the faithful, including a new heart and a renewed spirit, as well as the reality of a comforting interdwelling with God. The covenanter's blessings are bestowed through the righteousness of God. Most important of all, sins are forgiven and forgotten, never to be counted against us. Christ was wounded for our transgressions, and with His stripes we are healed (Isa. 53:5).

The covenantal curse is therefore shouldered entirely by Christ (see Gal. 3:13). In the *Journal of Evangelical Theological Society*, K. M. Campbell drew together Jewish ritual curse formulae, such as hungering and thirsting, banishing, death by hanging, as well as poverty, darkness, the presence of an earthquake, and helplessness. These curses are profitably compared with the sufferings endured by Christ, as per the following based on Campbell:

1. Hunger and thirst (Deut. 28:48. Isa. 65:13).

1. Christ hungered (Matt. 4:2, 21:18; Mark 2:25, 11:12; Luke 4:2). "I Thirst" (John 19:28).

2. Poverty (Deut. 28:31).

2. Poverty of Christ. (II Cor. 8:9)

3. The scorn of passers-by (Jer. 19:8)

3. Mockers of Christ (Mark 15:29-31).

4. Darkness (Isa. 13:10, Amos 5:18-20, Zeph.

4. Darkness curse at crucifixion (Matt. 27:45, 1:15; Luke 23:45).

5. Earthquake (Isa. 13:13; Amos 1:1).

5. Earthquake at crucifixion (Matt. 27:51).

6. Banishment (Ex. 12:15-19, 31:14; Lev. 7:25, 20:3-6; Jer. 44:7-11, etc.)

6. Christ was cut off from God (Matt. 26:69-75).

7. Death by hanging on a tree (Deut. 21:23).

7. Christ's cursed death on the cross (Gal. 3:13).

8. No help for the cursed (Deut. 28:31, Isa. 10:3.)

8. Christ helpless. (Matt. 26:14-16).

9. Heavens as brass to the cursed (Deut. 28:23).

9. As Christ died, heaven was unresponsive to His cry (Mark 15:34).

Similarly, the curse sanctions will come upon the immoral, idolaters, apostate children of God, and all who refuse to avail themselves of the escape provided by God through the redemptive blood of Christ, the Divine Substitute who fulfilled the eternal covenant of life (Rom. 10:1-4, Eph. 1:7). Even as Christ bore the covenantal curse as God laid our sins on Him (Isa. 53:6), we are counted righteous because Jesus' blood continually cleanses us from all sin as we walk in the light (I John 1:7). In this way, God keeps clean those He made clean through obedience to the gospel (Rev. 1:5b).

Summary

The eternal blood covenant is the foundation theme of the Bible. Beginning with Abraham, God progressively revealed His plan to disclose Himself by means of a covenantal relationship through additional revelation to Moses, David and various other prophets, with the ultimate and final fulfillment of all things realized in the life of the Messiah, Jesus of Nazareth.

Throughout all of these generations, various animals were offered for the remembrance of sins, all of which looked to the perfect sacrifice at Calvary. Christ is the gracious covenant victim who willingly told His father to give Him a body, and it was prepared for Him (Heb. 10:5), so that He could experience the earthly life and satisfy divine justice by ratifying the eternal covenant through the shedding of His blood.

The author of Hebrews recorded other reasons why Christ was made flesh and dwelt among men (John 1:14). He would taste death for every man (Heb. 2:9) so that we might be brought into ultimate glory (v. 10). Christ continually runs to our aid and renders help (v. 18), delivering us from the devil's power (v. 14). Especially, He is a merciful, faithful High Priest who unfailingly represents us before God's throne (2:17, 7:25).

In these expressions of grace, Christ serves as Heaven's spokesman, continually validating God's covenant (Heb. 9:16-

17). Without Jesus' perfect death and shed blood, there could be no remission for sin. His sacrifice on the cross was the substance, whereas the old Levitical arrangement in the tabernacle was merely the shadow (9:1-10). Through it all continuity of covenant is displayed.

In addition to eternal redemption (Heb. 9:12), the author of Hebrews assures us, as heirs of the Abrahamic promise (6:17), its fulfillment results in an eternal inheritance (9:15). To the heart–obedient, eternal salvation is secured (5:8-9) through Christ's offer of Himself to God as a "spiritual and eternal sacrifice" (9:14, NEB). Evidently, "eternal" is an adjective which the author of Hebrews intimately associates with all aspects of the eternal covenant (13:20).

The blood of Christ thus provides an eternal redemption and inheritance; and as an offering of the eternal spirit (9:14), the blood secured eternal salvation in the eternal covenant through the pleasing sacrifice of Christ. Such an overflow of grace and glory extends to faithful covenanters who are partaking of the heavenly calling (3:1); they are joint heirs with Christ, as explained by Paul in Romans 8:14-30 and Galatians 3:1 - 4:28.

In response to this wonderful display of mercy, man's obligation is to receive the covenant and abide in it. Despite all best efforts, everyone will break the agreement and thus be deserving of death, even as Israel of old had vowed to keep the covenant after receiving it (Ex. 24:4, 7-8), but ultimately violated it. Sin brought cursings which had to be expiated by the shedding of blood.

But the saints of old were not sentenced to destruction. David, for instance, violated the covenant, yet still had a relationship with God (Psa. 51, Acts 2:29 31). Other Jewish faithful also became transgressors and thus were in God's debt; nevertheless, they were not banished from the presence of God. Without a death (Heb. 9:17) and a shedding of blood, the eternal covenant would be meaningless, for according to its terms, when a man breaks it he must die.

The universally broken covenant could have been satisfied by the death of every human being, but such appropriate punishment would make God's agreement with man pointless. After all, God authored and then extended mercy to *save* man, and He knew beforehand that His created would break the covenant. Through this structure which demanded justice and the death of violators, God nevertheless legitimized the covenant through the voluntary death of His Son, as a representative from heaven in man's stead. Through this graceful act, the covenant would then remain consistent with divine justice, and not be invalidated.

Jesus Christ is indeed the covenant victim, as explained in Hebrews 9:15-18. When anyone injects into that text an interpretation which makes Him a will-writer, Christ's office has been effectually changed to one of a testator. But no such arrangement is found in Jewish history. Moreover, Christ Himself said that He did not come to do His own will, but "the will of Him who sent me" (John 6:38).

Thus, Hebrews 9:15-18 has a far deeper meaning than a description of a changing of covenants or the establishment of a new will. In historical, literary and social contexts, the writer of Hebrews in 9:15-18 explains that Christ as High Priest came to offer Himself as a covering for all sin through the mediating of a covenant. Christ did not experience the cross for the purpose of ratifying a new testament or establishing a new law.

The testament concept should therefore not be read into the text of Hebrews 9:15-18, as though Christ died to make a will effective. First and foremost, it is not Christ's covenant; it is God's, for He is and always will be the covenant author and sustainer. Also, Christ was not a testator, but a sacrifice. Significantly, there is absolutely no hint of an Old Testament type or shadow which corresponds to the idea of testator or will, as the King James Version and a few other translations allow.

The difficulty of the testament concept is simply summarized: if Hebrews 9:15-18 involves a testament, not a covenant; if the one who made the testament had to die (v. 16); if it was God's "testament;" *then* the conclusion is inevitable – that no one could ever have a covenant with Heaven, because God cannot die to validate it (v. 17)! More than that problem, how could Jesus Christ, after taking upon Himself the sins of the world, ever regain a covenant relationship with a deceased god, a "testator" who had to die (v. 16)? Surely, these are most unacceptable conclusions, are they not?

Instead, every idea throughout Hebrews 9:15-18 continues to describe the eternal covenant of peace (see 13:20), made secure by the willing sacrifice of God's Son on the cross. He was a lamb offered without spot or blemish (I Pet. 1:19). The covenant ratified by the death of Christ Himself, who suffered for us (I Pet. 2:21-24), as a lamb slain from the foundation of the world (Rev. 13:8), and as the lamb who took away the sin of the world through sacrifice (John 1:29) – not as a testator.

Chapter Four

⤳

The Covenant and First-Century Rabbinic Judaism

T HE VITAL BACKGROUND to a study of the New Testament is a familiarity with the "world behind the text," the socio-historical setting of the various writings. A vital part of this backdrop is the recognition of the extensive ecclesiastical power of first century Judaism, a Greek word meaning "the religion of the Jews." Indeed, a failure to recognize the length and breadth of this dynamic religious force, not only in Judea but also in the Grecian world as well, leads to serious misunderstandings as to what Jesus and Paul were responding in their public ministries.

Conversely, knowledge of the history and doctrines of the humanly devised Judaistic opposition, the vital spiritual milieu as described in the gospels, Acts, and Paul's letters, helps explain why Jesus and Paul preached in the ways they did about covenant, the reality of salvation, justification, grace, etc., and their firm opposition to anything resembling a works system to gain God's favor.

Israel's first century religious community, the Pharisees,

Sadducees, and about eleven other major parties, all strove to please God in regimented institutional systems with distinctive legalistic approaches. Each segment of Judaism equated its concept of covenant with the law, a particular doctrinal system derived from a mixture of scripture and human tradition, in a code called the Talmud. The orthodox professionals who thrived throughout the unstable spectrum of first century Judaism were truly the enemies of authentic covenantal religion, as expressed by most apostolic writings and those of the earliest church fathers.

The Origin of Talmudic Judaism

Centuries of religious evolution had taken place among the Jews to bring about the shameful, legalistic religion of Judaism of New Testament times. A "letter" approach to religion was evident within a few generations after God's people returned from Babylonian exile in the days of Ezra, about 445 B.C. Perhaps it started in the exile itself, when Moses' writings, as well as past traditions, were jealously preserved. Faithfulness to the prophets was redefined as "rallying around the law," which no longer merely regulated God's community but also created it. Rather than emphasizing covenant loyalty and relationship with God as an authentic basis for service to the Lord, form and structure, along with the law, became the sum and substance of religion.

Such an institutional emphasis ultimately produced an influential new class of religious leaders, the scribes. The Jewish dispersion which had organized synagogues in every locality (Acts 15:21) created a constant demand for copies of available prophetic records, and these professional copyists became legal experts, so that they might translate "the law" correctly. Certainly, by the second century B.C., the scribes had attained religious parity with the God-ordained priests, the ones whom God instructed "to keep knowledge," and the people "were to seek the law at [their] mouths" (Mal. 2:7; see also Deut. 18:1-8, 31:11, 33:10; Ezek. 44:15-23).

Around 196 B.C., with the creation of the 70-member Sanhedrin court in Jerusalem, wise teachers and scribes definitely helped determine what was perceived to be the will of God. This institutional approach to Old Testament writings amounted to a rejection of the sole authority of God's long-established priesthood. In the two centuries before the birth of Christ, the priests and scribes devoted an inordinate amount of time and attention to extracting doctrines and legalistic opinions from available scriptures, which to them had become the pedestaled "word of God." They read them, studied them, taught them, quoted them, administered them (as Sanhedrin judges), copied them, and preserved them . . . and ultimately fell in love with them. The scribes were regarded as experts in the law.

Highly judgmental religious parties arose, among them the Essenes, Saduccees, Zealots, and especially the Pharisees, each claiming to be the one true interpreter of written documents. In the Sanhedrin itself, scribes and lay teachers vied with the (now Hellenized) priesthood for religious and political authority, though all factions were fundamentally unfaithful to the prophetic writings.

By the second and first centuries B.C., ritual had long displaced covenantal relationship among these parties; form and structure smothered intimacy between God and man (see Hosea 6:6). Morality and holiness faded in favor of peculiar doctrines. Since the hundreds of Old Testament commands were perceived as being stated in black and white, once and for all, the documents were no longer thought of as merely *describing* practice in worship to God. They set forth rules and prescriptions for everybody in a structured Torah, a systemized law. God was no longer the way, truth and the life; rather, the religious leaders' law structure became the final authority and, essentially, the object of worship.

Each legal system was a mixture of commandments from

written records and man-made tradition. Some teachers claimed that their oral customs had been handed down from the time of Moses. The rapidly emerging Pharisees laid down laws to be observed apart from documents, in an oral Mishnah-form, a philosophical law code which ultimately became part of the Talmud, a religious commentary of the Jews consisting of a mixture of written records, tradition from oral teachings, legends, and embellishments of history. In this way they could enact new laws at their pleasure, and not even necessarily base them on tradition or scripture.

Jewish religious society, dominated by the teaching of the Pharisees and other religious parties, was torn with division brought on by differences on how to apply the law. The Talmud itself was a Pharisaic record of religious interpreters striving among themselves in legal and religious debates. Each thinker endeavored to convince others of the correctness of various religious ideas, rather than work harmoniously with others to carry out God's will. The Pharisees prided themselves on being people of the law, demanding that others meticulously obey their "jot and tittle" interpretations.

This institutional law-keeping mindset regularly manifested itself in second and first century B.C. literature. The book of *I Maccabees* staunchly defended and exalted structure, with a peculiar motive for observing the commandments of the Law (2:67-68), "for by it shall ye obtain glory" (v. 64; see also 2:21, 6:23; *II Macc.* 1:4, 2:2-3, and especially 3:1).

The unknown author of *IV Maccabees*, probably written a few decades before the birth of Christ, showed the continuing deterioration of authentic Jewish covenant thought. Religious practice was bluntly defined as education in the law (1:17), which regulated all aspects of living (2:8). The law could master affection (v. 10), govern lusts through reasoning (vv. 6, 9), and even conquer transgressions of marital love (v. 11). Defending the divine law was proudly described as virtuous (9:15; see also 9:1-3, 1:17).

This endless striving over words, interpretations, and doctrines continued unto the generation of Jesus. Clearly, by then, the scribes (the majority of whom were Pharisees) were potent figures in Jewish religious life. After all, when Herod wished an explanation of prophecy, he called together the chief priests and the scribes (Matt. 2:4), or lawyers – literally "men of the book" in Hebrew (Matt. 7:29; see also Mark 2:16, Luke 10:25). Their authority rested upon education and knowledge (see also Matt. 23:34).

Jesus and Judaism

The Pharisees and other authoritarian parties had assumed full control of Jewish religious life well before the time Jesus began His public ministry. The Master faced a spiritually decadent religious elite hemmed in by contradictory doctrines and a letter of the law approach toward worshiping God. The miracles and preaching of Jesus, such as the Sermon on the Mount, showed the common people that His spiritual approach was undergirded by even greater authority. The crowds were astonished at His teaching (Matt. 7:29). Conflict was inevitable with the entrenched scribes and Pharisees.

During repeated encounters with the Pharisees, Jesus constantly had to fend off Talmudic legalism. Mark 7:1-11 shows the demarcation between godly covenantal Jews adhering to Moses, and Judaism's law-based sects and parties. Such human systems made void the word of God – the mind and will of God – by their tradition "which you have handed down . . ." (v.13). Clearly, Moses was saying one thing as his writings unfolded the plan and mind of God in a covenantal relationship; the Pharisees and other denominations practiced something else entirely by imposing man-devised tradition upon one and all (Matt. 15:9), thereby breaking the law of God and working against His will and purpose.

Matthew 15:1-20 further shows how these Jews had freely bound themselves to the elders' instructions. Such *external* observances made them indifferent to the stains and sins of the heart. They had entirely neglected the inward man. Jesus bluntly called these Pharisees "hypocrites" (v. 7), "blind guides" (v. 14; see also Matt. 23:16, 24), a people "lacking in understanding" (v. 16).

In almost every discussion with the Pharisees, Jesus moved on a confrontational course with these self-styled guardians of true religion. To such people, who read the law and the prophets and built from them a legal structure, Jesus said, "You search the scriptures, for *in them* you think you have eternal life, for these are they which testify of Me" (John 5:39). Lacking a personal approach with Heaven, the Pharisees likely regarded all of God's laws as equally important (Matthew 23), but the Master spoke of "weightier matters" – mercy, justice, and faith – as superior to meticulous tithing and certain other duties (v. 23). Jesus was clearly *not* like any of the scribes – Judaism's self-styled custodians and interpreters of available scripture (Matt. 7:28-29).

During His final weeks of preaching in and around Jerusalem, Jesus' several discourses dramatically contrasted God's way of repentance, righteous living, equality, judgment, and proper respect for the law and the prophets, with the prevailing authoritarian approach toward religious life. The parable of the wicked husbandmen (Luke 20:9-18) directly slapped the face of evil Jewish leaders, and their impersonal treatment of brotherly relationships. In the story, the kingdom of God was taken from the rejected tenants, the prevailing religious politicians, and given to covenant people who would bring forth spiritual fruit – repentant Jews and Gentiles who would join the longstanding faithful covenant remnant (see Chapter Six).

The Master left no doubt as to the Jewish leadership's spiritual depravity, their rejection of God by inordinately glorying in the letter of scripture. Concentrating on ceremony and outward appearances, these partisans had neglected the heart which nurtures the inward man. The cleansing of the temple (Mark 11:15-18), the condemnation of the unproductive fig tree (Mark

11:12-13, 20-21), Jesus' entry into Jerusalem mounted on a donkey (Luke 19:29-40), and similar incidents, all declared the unworthiness of these rebellious religious leaders, who were fundamentally untrue to God and blind to Jesus' miracles and kingdom preaching. Their faith resided in their unemotional understanding of religious documents and abiding in human tradition.

As spiritual adulterers, these partisans slowly guided the Jewish nation into physical and spiritual destruction. "How can ye escape . . ." said Jesus (Matt. 23:33) at a time when He talked about the end of the nation in AD 70. On another occasion, when Jesus met the Pharisees and the Sadducees head on (John 5:37-47), He rebuked them for the lack of love in their hearts (v. 42) and their exaggerated interest in acquiring knowledge and facts: "You search the scriptures, because you think that in them you have eternal life . . ." (v. 39).

Ostensibly, these blind guides ignored God's truth that Jesus was indeed the Christ. Instead, they freely accepted praise from one another (see v. 41). They were unwilling to come to Him, regarding the scriptures themselves as the source of eternal life. This action constituted idolatry, just as much as the setting up of a golden calf or carving out a wooden image and bowing down to it. Their religion of the book was in vain, unprofitable and unacceptable to God.

Paul and Judaism

During the generation after the cross, the apostles battled the same authoritarian approach toward religious life that Jesus faced during His ministry. In Galatians 1:11-17, the apostle Paul clearly differentiated between God-dependent, faithful Jews, the *ekklesia* (church) looking to the Christ, and tradition-based Judaism, which leaned heavily upon adherence to the strictness of ancestral law (Acts 22:3). In Galatians 1:13, Paul clearly regards this Judaism of the majority as a different religion from covenant faith, even as in John's gospel "the Jews" were essentially synonymous with opposition (1:19, 2:18, 5:10, 6:41, 7:1, 8:48, 10:31, etc.).

In II Corinthians 3:4-18, Paul employed a very pointed term to describe spirit-killing Judaism, calling it "the ministry of death . . . an old covenant" (see Chapters Eleven and Thirteen). The leaders of such man-devised faith would lord it over others with toe-the-mark scripture interpretations which they mixed with their own tradition. The apostle had already taken up this theme in the province of Galatia. In a letter to those *ekklesiai*; Paul bluntly outlined a clear choice: either remain under bondage to a human-authored Judaistic sect or enjoy freedom through Jesus Christ in a promise-filled, authentic covenantal relationship (Gal. 4:23-26, 30-31; 5:1).

Paul indicted Jewish partyism as a disturbing force and a stumbling block that was unsettling many because of an insistence on being justified by the keeping of the law of circumcision (Gal. 5:2, 4, 6, 11). In a graphic response to their zeal for that ritual, the apostle wished that these troublemakers would lower their knives just a little and castrate themselves! (v. 12).

For years, Paul had been a purblind follower of Judaistic tradition, a zealot determined to stamp out all who followed Christ, for they were not of his party. Later, after baptism into Christ, he never persecuted kinsmen of the flesh, and for almost a quarter century actively preached and worshiped with them in the synagogues (see Chapter Eight).

In Romans 9:31-10:4, 11:28-32, Paul staunchly condemned all works-entrenched Jewish religion. Institutional Jews had pursued a "law of righteousness," miserably failing to see it as it was, because of failing to approach God through a relationship based on covenant, i.e., by faith (9:32, 10:6). They stumbled because they sought self-righteousness (10:3), trusting in obedience to a law structure, as explained in II Corinthians 3:15-16 (see Chapters Eleven and Thirteen). In thus rejecting Christ, those unbelieving, disobedient Jews (Rom. 3:3-4) had a veil over their minds which could only be removed by abandoning their faction-inspired law patterns which they taught and lived by in attempts to make themselves right with God.

Such misguided zeal, based on meticulous obedience to an ecclesiastical system, centered upon man earning favor with God by piling up a credit balance, through good works. In response, Paul declared that – in the way of faith – Christ is the end of the law (10:4), fulfilling it in every detail through His life and teaching. The apostle further contrasted Judaism's warped view of righteousness (v. 5; see Lev. 18:5) with the preaching of the word of faith (v. 8).

Paul pleaded with all zealots to abandon their formalistic mindset toward God, in favor of gracious faith, which involved confessing with all their being Jesus as Lord (v. 9). In precisely this way, the Jewish faithful remnant was true to God (Rom. 11:5), being justified through grace and not works (v. 6). These covenanters trusted in God (not themselves) in ways far more meaningful than poring over scripture to find laws to obey "to make one right with God." This manner of life, or true visible faith, is precisely what the prophets of Israel and Judah had continually declared to the people as the proper motive to serve God.

Formal Judaism forever sought to put the Lord as a debtor, trying to secure salvation by "doing things for God." Unhesitatingly, Paul called such disobedient Jews enemies of the gospel (Rom. 11:28-30). Meanwhile, the covenant faithful were content to be in God's debt, continually amazed at what He had done for them. The works approach, centering upon man-devised law systems, pales in comparison to simply trusting in the One who blesses and sustains us in a covenant relationship.

In Philippians 3:2-6, 17-19, the apostle warned the brethren against a possible invasion of Judaizing teachers, men who would lean upon their glorious ancestral heritage and fleshly circumcision along with other ordinances. To Paul, reliance upon these things was but rubbish (see Chapter Twelve). Partisanship was also reflected in Philippians 1:15-17, 28, wherein

Paul could still rejoice during those times when less fanatical Jews did preach Christ, though insincerely, even if their motive was to injure him. Far more often, various Jews tried to keep the gospel of Christ from being taught, not only to truth-seeking kinsmen but to Gentiles as well (I Thess. 2:15-16). In all, Paul had been beaten with stripes five times at the hands of excisive Jews (II Cor. 11:13-15, 20, 24-29).

In Romans 16:16-17, Paul described his opponents as separationists, earthly-minded "gluttons" who were promulgating contrary doctrines and serving their own bellies. These Judaizers were bent on deceiving innocent, guileless hearts (v. 18, see also Phil. 1:15-28). The "children of disobedience" at Ephesus might also be those same unbelieving Jews (2:2; comp. Isa. 65:2). These contumacious Jews, who knew the "crafty ways of the devil" (6:11), stood before God in sharp contrast to covenant messianic Jews who were being saved by grace through faith (2:8).

At Colossae, Judaizers also had mingled with the *ekklesia*, insisting upon the maintenance of the law of Moses with its ordinances of fastings, sacrifices, and purifications (2:14-16) as the means of procuring the pardon of sin. These teachers erred in insinuating that the ministry of angels (2:18) was the more perfect revelation, rather than God's Christ who alone possesses "all the treasures of wisdom and knowledge" (2:3).

To counter the opposition, Paul told the Colossians not to be judged in respect to foods, festivals, and the Sabbath (v. 16), all of which were a shadow of things to come, when the reality was to be found in Christ (v. 17). One purpose of the Colossian letter was to silence the Judaizers, who insisted that the Levitical sacrifices were obligatory, since they saw no covering of sin in the propitiatory offering of the Christ at Calvary.

Paul's man of lawlessness (II Thess. 2:1-10) probably addressed the activity of factions in Jerusalem, among them the Zealots, just prior to the fall of the city in AD 70, noting that these Judaizers were already at work (v. 7). The setting for the lawlessness was God's temple (v. 4), where apparently one

Jewish leader had usurped the high priest's position. This lawless one's seditious acts took place in the temple sanctuary, the very location of the "abomination of desolation" (Mark 13:14), a phrase which Jesus had applied to the future sacrileges which would be perpetrated by rebellious Jewish factions that perverted the eternal covenant at the time of the end of the Jewish age (Dan. 11:32; see also 9:27).

In mid-first century at the Jerusalem Conference, certain Pharisees sought to bind Jewish ceremonial aspects of law onto Gentiles in Christ (Acts 15:1-2), but these things along with Moses' types and shadows were meant to pass away (Heb. 8:13). In that same time frame, the apostle Paul devoted much of his Galatian and Roman letters to this same distorted gospel. They were the "false brethren" of Galatians 2:4, who argued for righteousness based on performance (vv. 15, 21), an approach to serving God which actually puts worshipers in spiritual bondage.

To the Romans, Paul wrote that Jewish pride rested squarely upon reliance upon law (2:17) wherein they taught others scripture and tradition, but did not develop in themselves inner righteousness. Not the hearers but the doers of the law, God justifies (v. 13). Judaism's many sects had missed the very *purpose* of the teachings of Moses and the prophets, failing to put them in their proper place, as instructors of righteous living.

Such Jewish people in Christ caught up in external religion were not alone in insisting upon imposing a formal, structured religious system upon fellow saints. Near the close of the first century, John described the Ephesian *ekklesia* of lawkeepers as having "left their first love" (Rev. 2:1-7) – a stinging indictment of the law-works mindset.

Revelation's letters to Pergamos and Thyatira also indicate that various Gentile believers aligned themselves with the thinking of Judaism's failed carnal religion. New divisions and emerging parties and sects in the second century centered upon disputes about what Christ and the apostles might have taught.

See also Titus 1:14, a scripture which admonishes the faithful not to give heed to Jewish fables.

The Second Century: The Rise of Power of Bishops

Legalism continued unabated among Christians past AD 100-110. Conflict and tension among God's people was also especially evident in such writings as Clement's *I Clement* and the *Shepherd of Hermas*. Such a mindset paved the way for late second century institutional hierarchalism among the people of Christ, and an even more structured belief system than the Jews of old had contrived.

Though the apostles and gospel writers had written most of the letters and gospels of the present New Testament by AD 96, by no means were they soon collated into a closed collection, a canon. Around the year 140, one religious leader, Marcion, collected Paul's work, and Irenaeus in AD 180 isolated the four gospels that eventually became canonical. Throughout the Roman Empire, rival lists of New Testament books appeared, compiled by orthodox and even heretical religious leaders who took it upon themselves to decide what were the authentic scriptures. Very often they chose some particular writings over others because with them they could justify their various doctrinal positions and defend their hermeneutic, their system of interpreting scripture.

While the scripture-worthiness of various apostolic writings was being considered in the first four centuries, a three-tiered system of ecclesiastical authority – one bishop per city, elders and deacons below them, and then members – began to develop, in attempts to bring about organizational unity. But power-driven rival Christian sects arose, all claiming to be God's exclusive chosen people.

Each group revered their collection of scriptures and believed that the writings gave their sect superior faith, based on their peculiar doctrines, separatism, and hermeneutics.

Every authoritarian religious sect fell into the same damaging legalistic traps that had snared Jews of the late Old Testament period. Now, however, acceptable faith would be based on rules and works systems derived from interpreting tradition and available apostolic writings which later were collected into a canon, the New Testament.

Further debate centered on who would occupy the chairs of authority to give clear guidance to the flock. As with Judaism, the question was, who would be in charge? Very early, the church bishops (the head elders) seized the moment by proclaiming themselves successors to the apostles. They took it upon themselves to direct God's people in all aspects of spiritual life, since they believed they were more gifted than the rank and file and could "handle aright" extant scriptures better than others.

The second century bishops' rule-making and interpretive systems were presented to their followers as a focal point of unity, and as the best way to fight rapidly emerging heresies, especially Docetism, multiple Gnostic sects, and Montanism. Instead of holding the saints together through uniform practices and doctrines, even more confusion and division resulted. In actuality, there existed a considerable amount of healthy diversity of thought among first century people of God in various assemblies, sometimes even those founded by the same apostle. The authoritative bishops clearly deemed such situations undesirable.

Ecclesiastical officials of the second, third, and fourth centuries very quickly developed the formal Jewish-style religion. The bishopric controlled what doctrines would be taught and what writings were "inspired," encoding their beliefs into creeds, which they also considered inspired. Generally, they succeeded because they claimed to be the apostles' spiritual successors.

These leaders' beliefs were directly equated with an institutionalized "one true faith," an otherwise valid concept if expressed by spirit-filled saints seeking to unite God's people on the basis of grace and love, and guided by divine wisdom. Since religious people came from various educational and social backgrounds, and all based their doctrinal systems on "that which is not seen" (Heb. 11:1), the faith which people held was merely what they perceived as truth – that which was thought to be the "right teaching." But such was nothing more than their subjective statements of personal faith, adequately justifying and serving them in their religious practices.

Various patterns of belief may or may not have satisfied a religious neighbor, and items of faith may not even have coincided with God's revelation. As with Judaism, authoritarian Christians equated their positions on various matters with the correct interpretations, and obviously did not allow room for personal differences or other statements of religious practice. But as bishops forced their doctrines on others as the basis for acceptance, disputes inevitably arose, leading to shameful factionalism and ultimately physical division.

Institutional religion truly hit its stride early in the fourth century when the organized church became fully intertwined with the Roman Empire's political structure. Because a great number of Emperor Constantine's constituents had adopted visible Christianity in one of its many forms, Constantine saw an advantage to Christianizing himself as an additional way to control his empire. Consequently, church bishops and other leaders more than ever could enforce their ecclesiastical authority, since political power was available to them. It was a convenient marriage for both.

The Covenant Remnant

Apart from the all-powerful monolithic church, which functionally defined itself as an organization apart from people, a faithful remnant throughout the ages has maintained the simplicity of pure religion by emphasizing positive relationships, moral behavior, reason, and personal responsibility. They had been more or less united under one man, Jesus Christ, as a guiding principle of life.

First and second century faith stressed mutual service and submission, with all disciples working as equals, not one above another, "for ye are all brethren" (Matt. 23:8, 20:25-26). This principle ruled out entirely all hierarchical notions. No one was in charge, barking out orders. All were called to service, in a fellowship that emphasized helping "one another," a phrase which occurs about 87 times in the New Testament.

Similarly, Paul consistently rebuked all claims of religious superiority, properly stressing godly, covenantal moral living in a grace-through-faith relationship with God, speaking the truth in love, and avoiding factionalism. A right-standing be-fore God through grace means that salvation and justification arise, not from what Christians do in response to biblical com-mands, but from what God has already done at Calvary. Though some may have called this heresy, most faithful saints recog-nized it as the good news.

In a real sense, these godly people did not have a "biblical" faith. On the other hand, the late fourth century *ekklesia*, which more or less possessed the completed Bible and various creeds, was rife with strife and speculative reasoning and interpreta-tion of religious documents. What a paradox! It was in a scripture-conscious environment that church hierarchism de-veloped with super bishops at Alexandria, Antioch, and Rome, with the universal bishop (Pope) at Rome installed in the year 606. In contrast, righteous covenanters, who respected God's special (biblical) revelation, did not deify the scriptures, for their faith rested squarely upon a relationship with a Person.

The prominent issue was always authority – who would lead and what would be taught to the brethren. Various power-conscious leaders succeeded in imposing their will on others, claiming superior knowledge and experience, especially in determining an exclusive interpretive procedure for "rightly dividing" scripture, and securing what they perceived to be the correct doctrine to teach and govern others.

Just as the first century Pharisaic society was filled with strife and doctrinal division, church leaders contended among themselves by debating word meanings and interpretations, each trying to convince others of the correctness of his belief system. There was no inclination to work harmoniously to seek God's will together to please Him. The vast majority trod the same well-worn path which the first century Pharisees and other Jewish sects before them had taken.

Allegedly, these "people of scripture" very often read their own interpretations into religious writings, professing to please God by strident obedience to what they thought was God's will, a contrived legal system. Against this prevailing external religion, God's covenant faithful always pled for His magnificent eternal covenant of grace, which saved in a relationship with God, and contended against all regimented religious systems which emphasized conformity to various man-devised patterns which could only stifle and enslave.

Summary

Throughout the historical stream of nearly 2000 years of organized Christian religious thought and practice, and in Judaism for hundreds of years before that, two distinct approaches toward serving God have coexisted, even in the same families and in common assemblies. First, there are the covenant faithful who find their strength and power, not in their performance directed by a belief system, but rather in an active positive relationship with the living God. These people cultivate and develop the inner man – honesty, ethical behavior toward others, and fundamental fairness – while actively helping others, through promoting the general welfare and the common good.

In a second way, various religious people seek to be right with God externally through ritual, by performing various works in response to commandments and carefully selected Bible statements. This mindset rests squarely on a foundation of constantly acquiring knowledge of biblical facts and, through legal and polemical processes, formulating carefully systematized doctrines to obey, as a way to maintain favor with God. Worse, such people presume to possess from within the ability to pull themselves up spiritually by good efforts, especially in an attitude of law keeping which would place God into their debt.

These non-spiritual concepts find their way among God's people when religious leaders oriented to law and works consistently use the Bible to override the flexible, expanding, powerful, oral/written expression of the word of God. Peculiar perception and reverence for law have brought about an ungodly imbalance, demanding that man fit the law. Such an emphasis almost always rose above personal holiness and the practice of morality in common relationships.

In bold contrast, God-fearing, faithful covenanters throughout the ages regard the prophetic and apostolic writings as a teacher containing the revelations of God given for man's guidance. Many first century Jews and Gentiles who ultimately accepted Jesus as God's Christ possessed in their hearts a foundation of love and faithfulness upon which to build authentic faith in heavenly things. These covenant people of peace and godly disposition are represented in the figures of Paul's olive tree (Rom. 11:15f) and John's heavenly woman (Rev. 12:lf) as developed in Chapter Six. Their faithfulness insured that the God of heaven would always continue to own a people, who are called a kingdom, a called out assembly, a family of God, and a holy nation.

FISHING BOATS AT TIBERIUS

Chapter Five

The Primacy
of Covenant

VARIOUS RELIGIOUS THINKERS see as many as seven distinct
and often unrelated covenants, expressed in scripture between God and man. Some of these are the Abrahamic,
Davidic, and the old and new covenants. Contrary to such
notions, this chapter and those following develop a doctrine of
one eternal/everlasting covenant for God's people, initiated
with the patriarch Abraham and extending to the present and
into the future, forever and ever. This peace treaty rests squarely
upon God's timeless moral law, also called natural law.

The eternal covenant shows an uninterrupted continuum
of firm relationships between God and His people through all
man-devised "dispensations" – Patriarchal, Mosaic and Christian. Certainly this everlasting covenant has undergone changes
and renewal, in the same way that the moon passes through its
various monthly phases. Whether it is the quarter, half, full, or
new moon, it is always the same eternal moon, as embedded
in Hebrew thought. It is thus with the eternal covenant, as in
the following chart:

God's Everlasting/Eternal Covenant with Man:

Abraham   **Moses**   **David**

★ *Genesis 17:7, 13, 19 (see I Chron. 16:15)* ─────────────────────────────

Everlasting covenant described generally in land and redemption promises, with few details. There is no specific

★ *Psalm 105:8-10 [see: 11-45]; (comp. I Chron. 16:17)* ─────────
Everlasting covenant visible in Ten Commandments to Israel, in
18:19) land promise, etc. Promises made to Abraham renewed,
of priests (Ex. 19:5-6).

★ *II Samuel 23:5; I Chronicles*
**Through David's seed would
kingdom (II Sam. 7:11-17) in
crowned in Psalm 2:8-9;
Abraham and/or Moses,
salvation retained in his**

NOTE: Three, and perhaps four, stages of everlasting covenant are found in I Chronicles 16:15-17;
Jeremiah 32:36-40; Ezekiel 37:15-27. The "old
covenant" is not old in the sense of inferior or
wanting. The new covenant of Hebrews 8:8f is
not different from or superior to any previous
historic stages of covenantal development. Because of a realized Christ, the eternal covenant
now is better in every way.

The Plan of Redemption Unfolded

The Prophets	Jesus Christ

Galatians

mention of the law in heart, or of a new spirit; there is no mention of Christ ruling over an eternal kingdom.

Romans

the covenant of everlasting pristhood (Num. 25:13), and in ceremonial laws, (Lev. 24:8; Num. extended, enlarged upon, made fuller, in lovingkindness (Ex. 20:6, 34:6), through a kingdom

16:15-17 ———————————————————————— Acts, Hebrews

come the Anointed One (Psa. 2:2), Israel's salvation, ruling over an everlasting righteousness, mercy, and faithfulness (Psa. 89:1-4, 14, 28-37; 132:11-18), and 110:1-6. Covenantal development now more specific, better, than at the time of legitimately "new." David's kingdom (nation of Israel) would end, yet promise of family (I Chron. 17:11-27), through the everlasting covenant.

★ *Jeremiah 31:31, 32:40, 50:5* ———————————— Hebrews
★ *Ezekiel 16:60, 37:26; Isaiah 54:10, 55:3, 61:8*
Jeremiah 31:31-34 describes the everlasting "new covenant" with the law in the heart. Idols are removed as Judah returns from Babylonian exile with a new spirit/heart. Sins are not remembered as Jews are cleansed/washed in a renewed relationship with God. Everlasting covenant (Psa. 111:5,9; comp. I Chron. 16:15-17, written at this time) ultimately to be enlarged upon in the Christian era with the prophetic "David" (Christ) ruling over righteous hearts in the eternal kingdom, which would be renewed and consummated as shown in Acts I.

        ★ *Hebrews 8:8f, 13:20; Luke 1:72-73*
        Luke describes the eternal holy covenant, about to be gloriously fulfilled and renewed in Christ (1:32-33, 54-55, 72-73), reaching its final inevitable development, which would include the Gentiles (Heb. 8:6-10, 18). "New" also because of ultimate passing of tutorial types and shadows and Moses' ceremonial duties and sacrifices. Christ restored and reaffirmed all terms of eternal covenant in ways far beyond Abraham or any renewal under Moses, David, or the later prophets.

As shown by the preceding chart, from the time of Abraham through Moses, David, and the prophets, the eternal covenant evolved toward its fuller and more complete and glorious state under Jesus Christ, in which there is the ultimate forgiveness of sins because of His perfect sacrifice (Heb. 10:1-10). In this grand fulfillment, all things are thus made "new." Christ is the better mediator, far surpassing anyone else.

The eternal covenant in the first century is not described as *different*, for all people of faith from Genesis to the generation of Christ and the apostles and beyond were saved precisely alike, by the grace of God through a living faith in His ever-lasting (Gen. 17:7-19), holy (Dan. 11:30), confirmed (Dan. 9:27) covenant of peace (Isa. 54:10; Ezek. 34:25, 37:26; Heb. 13:20a).

It was originally made with the distant Hebrew fathers (I Chron. 16:16, Luke 1:55, 73), then renewed among chosen people during the time of Moses (Psa. 105:10), David (Psa. 89:34), and the prophets (Isa. 55:3, Jer. 32:40, Ezek. 37:26), and now to all the nations under Yahweh, where the everlasting covenant under Christ has been made "new" and "better," (Heb. 8:6-13). But every essential term of the agreement is as old as the promise to Abraham, and its benefits, including the reality of present salvation and acceptability before God, have remained constant.

Many important biblical concepts are spoken of as "old" and "new," evidently to heighten and bring attention to the idea of renewal in continuity. In John 13:34-35, Jesus gave His disciples a new commandment to "love one another," even though such an order had been around since ancient times, hence is an *old* one (See Lev. 19:18). Late in the first century, the apostle John declared that "I am writing a new command-ment" (I John 2:7-8, II John 5) in a context of loving and not hating one's brother, and abiding in the word they had already received. John himself was the first one to say that what he had set forth was *not* new (v. 7); commentator R. C. H. Lenski says that John was writing nothing different.

John's use of the word "new" draws special focus upon love and other subjects at hand, calling them commandments which are at once "old" and "new." As in John 13:34-35, Jesus elevates love to a loftier standard, a higher motive; followers of Christ may be assured that they are walking in the light by keeping these "old" commandments which have become "new." In the same manner, the everlasting covenant functioning in Old Testament times is legitimately described as "new" in the present era, even though it had undergone advances and changes from the time of Abraham through renewals to Israel in the days of Moses, David, and the prophets.

Revelation 21:5 states that in the New Jerusalem all things were being made new. No matter in what "all things" consist – whether the people of God, a new song (Rev. 14:3, 5:9), a new man (Eph. 4:24, Col. 3:10), and heaven itself (Rev. 21:1) – they are not new in the sense of never having existed before. Rather, the newness of "all things" now has been restored, renewed, and made new again (see Chapter Ten). Such concepts as "new moon" (as presented above), the "new creation in Christ" (II Cor. 5:17), new heart and new spirit (Ezek. 18:31, 36:26) similarly convey the idea of renewal, even as the Lord's compassion is made over every morning – renewed and refashioned (Lam. 3:23).

One Eternal Covenant Throughout Time

God's gracious, saving relationship with His people has always been within the context of the everlasting covenant, sealed by the blood of the One who has entered the holy place (Heb. 13:20, 10:29), and binding the two parties together by grace through faith. It needs no other sacrifice nor intercession, for all covenant people are equipped with everything good, so that we may do His will and be pleasing to Christ.

In this way, salvation is absolutely assured and is a present reality, for God seals us in and by the covenant. Earthly forces cannot take this relationship from us; no, not civil government, other powers, or any created being can separate us from God (see Rom. 8:35-39). Only our personal renunciation of the Lord or our continual willful sinning disrupts our standing before the Father. By virtue of this covenant relationship, all sins we commit are covered – continuously cleansed, forgiven, and forgotten. We are saved!

Continuity of covenant is a unifying Bible doctrine. The promises and the oath God made with Abraham and Jacob were renewed under Moses, David and the prophets, finding their complete fulfillment in Jesus Christ. The God who pardons iniquity and delights in forgiveness (Mic. 7:18-19; see also Ex. 34:6-7, Neh. 9:17b, 9:32), renewed to His people Israel what He had sworn to the fathers from the days of old (v. 20). At the dawn of the era of Christ, Zechariah prophesied significantly that God had shown mercy toward our fathers as he admonished the people to remember His holy covenant, the oath which he swore to Abraham, our father . . . (Luke 1:67; see also I Chron. 16:16).

Note that according to Micah and Zechariah the covenant was an *oath* made to Abraham and to Jacob. In numerous places Moses inextricably bound the patriarchs in covenant with the Israelites after the events at Sinai. In Deuteronomy alone are more than forty "our father" passages, viz. "Go . . . possess the land which Jehovah swore unto your fathers . . ." And who were these fathers? Deuteronomy 1:8, 6:10 and many other scriptures identify them as not only Israelites in Egypt but also Abraham, Isaac, and Jacob, for they are expressly named. Thus, the covenant enjoyed by Abraham, Moses, and the people at the time of Christ is the same agreement, the same peace treaty. It is the eternal agreement spoken of first by Abraham (Gen. 17:7-19), by several other holy men throughout the ages, including King David, Isaiah, Jeremiah, Ezekiel, and finally by the writer of Hebrews at the beginning of the Christian era (Heb. 13:20; see also Luke 1:67-75)

King David's last words thoroughly intertwine the covenantal promise made to Abraham, Israel (Moses), David, and fulfilled in Jesus Christ. He fully realized that salvation would not come through any member of his immediate household (II Sam. 23:5a), but only through a future King who would preside over an everlasting kingdom (II Sam. 7:11-14), not bound by geography or time. In his next breath David declared that God had made with him an everlasting covenant (II Sam. 23:5b), an agreement which would benefit all of Israel (v. 3).

This truth is also emphatically taught in I Chronicles 16:7f, a passage which describes the eternal agreement as flowing from Abraham through Isaac to Israel (vv. 16-17). In verse 15, David admonished all to "remember His [God's] covenant, the word which He commanded to a thousand generations," expressing a concept of very long duration. It was the agreement made with Abraham, Isaac, and Jacob – an everlasting covenant for Israel (v. 17; see also Psa. 105:8-15). Thus, salvation was securely vested in this eternal covenant which began with Abraham (v. 16) and endured through David, finding glorious fulfillment in Christ (II Sam. 7:11-14), the King over the ideal kingdom that would last forever.

Ezekiel 37 – Jeremiah 33

Ezekiel 37:15-27 binds the Jewish and the New Testament eras under the same covenant, culminating with God's promise that He "will make a covenant of peace with them (Israel and Judah united] . . . It shall be an everlasting covenant with them . . ." (v. 26; see also Ezek. 34:25). Further, "David [Jesus Christ] shall be king over them . . . David my servant shall be their prince forever" (37:24a-25b).

Between these passages, God promised the reunited nation that they would "dwell in the land that I had given unto Jacob my servant, wherein your fathers dwelt, and they shall dwell therein . . ." (v. 25a). This restoration of farms and villages took place in about 536 B.C., after the 50-year Babylonian captivity, when the Jews reclaimed their former land. It was a promise sandwiched between the renewal of David [Jesus] as their king (v. 24) and the fulfillment in Christ of the everlasting peace covenant (v. 26). The people of Moses would then become the people of Christ.

Jeremiah 33:14-26 also spoke of the Branch unto David, who, as in Ezekiel, is Jesus Christ. Jeremiah promised that there would be no lack of a man to sit on David's throne (v. 21), or a covenant day and night (v. 20) which would never fade. This is the very covenant that was made with Abraham, Isaac, and Jacob (v. 26), the same gracious agreement between God and all of His people in all "dispensations" of time. Jeremiah introduced all of these concepts in such a way that, as in Ezekiel, it is impossible to isolate a distinct "old covenant" from a "new covenant." Rather, both Jeremiah and Ezekiel showed a continuity of covenant people throughout time. Those whom God has joined together, let no man put asunder!

The eternal covenant mentioned by David, Jeremiah, and Ezekiel inextricably binds all of God's chosen people in one gracious saving agreement, whether they lived before or after the cross, and makes them into one body of called-out people, one *ekklesia*, one family, one house, one flock of God, one kingdom under one law, one Zion! (Heb. 12:22f), one city of God (v. 23), one Israel, one olive tree (Rom. 11), one heavenly woman (Rev. 12), and one beautiful bride of Christ (Eph. 5:23f, Rev. 19:7f), even as the Jews were in the Old Testament God's wife of old. In the consummation all will live in one location – the New Jerusalem (Rev. 21-22).

All who possess Abraham as their spiritual father, whether circumcised or uncircumcised in the flesh, comprise a common priesthood of believers (Ex. 19:6, I Pet. 2:9), one holy nation, one elect race, one community of the saved, and one perfected spiritual group in covenant with Yahweh. All enjoy God's loving care in His one plan or way of redemption, and are saved in precisely the same manner – by grace through a living and abiding faith (Eph. 2:9, 4:4).

God has harvested these people of faith – Abraham's seed – into a common granary holding His people, both the Jews of old and the people of Christ. All of these saints benefit from the one promise, first given to Abraham and made good in Christ (Rom. 9:8, 15:8; II Cor. 1:20; Acts 13:32), a promise inseparable from the gospel. All are equal partakers of spiritual things, especially in the one hope of the one resurrection taught by both the prophets and the apostles (Acts 26:22-23, 24:14-15). The continuity of the eternal covenant enjoyed by all of these faithful is, therefore, the backbone to which all other Bible truths and commandments are appended. It is indeed the gospel itself, for God entering into covenantal union with man is exceedingly good news!

One Spiritual Assembly
One Group – One Body – Throughout Time

The continuity of God's covenant people throughout the ages is heightened by the events of the Pentecost of Acts 2, when about 3000 faithful, repentant Jews learned of the gospel of Christ. These first respondents to the preaching of the resurrected Christ were described as being "added to the church" (KJV) or *ekklesia*, or more properly, as in virtually all Greek texts, "added unto them" (Acts 2:47). Unto whom? The Lord did not add something to nothing, some people to no people. The Pentecostians therefore joined John the Baptist's disciples, Jesus' 120 close followers (Acts 1:15), and an indeterminable number of faithful, devout covenant Jews and Gentile proselytes (I Peter 1:1) scattered throughout the Roman Empire (Acts 13:16, 26, 50; 16:14; 17:4, 17; 18:7).

Pentecost, together with the resurrection of Christ only days earlier, represented a milestone in God's dealing with man, a watershed in covenant history, for thereafter God's redeemed body of saints had Christ as head forever. In earlier times God, as the Rock of Israel, had ruled a covenant assembly of people who followed Him even in the wilderness (see Acts 7:38). These same faithful abide in the eternal kingdom which, according to prophecy (Dan. 2:44), would be "set up" forever, without end, during the period of time surrounding that same Pentecost, with Jesus the new foundation stone or corner stone.

The phrase "set up" does not necessarily mean establish as a *beginning* point, any more than Jesus' statement "upon this rock I will build my church" (Matt. 16:18) announced that this church-body would be some future institution to appear as something entirely new. These elect of God date from Genesis, for it was then that God began to gather faithful people into a spiritual assembly, and also ruling as King in their hearts.

Rather, Matthew 16:18 conveys the idea that "upon this rock [the revelation of Jesus as Messiah] my people will stand," evidently a renewal of the oft-repeated, long-established covenantal expression, "I will be their God and they shall be my people." These saints of God were built upon the promised foundation of Jesus the Christ, and on the ruins of spiritually decadent formal Judaism which, by the early first century, had splintered into carnal sects, each burdened by human law-making, embodied in numerous traditions. But a legitimate Messiah-oriented remnant of believers was always in place, for Jehovah as King was never without a kingdom, and as Head of an assembly of believers He was never without a called-out body of faithful people (as God pointed out to a despondent Elijah in the wilderness).

The future tense of Matthew 16:18, "I will build my church," should be understood in the same sense as Luke's statement, "I appoint unto you a kingdom . . ." (22:29). Both were already in existence before headship had been given to Christ. In the phrase "Ask of me and I will give thee the nations for thine inheritance . . ." (Psa. 2:8), God spoke while relinquishing Headship and Kingship to the Son, thus initiating the reign of Yahweh's anointed after His resurrection (v. 8b).

Building a renewed people of God on a sin-filled failed

economy is a common theme in the prophets. God promised Amos that, in the day of Messiah, He would raise up the fallen tabernacle and dwelling of David. " . . . And I will build again the ruins thereof and I will set it up as in the days of old" (Amos 9:11b). At the Jerusalem conference James quoted this statement and applied it to the time when Gentiles would be called into the covenant family of God in this era after the cross (Acts 15:16-17).

Jeremiah spoke of God painstakingly destroying the nation of Judah, yet He would carefully build it up after the Babylonian captivity: "The days are coming . . . when I will plant . . ." (31:27-28). Note the similarity of the construction in this verse with Matthew 16:18: "I will build . . ." The fortunes of Judah's captives would be reversed after being in exile: "I will build them up and not tear them down; and I will plant them and not pluck them up" (24:6). "I *will build* thee [a remnant]" is recorded at 33:7 and 31:4, though it was *already* in existence (see 31:7, 43:5, 44:28; see also Isa. 46:3; Ezek. 5:10, etc.). Additionally, Luke 2:34 declared that Jesus was set for the falling and the rising of many in Israel.

F. F. Bruce sees the called-out people as existing throughout history. "If the church excludes Abraham [as if from another "dispensation"], we should be well advised to look at our definition [of the church] again and see what is wrong with it." Bruce sees a vital continuity between God's people before and after Christ. "But after His coming the people of God underwent a fresh beginning by dying with Him and rising with Him to new life, hence the future tense [of Matt. 16:18] ' I will build.'" God had "built again" Israel several times in their 2000 year history, both before and especially after the giving of the law at Sinai, considering each occurrence a "new beginning" for His chosen.

Indeed, Abraham heads up a people consisting of both Jews and Gentiles who have faith in God of the quality Abraham possessed. Abraham had the gospel preached to him (Gal. 3:8; see also Heb. 4:2). He believed God and it was counted to him for righteousness (Gen. 15:6). He received the promises and rejoiced over the day of Christ (John 8:56). In 1887 B. W. Newton pointedly asked, "Are we to say that Abraham hath the promises and yet that the chiefest results of those promises he hath not? Are we to say that Abraham belongs to that heavenly city whose maker and builder is God . . . and yet that he hath not the blessings which pertain to that city?" Abraham is therefore the father of the faithful.

In view of evidence in scripture and the testimony of religious scholars, Matthew 16:18 is best understood as "upon this rock (Christ) I will *continue* to build my assembly," my people. After the apostles began preaching the gospel of Christ, the fragmented congregation of Israel would become the called out body of Christ, as good-hearted Jews embraced Jesus as Lord and responded to God through their repentance and baptism. The stony hearts of many Jews etched in sin (Jer 17:1) would now be softened to allow the renewed covenant law of God to be written thereon. Within that same generation, myriads of Gentiles would join these Jews in Christ's body and kingdom as unified, justified saints following God.

Continuity of Covenant in Jewish Hope and Promise

Nathan's significant prophecy concerning the House of David, as recorded in II Samuel 7:11-17, restated God's covenantal dealings with man, which date from the time of Abraham. Since this prophecy also looked forward nearly ten centuries to the era of Christ, and the further development of His kingdom, II Samuel 7 demonstrates the continuity of covenantal promises throughout God's dealings with Abraham, David, and Christ.

The prophet disclosed that through David the God of heaven would establish "the throne of His kingdom forever" (v. 13). David's seed (progeny) would bring forth the anointed One

(Psa. 2:2). This seed, which was first mentioned in Genesis 3:15 and spoken of by Abraham, would establish His rule just before the Pentecost of Acts 2 over a kingdom that would have no end (v. 16). Between these marvelous promises are statements of further covenantal bonding: "I will be his father and He shall be my son . . . God will not take His steadfast love (*chesed*, or lovingkindness or mercy) from Him" – that is, Jesus (vv. 14-15).

A parallel to II Samuel 7, Psalm 89 declares that God had made a covenant with His chosen, King David (vv. 4, 20). In faithfulness, mercy, and lovingkindness (vv. 1-3), God would make David's seed, the Christ, reign forever (v. 36). Nothing that Israel might do would stop this kingdom (reign) from coming to pass; all eyes in the coming generations would focus on this Seed and His dynasty.

This promise of God's absolute, immovable, unchangeable faithfulness to His covenant would supremely comfort Israel. God's manifold mercies and lovingkindness would thus never depart from His people. This covenant sworn by God's holiness (v. 35) would endure as long as the created world would last (vv. 36-37), just as the sun, moon, and other celestial witnesses are described as being established forever. None of these would ever be desecrated.

In I Chronicles 17:11-27, an ecstatic King David could hardly contain himself over the prophetic reality that through him would come the One who would in time establish an everlasting kingdom (vv. 12, 14), secured by the terms of God's covenantal oath: "I will be his father and he shall be my son" and "I will not take my lovingkindness away from him [David]." He would be bone of his bone and flesh of his flesh and, simultaneously, a descendant of the God of heaven.

This wonderful covenantal promise constantly occupied David's meditation and thought, as he wrote nearly a score of Psalms which specifically declare God's lovingkindness, precious relationship with Israel, and mercies extended toward His people. All of David's descendants relied on these comforting words while focusing their hope on the Seed (Christ), ruling a kingdom from His heavenly throne (vv. 17, 23).

David's salvation resided in this everlasting covenant (II Sam. 23:5), which would have its glorious inevitable fulfillment realized through Yahweh's "anointed" (Psa. 2:2), the Christ. In Psalm 110, David looked ahead ten centuries to the crowning of this One as the King of Righteousness (see also Psa. 2:8), ruler over a universal eternal spiritual kingdom, Zion. Verses 1-4 describe how God would give this dominion to the future King: "The Lord (Yahweh) said to my Lord (*Adonai*) Sit on my right hand until I make thine enemies thy footstool . . . Rule thou in the midst of thine enemies . . . Thou art a priest forever after the order of Melchizedek . . ."

That the coming Messiah would reign from God's right hand denotes great favor (see also Matt. 26:64; Heb. 1:3, 8:1). His royal rule over the hearts of covenant people began with His teaching before the first Pentecost after His ascension (Acts 2:22-36), through God installing Jesus as both priest and king forever (Psa. 110:4, II Sam.7:12-15) with an oath that was of equal force to the covenant when it was first made with Abraham (Gen. 15:9-18).

Among those who lived after David were many godly prophets who, during the time of the divided kingdom, further developed the truth of the son of David sitting upon his throne. Jeremiah 23:5-8 spoke of Judah and Israel renewed under divine rule which Zechariah said would extend from sea to sea (9:10). Hosea placed the time of this rule in the "latter days," in this case the first century Christian era (3:5, see also 1:11). Micah concurred (4:3), while Amos prophesied of the renewed tabernacle of David which James of Jerusalem applied to his day, the mid-first century (Acts 15:13-18). Jeremiah 33:15-18 and Ezekiel 34:20-24 (and 37:24-27) identify "David" (or Christ) as the Shepherd who would reign forever over a universal kingdom (see also Dan. 2:44 and 7:14).

Isaiah especially foretold of this particular Seed of David's family, who would be born of a virgin and reign forever over the House of David (7:14). The prophet further defined this eternal rule which is upheld with justice and righteousness (9:6, 7b; comp. with II Sam. 7:13-17). As the Root of Jesse, He came with a spirit of wisdom and understanding (11:2) to break into pieces the nations (v. 4; see also Rev. 1:5, 12:5). Isaiah 11:6f describes the peaceful nature of the remnant of grace (v. 11) under the Root (Christ), who would establish His eternal reign over a spiritual kingdom (vv. 12-16), from the throne of David (9:7).

This point was precisely the one in David's Second Psalm which prophesied of the Anointed One (v. 2c) who has a divine relationship (begettal) with God (v. 7c; see also II Sam. 7:12f). His worldwide rule from Yahweh's throne in spiritual Zion (v. 6a) would be over an everlasting kingdom (v. 7b). All would recognize this Messiah when various kings and religious rulers would reject His authority by plotting against Him, as did Herod and Pontius Pilate (Acts 4:25-27) and the Pharisees (Matt. 21:33-44).

But God would laugh at such puny plans (Psa. 2:4), keeping His covenant with man by installing Christ on His throne, where He would, as the Son, rule forever – an unmistakable sign of covenant (v. 7a). His universal dominion would be over all nations (v. 8), ruling them with a rod of iron, smashing them decisively in judgment as if they were mere clay pots (Rev. 1:5, 2:27, 12:5, 19:15-16). Coincidentally, His spiritual rule would be over a multitude of joyous covenanted ones, as He bathes them with continuous protection and every kind of blessing. Here was God's faithful promise of mercy (*chesed*) to the covenant faithful in the house of David.

Just months before the birth of Jesus (Luke 1:27f), the angel Gabriel appeared to Mary, restating the many marvelous covenantal promises given to David concerning the anointed One and reporting that all was about to be fulfilled in Jesus. Gabriel declared that "He will be great, and will be called the Son of the Most High, and the Lord God will give Him the throne of His father David; and He will reign over the house of Jacob forever, and His kingdom will have no end" (vv. 32-33).

In this declaration, God was keeping His word to Israel's covenant remnant. The One born of Mary and a descendant of David would be given "dominion, and glory, and a kingdom" everlasting (Dan. 7:14) to be "set up" or established in the latter days (Dan. 2:44). Christ acquired this kingship from God (see below); it was an everlasting kingdom, bringing the sure blessings of Abraham. At the same time, Zechariah, the father of John the Baptist, prophesied that God was now visiting His people Israel, keeping His covenant word made with an oath to the fathers (Luke 1:72-73). This oath, first sworn to Abraham and renewed in David, was about to be fulfilled in Jesus in a glorious unfolding of the "knowledge of salvation," by the forgiveness of sins (v. 77).

Thus, throughout the centuries of Old Testament times, God had this special mission among the people of Abraham, but not all of them, for only through one of His descendants, Israel, did God extend the formal covenant. Further, the nation was carrying the Seed who would satisfy everything which holy men of old had been saying about Christ's rule over the eternal kingdom. Various prophets taught that out of Israel a remnant would remain faithful to God and preserve the seed, the lineage of Abraham (Isa. 11:11; Ezek. 37:21f; Jer. 23:5-38, 30:9-10; see also post-exilic prophets). And so, God had been protecting His pregnant bride, the covenant remnant which is graphically revealed as a heavenly woman in travail in Revelation 12:1-6.

By the time of the Pentecost of Acts 2, Jesus, the Seed of Abraham, already had initiated His spiritual reign over a people of faith whom Paul later called the seed (sons) of Abraham (Gal. 3:29). John referred to these blessed people as the progeny of the heavenly covenant woman (Rev. 12:17). Such a designation had nothing to do with being a Jewish blood descendant of Abraham. Instead, the word "seed" referred strictly to born-again covenant ones, each of whom possessed the faith of Abraham.

Just as Abraham believed and it was accounted to him for righteousness, the covenant people of God today are blessed in the same way with a right standing before God based on faith. All have the gospel (Gal. 3:8) and enjoy a gracious saving relationship, demonstrating covenant in continuity with God.

Peter's sermon on Pentecost (Acts 2:22-36) announced again the crowning of King Jesus on His throne in heaven, exactly as foretold by David a millennium before (Psa. 2, 110). Evidently, God had kept His word that through a covenant oath to the family of David a particular Descendant would reign forever over the house of Israel. This holy one would not be held down by His crucifixion (vv. 23, 27, 32) but would, through His resurrection (being raised up by God), demonstrate His ascension to the throne of David at the right hand of God, the coronation (*not* the inauguration) of Christ's reign in heaven.

After all, King David of old did not ascend into heaven at any time, "for his sepulchre is with us to this day" (v. 29), but he anticipated the victorious One who would prevail against earthly rulers who had gathered against Him (Psa. 2:2). A few days after Pentecost, Peter and John openly declared that Jesus had overcome Pilate and Herod and other enemies (Acts 4:25-27). In doing so, David's words of Psalm 2:1-2 had been fulfilled in those very recent events involving the Anointed One, Christ, in the city of Jerusalem. Even in crucifying Him, they failed to get rid of Him.

In verse 36, Peter reached a conclusion. Because Jesus had been exalted to God's right hand and had received David's ancient promise of Psalm 2, the whole house of Israel could know assuredly that God has declared Jesus of Nazareth both Lord and Christ, fulfilling every hope and promise of Him held by holy men of old.

Here is the climax of long-anticipated covenantal blessings. The focus is on Israel only. Because they had rejected their Prophet, they are called to repentance. Those baptized would receive the Holy Spirit (v. 38) according to the Abrahamic promise (v. 39), which would extend to their children also. The 3000 or so respondents comprised a restored people of God, part of a body *already* having universal character, inasmuch as it included Jews from at least 15 nations from throughout the Diaspora (Acts 2:5-13, I Pet. 1:1). God indeed was keeping His covenantal oath made with Abraham, that through his seed all nations would be blessed.

Thus, in Acts 2:37, the Jews in Peter's audience were not asking about salvation, but rather what they should do about the fact that they participated in crucifying the Messiah. Far from being totally out of favor with God, these devout of Israel and spiritual brothers of Peter (vv. 5, 22, 29, 37) were the pick of God's covenant people at that time. Nevertheless, they needed to turn from their sin and be baptized, so that they would *continue* to enjoy the covenantal blessings. In a sense, Peter's Pentecostal baptism was an extension of John the Baptist's baptism even unto remission of sins – a call to repentance and an occasion for covenant renewal.

Christ's divine right to give the Holy Spirit on earth was a sure sign that the kingdom promise made to Abraham and David had indeed been fulfilled – that He would reign forever over covenant people from throughout the earthly nations in righteousness, joy, and peace in the Holy Spirit (Rom. 14:17). Further, each of those 3000 Jews who became part of God's renewed reign on Pentecost, and others who would follow them (Acts 2:47, etc.), comprise a covenant house of living stones which, nearly 2000 years later, is still being built. All who are a part of Christ's spiritual dwelling await the final return of Christ, and the glorious consummation of the kingdom.

Many days thereafter, Peter preached another sermon which climaxed with the assurance that all who identified with Christ would participate in the "times of refreshment from the presence of the Lord ..." (Acts 3:19). This period of revival or "time of restoration" (v. 21) was something about which God had spoken through His prophets from ancient times.

These renewed people of God all benefited from the everlasting covenant which God had given to the Jewish fathers, saying to Abraham, "And in your seed shall all the families of the earth be blessed" (v. 25). Over the next several weeks, numerous other Jews renewed their participation in the Abrahamic blessings by responding to the gospel of Christ (Acts 4:4, 5:14).

Evidently, visible religious "authority" over Israel was quickly passing from institutional Judaism's Sanhedrin to the apostles, who since Pentecost had begun to participate in a spiritual reign from Jerusalem over the restored twelve tribes but also ultimately over the Gentiles, a people who were more than artificially connected with Abraham. In fact, they were the logical extension of God's blessings promised to the ancients from Abraham onward. Thus, believing Jews and Gentiles this side of the cross together made up Israel as part of the covenanted people of God in continuity throughout the ages.

Years later in a synagogue in Antioch, Paul preached the good news that God had fulfilled the promise made to Abraham, Isaac, and other fathers, as well as Moses, David, and later prophets about the resurrected Jesus (Acts 13:33–34). As Peter did on Pentecost, Paul referred to David who underwent decay, and to Jesus who did not. Through Him the apostle could proclaim the forgiveness of sins through faith. Those submitting to Christ share in a covenant with Old Testament people and enjoy the sure blessings of lovingkindness (*chesed*), as did David. Here is a clear demonstration of Jesus reigning as King over His kingdom.

Before King Agrippa, Paul declared that he was on trial because of the promise of the resurrection made by God to the fathers, "something which our twelve tribes hope to attain" (Acts 26:6–7). The apostle was defending himself on the basis of the blessing of Abraham and the resurrection of Jesus from the dead (v. 8; see also 24:21). These things brought the promise and coming of the Holy Spirit.

Paul told the Galatians that Jesus put away any curse "in order that in Christ Jesus the blessing of Abraham might come to the Gentiles, so that we might receive the promise of the Holy Spirit by faith" (Gal. 3:14). As the Anointed One, Jesus was worthy to be the covenant Redeemer and sit on David's throne over the everlasting kingdom, because He had emerged victorious from the dead.

And so, through prophetic utterances of old, and their fulfillment in the events surrounding the resurrection of Jesus Christ and Pentecost, and for at least a generation afterward, there is a continuity of God's unfailing promise and His mercies incorporated into the everlasting covenant. The Messiah would reign from His heavenly throne over an everlasting kingdom, embracing also four millennia of covenant faithful, extending from the family of Abraham into the era of Christ. All of these people of God comprise one body and one kingdom. In particular, II Samuel 7 and Psalm 89 are a marvelous reaffirmation to David of bold promises made earlier to Abraham that God would fulfill all truths promised to His people, establishing divine rule over righteous people through the resurrected Christ.

Since these matters of covenant which extend from Abraham past the time of Christ to the present are so harmoniously intertwined, it serves no useful purpose to separate them into old covenant and new covenants, indicating a total passing away of an old order (and law system) in favor of inaugurating another. Rather, throughout the ages, there is one eternal covenant wherein the first century era of preaching was the time of the blooming spring flower which for many centuries before had been a life-containing bulb embedded in the soil of Jewish covenant faithful.

The writings left behind by the prophets and the apostles disclose one glorious unfolding of God's plan of redemption – the revelation of His grace and blessing – to receptive hearts who have made peace with God by entering into covenant with Him. There are not two peoples of God, Israel under an old covenant governed by the law of Moses, and Christ's church or *ekklesia*, said to be under a different law. Rather than replace or otherwise do away with the truths taught by the prophets of

Israel (Matt. 5:17-18) Jesus Christ came to fulfill and amplify them, to give them the full substance and meaning.

As the ruling King over one holy nation, Christ is ever building for the Father a spiritual house whose foundation, Jesus Christ (I Cor. 3:11) was laid by the apostles and the prophets and He Himself now the cornerstone (Eph. 2:20-22, I Pet. 2:5-6). It consists of the one body of God's people who have served him on either side of the cross. Thus, continuity is the essential element of covenant, instead of a contrast of agreements between God and His people of old, and, after Christ came, between Him and the people of the way – Christians.

Continuity of Covenant Among the Church Fathers

When many of the early church fathers fused the teaching of the apostles and the prophets, they indirectly demonstrated continuity of covenant. Early leaders among the saints in Christ appealed to Old Testament books as the background for church order and mission and especially as a predictive witness to Jesus of Nazareth as the long-awaited Christ. The moral precepts embodied in Moses and the prophets served as the authoritative standard of Christian faith and life.

In his treatise *To the Philippians*, Polycarp, in about AD 140, saw the prophets as inseparable from the apostles: "Let us then serve Him . . . as did the apostles who brought us the gospel, and the prophets who foretold the coming of the Lord" (6:3). The dean of early church fathers, Irenaeus, concurs, proclaiming a three-fold source of authority for the church when he wrote in about AD 180: "The Lord doth testify, as the apostles confess, and as the prophets announce . . ." (*Against Heresies* 3.17.4). In that same work he contended for the unity of the Old Testament and the as yet uncanonized New Testament, in a relationship he saw as progressive development in moral education.

Clement's late-first century *I Clement* drives home with

Old Testament citations almost every point of faith and morals to Christians. The author of II Peter elevates Paul's corpus of epistles to the status enjoyed by Old Testament writings (3:15-16). The *Epistle of Barnabas* (dated variously from about 98-125) rests its entire case for the validity of the entire Christian faith on Jewish writings.

The unknown author of *II Clement* acknowledged as authoritative the Jewish scriptures and the "books of the apostles" (in oral and written tradition), further noting that the "church is not of the present" (that is, in about the year 130), but had existed "from the beginning" (14:2; see also 2:4 and Gen. 2:24). Ptolemy's letter to Flora (AD 160) appeals to the integrity of both the Jewish scriptures and the "words of the Saviour" (3:6).

In *I Apology* 67, Justin Martyr noted that a mid-second century assembly of believers featured both a reading of the apostles' memoirs (the gospel of Christ) and the writings of the prophets. In about the year 190, Clement of Alexandria saw in the canon or "rule of faith" a harmony between the law and the prophets (scripture) on one hand, and the "apostles, the unwritten rendering handed down to us" on the other, (*Stromata* 6.15). Early in the third century, the prolific Tertullian noted that the church drinks its faith from the law and the prophets, united with the writings of the apostles and evangelists (*Prescription Against Heretics*, 36).

The heretic Marcion in about AD 140 expressly rejected the authority of the Jewish prophets by promulgating a fixed list of Christian documents, specifically ten writings of Paul and portions of Luke, viewing them as something quite distinct from Moses and his law. Among early church leaders he perhaps stood alone, for almost all other fathers liberally borrowed from the God-centered writings of Isaiah, Jeremiah, and others among the prophetic band for teaching on faith and morals.

Not until AD 180-200 did these Christian fathers in their noncanonical writings do much quoting from the present New Testament scriptures, for until that time the exclusive sources of church doctrine and practice came from apostolic oral tradition and the writings left by Moses and the Jewish prophets.

Language resembling the two covenant theory appears in the *Epistle of Barnabas*. While arguing for the abolition of Jewish sacrifices, the author saw a "new law of our Lord Jesus Christ," further described as a "human oblation" – a dedication of man himself to God (Ch. 2). From the context, his use of law has absolutely nothing to do with a structured doctrinal system, as developed by Christians a century later.

The author of *Barnabas* further stated that the broken Mosaic covenant allowed the "covenant of the beloved Jesus" to enter our hearts, though this phrase does not imply a separate Christian "new covenant" (Ch. 4). In context, the author quoted material in Ezekiel 16, 36, statements fulfilled in the Jews' return from Babylonian captivity (see Chapter Ten), and applied it to the era of Christ, thus actually showing continuity of covenant. *Barnabas* chapter six significantly states that God's people this side of the cross have been "refashioned" – renewed and recreated – in the "good land of milk and honey," imagery borrowed from Moses. Thus made perfect, the people of Christ are "heirs of *the* covenant of our Lord" (Ch. 6).

Stated another way, the author of *Barnabas* believed that "the covenant belongs to us [Christians] and not to them [the institutionalized Jews]" a teaching parroted by Justin Martyr in about AD 160 (*Dialogue with Trypho*, Chs. 10–12, 67, 118). In chapters 122–123, Justin identifies this "new covenant" through metonymy as Christ, precisely as Isaiah had done (42:6, 49:8).

In writing about an old law given at Horeb and an eternal and final law – namely, Christ – given to Christians, Justin became the first church father to make such a contrast. But as with the author of the *Epistle of Barnabas*, law to Justin was not at all a legal system of rules, for he also personified Christ as the "new law" (*Dialogue*, Ch. 11). Further, he saw in Jesus' teaching in the Sermon on the Mount an ethic of universal validity, in accord with the covenant Jewish religion, but freed from the shackles of its ceremonial laws (*Dialogue*, Ch. 14).

Finally, it was bishop Irenaeus of Gaul in AD 180 – nearly 150 years after the cross – who clearly taught that there was an old covenant and its law, under which the Jews lived, contrasting it with a Christian new covenant of liberty (*Against Heresies*, Book 4, 9:1-3, 33:14, 34:3-4). The latter canceled the statues and judgments peculiar to Moses, but even Irenaeus, who believed that the Decalogue had never been blotted out (4.16.5), declared that "such noble and natural laws common to all were increased and widened by Christ."

Irenaeus' understanding saw currency in the northwestern part of the Roman Empire around AD 200. In North Africa shortly thereafter, Tertullian cited Jeremiah's famous promise of a new covenant in 31:31-34 as a present one of mercy and peace, against the "temporary" law and covenant of the Jews (*Answer to the Jews*, Ch. 3). Evidently, these leaders among the later second and third century hierarchal institutional church could not separate the spiritual term "covenant" from a *legal* frame of reference.

But throughout the eastern Roman Empire, the legalistic teaching did not surface. In fact, Clement of Alexandria specifically saw an inextricable relationship between the concepts of one covenant, salvation, and unity: "For, in truth, the covenant of *salvation*, reaching down to us from the foundation of the world, through different generations and times, is *one*, though conceived as different in respect of gift. For it follows that there is *one* unchangeable gift of *salvation* given by *one God*, through *one Lord*, benefiting in many ways. For which cause, the middle wall which separated the Greek from the Jew is taken away, in order that there might be a peculiar people. And so both meet in the *one unity* of faith; and the selection out of both is one" [emphasis supplied] (*Stromata*, Book 6:13; see also 7:17).

Origen, in his *Commentary on Matthew*, also said it well, declaring in about AD 300 that all of the sacred writings were in fact one book, "one perfect and harmonized instrument of God" (Book 2; see also his *Commentary on John* 5.4). It was the person of Christ, according to Origen, who was the key to the unity of scripture – the Old and New Testaments.

Summary

The continuity of the eternal/everlasting covenant from Abraham through Moses, David, the era of the prophets, and the Christian age is amply shown in such passages as II Samuel 7:11-14, Ezekiel 37:15-27, and Jeremiah 33:14-26. These and other Jewish prophets intertwined God's gracious, saving agreements throughout the ages, effectively placing all of God's covenanted ones in one spiritual body or *ekklesia* throughout time.

The varied descriptions of covenant were part of the larger messianic expectation that burned within the bosom of Israel. This hope, and the many other promises made to its prophets which were fulfilled in the apostolic era, further demonstrated covenant in continuity among all of God's children. In fact, the early church fathers for the first 150 years after the cross understood the concept of continuity as something which began even before the era of the prophets, and did not teach that a new-in-kind covenant had been established with Christ's death. The Christian people of God are therefore a *continuation* of the faithful of Israel through covenant renewal.

And a great sign appeared
in heaven, a woman clothed
with the sun ... and on her head
was a crown of twelve stars ...

Chapter Six

New Testament Figures Denoting Continuity of Covenant

IN ADDITION TO specific Old Testament scriptures which show covenant in continuity throughout the traditional "dispensations" – Patriarchal, Mosaic, and Christian (as shown in Chapter Five), the apostles Paul and John, after the cross, employed two striking figures, in Romans 11 and Revelation 12 respectively, to show that the people of God have enjoyed the blessings of the same eternal covenant throughout time.

The Olive Tree of Romans 11

In Romans 11:13-24, the apostle Paul introduced the lofty concept of the domestic olive tree to symbolize covenant people from the time of Abraham to the Christian era. In the days of Abraham, God had planted the true green olive tree with its smooth gray branches, representing God's beloved Israel (Jer. 11:16-17; see also Psa. 52:8). The olive tree has stood for prosperity in the Lord since the time divine blessings had been given to Abraham, Isaac, Jacob and his sons. These individuals (first fruits), the root of the salvation tree (Rom. 11:16), held in place the essential trunk and its many branches.

After those days God still nurtured His people, comforting and cultivating them in lovingkindness. Believing Jews were natural branches because they had made peace with God in the covenant God initiated with Abraham and extended to Moses and David. To carry out God's promised blessings to all people through the Christ, God had chosen the Jewish family (Rom. 9:4-5, Eph. 2:12) to be "heirs of *the* covenant" (Acts 3:25) and "sons of *the* kingdom" (Matt. 8:11-12).

Whenever apostasy set in among the Jewish people, God pruned the unbelievers; they never participated in the ongoing spiritual blessings that culminated in Christ. This amazing tree of saved people embraced all of the faithful among the generations from Abraham to the time of the Christ. Meanwhile, a nearby wild olive tree represented the Gentiles.

At the onset of Jesus' mission, the trunk and the branches of the domestic olive still stood for saved, covenant Jews, though the book of Acts shows that the long-despised, unpruned wild Gentile branches ultimately would be grafted into the covenant tree according to promise. All faithful people would then be sustained by the Jewish root of the domesticated tree, even those Gentiles subsisting before the cross on the wild olive tree.

Throughout the New Testament era, Jews and Gentile branches thrived side by side in fruitful unity. To both groups and with equal force, Paul developed the marvelous illustration of the true olive tree to show that there has been continuity among God's covenant children throughout time.

Since the root of the tree (the family of Abraham) prospered by faith, then the natural branches – covenant Jewish descendants over the centuries and the grafted-in Gentiles from the first century onward – would also be accepted before God through faith (Rom. 11:16, 24). God's grace saves all of the redeemed, past and present, precisely in the same way in the eternal covenant. All are consecrated before the Father, as shown in the companion illustration of the baker's flour which, if pure, would result in an acceptable finished loaf of similar quality (v. 16a).

By the time of Christ, the olive tree had lost much of its size and had become less productive. Untold numbers of Jewish people had turned from God's ways, and He had to cut them off because of unbelief (v. 17a). The process of the stone builder's rejection of the head cornerstone had begun to take place (Matt. 21:42-44). In their stead, sometime after AD 33, God would ingraft wild olive shoots, Gentiles who would enter the covenant through Christ. He made them joint partakers with believing Jews (from the contemporary back to Abraham) of all the privileges of God's eternal covenant, symbolized by the domestic tree.

These two together ultimately comprised one invigorated body, one called-out group faithful to Christ, one people sharing in the same fatness (fruit) of the covenant tree. What a marvelous concept! Since all of these children of God sprang from a Jewish root, Jews and Gentiles share Christ's eternal life in common and are organically one. Thus, the domestic olive tree shows that all those good-hearted covenant people, who put their trust in God and His Christ are saved and gathered into a spiritual corporate whole, the one body. This tree of salvation is evidently not bound by geographical or temporal limitations. To partake of the tree's blessings, all man needs to do is take God at His word, trust Him, and accept the place He offers to everyone in the eternal covenant.

To such a display of God's grace and His election, covenant Gentiles offer faith with gratitude and a sense of awe. Their grafting into the tree did not call for pride on their part but for a certain wholesome fear. Nevertheless, the ingrafted Gentiles invigorated the long standing Jewish olive tree, influencing it positively, just as ancient farmers spliced young branches into an old tree to bring it renewed life.

But God's mercy and grace did not stop with these faithful

covenanters. The fallen Jewish branches strewn about the great tree could be restored. Through covenant renewal, these obstinate unbelievers could be grafted back into the parent stem and be incorporated afresh, to serve God in a new spirit when joined to Christ, once again becoming an essential part of the whole.

The root was the source of all blessings. Since God provided the tree's nourishment and cultivated it, insuring its fruitfulness, it is His cash crop (compare with John 15:1-8). Covenant relationship by attachment to the tree was not at all by works or merit, but by the grace of God (Eph. 2:8-9). Apostasy was a reality, and Jew and Gentile alike were cut from the salvation tree for unbelief and continual rejection of God and His ways. But all covenant people who sincerely follow the Lord to the best of their ability, and according to their current understanding of truth, will never be cast out (John 6:37).

All of God's chosen since the call of Abraham (Gen. 12-15-17) continually abide in God's goodness, favor and lovingkindness (*chesed*), a term which can describe a relationship between parties in a covenant. As demonstrated in the metaphor of olive trees, domestic for the Jew and wild for the Gentile, God has sustained all the faithful, in due time combining the faithful branches of the two onto one tree, bringing long-desired peace and maturity among God's people.

The Mystery of Christ

The beneficial amalgamation of God's covenant people in unity, clearly foretold by various Jewish prophets, became a confirmed reality under Christ in the generation after Pentecost as a "mystery" being revealed (Rom. 11:25, 16:25). The mystery became known when the Gentiles became covenant people of God with the Jews. It was hidden to covenant people of old, even though the prophets had searched diligently for such blessings (I Pet. 1:10).

Before the coming of Christ, Jews and Gentiles were two

distinct groups. Peculiar Jewish ordinances and sacrifices functioned like a twentieth century Berlin Wall separating covenant Israel from the Gentiles round about. In this way, God kept the Jewish nation pure and distinct, so that the promised Seed (Christ) should come untainted (Gal. 3:15-22). But the mission of Christ was also to break down the middle wall of partition and do away with separation between Jew and Gentile, so that "all may be sons of God by faith in Christ Jesus" (Gal. 3:26-28).

A major part of God's eternal purpose was this gathering together of two groups to create one covenant man, thus making peace in a joint assembly of Jew and Gentile, so that they all may be fellow-heirs in one body, all partaking of Christ's promises. Salvation would be for all people through belief in and union with Christ. Everyone thus saved would be in one body (Eph. 4:4), an assembly which reflected the manifold wisdom of God (3:10).

Now under a single Head (Eph. 1:10), both Jews and Gentiles would be united forever, partaking of the covenantal blessings that Israel of old had uniquely enjoyed. All received citizenship in Israel, and could rejoice in the same hope (Eph. 2:12, 4:4b). Because of the gospel of Christ, Gentiles could also enter the eternal covenant and become heirs *together* with longstanding Israel, members *together* of one body, sharing *together* in the promise in Christ Jesus (Eph. 3:6). The threefold stress of "together" originates from a common Greek stem, further accentuating the equality of Jewish and Gentile people of God.

Paul's use of "mystery" in Romans and Ephesians therefore refers to the fellowship of covenant peoples from all nations in one spiritual group (Gal. 3:28). Two previously separated segments of the human race are reconciled by the cross, made into an organic whole; Jew-Gentile differences are therefore forever abolished in and through union with Christ. Now they are in the same body (Eph. 3:6), not one "church" or called-out people consisting of Jews and another of Gentiles, not two separate people with different destinies, but one (I Cor. 12:12–13, Eph. 2:14–15), realized through the cross (v. 16).

The Perfect – The Mature – *To Teleion*

Paul's famous phrase, "When that which is perfect has come, that which is imperfect will be done away . . ." (I Cor. 13:10) has been the touchstone of much speculative discussion centering upon the word perfect (Greek *teleios*), which is variously translated "completeness," "fullness," or "maturity." Contemporary charismatics associate the coming of the perfect with the "second coming of Christ," arguing that tongues and other gifts will always be available to God's people until that time. Answering simply, the perfect cannot refer to Christ or any other person, because *to teleion* is singular in number and neuter in gender.

A second view assumes that God gave various gifts of the Spirit to confirm the delivering of the complete revelation of facts and doctrines which ultimately were embodied in the 27 books of the New Testament. After God's entire revelation had been set forth and the last epistle was written early in the second century, it is argued that charismatic gifts were then no longer necessary and "done away" (v. 8b). The various gifts, it is reasoned, served the same purpose that scaffolding accomplishes for a building under construction: when it is finished, the scaffold becomes superfluous and is torn down. Thus the gifts allegedly ceased, along with the offices (works) of apostle and prophet.

This theory suffers because it imposes a meaning on *teleios* that is not justified by the context of love in I Corinthians 13. Paul could not have had the spiritual gifts themselves in mind in the "perfect" *(teleion)*. Otherwise, the apostle is saying that his own gifts of knowledge and prophecy were inadequate. Such could not be. Further, neither first century revelations to various churches and saints, nor knowledge itself, is under consideration, because a person could have a pattern of spiritual truths, facts and biblical doctrines committed to memory and still not "know fully even as I have known" (v. 12).

Except for an all-knowing authoritarian, who would dare to assert that anyone, then or now, can know fully? Could any mid-first century Corinthian conceivably have understood that "the perfect" might be referring to a written, collated body of knowledge and instruction in righteous living, as embodied in histories and epistles which, not until late in the *fourth* century, would finally be assembled into a closed canon of scripture, the modern New Testament? Was Paul *really* trying to convey this notion? Therefore, neither a collection of Christian writings nor their initial revelation in the first century has contextual support in "the perfect." Actually, such a theory has its roots in institutional religion.

I Corinthians 13 does teach that spiritual gifts would at some time come to an end, but that love would continue. A comparison of "that which is perfect" (v. 10) with the "perfect manhood" *(to teleion)* of Ephesians 4:12-16 provides a vital clue to understanding this much-abused passage. In both instances, "perfect" carries the idea of attaining a certain end, or becoming finished, mature, reaching a full age. Further, the context of Ephesians 4 is unity and the context of I Corinthians 13 is love.

Tying it all together, "the perfect" best refers to people coming together in mature loving unity. The process of gathering all of God's elect finally came to pass, *teleios*, when in the AD 60's both Jews and Gentiles were firmly entrenched in the body of Christ, growing side by side as branches on the olive tree, so that all of God's covenant ones would be forever fused in one body. Paul's measurement of the fullness of Christ in Ephesians 1-4 in a perfect man (4:13) coincides with his man/body illustration in I Corinthians 12:12-27 and 13:10-12. Each passage culminates in *teleios*.

John McRay in *Restoration Quarterly* conclusively shows that *teleios*, though translated "perfect" in I Corinthians 13:10

and "mature" in Ephesians 4:12, refers precisely to the same situation. Note the development of Paul's thought in each instance, as evident in the following chart adapted from McRay:

I Corinthians 12–14		Ephesians 4:7–16
Gentiles 12:2; Greeks 12:13, 2:11	– 1 –	Jew–Gentile discussion 3:1, 4:17, (22)
"All in all" 12:6, 12	– 2 –	Emphasis on "all" 4:6
Emphasis on "one, one and the same" giver of the gifts, 12:4, 8 same Spirit 12:5 same Lord 12:6 same God, 12:9, 11, 12, 13 one spirit, 12:12 one body	– 3 –	Emphasis on "oneness and unity" 4:4-6, 2:16ff 4:2 unity of Spirit 4:5 one Lord, 4:6 one God 2:18 one Spirit, 4:4, 2:16 one body
DIVINE GIFTS 12:4 to 14:40 To pass away, 13:10 Cease when perfect comes 13:10 Then have completed knowledge [about love]. 13:10-12	– 4 –	DIVINE GIFTS 4:7-8, 11 To be done away 4:13 End when come to the unity of the faith 4:13 Then have completed knowledge [about perfect] 4:13
Human body Illustration 12:12-13, 14ff.	– 5 –	Human body Illustration [of unity] 4:12-16
Paul's growth illustrates Corinthian's progress, 13:11	– 6 –	Human growth illustrates progress of spiritual body, the church 4:13-16
Teleios 13:10	– 7 –	*Teleios* 4:13
The body a child before fulfillment 13:11	– 8 –	The body a child before fulfillment 4:14
The body a mature man when divine gifts ceased 13:11	– 9 –	The body a mature man when divine gifts ceased 4:13

This perfection and maturation of faith in the much desired unity of Jews and Gentiles in one spiritual body was a prominent part of first century apostolic preaching and teaching, as a natural response to the Jewish prophets. Isaiah foretold of the Gentiles' inclusion in God's spiritual house (11:10-16); Paul said that such promises to the fathers were being fulfilled in his time (Rom. 15:9-12; see also Acts 15:14-18, 13:47, etc.). Ephesians 3-4 illustrates how God planned to bring salvation to the Gentiles, add them to the one eternal covenant body, metaphorically one new man designated mature, or *teleios* (v. 13).

To assist in bringing the Jew and Gentile together in the salvation tree of Romans 11, God gave Jewish saints of the mid-first century charismatic gifts (Acts 2, etc.); Gentiles received similar favors (I Cor. 13:8-12). The generation of God's covenant people which experienced these charismata was the first one to participate in the unity of the long-estranged Gentile and Jew under Christ in a *teleios* (complete) body.

The bringing together of Jew and Gentile in one location also seems to be Paul's point of the gathering in II Thessalonians 2:1; it is an event that would take place just prior to the "coming" of Jesus Christ in judgment against the "man of lawlessness" (v. 3) and the Jewish nation in AD 70. This gathering had nothing to do with various city churches or *ekklesiai* (though the "bringing together" likely does in Hebrews 10:25). It is rather the empire-wide call of Jews out of Talmudism and the Gentiles from the worldly society to become one people – a spiritual assemblage of God's elect into a holy nation, transcending time and geography.

Thus, it was the mid-first century saints who first saw the realization of "that which is perfect" (I Cor. 13:10), the reaching of the "mature man" (Eph. 4:13). Forevermore, there would never again be separate Jew and Gentile groups, for they would be indistinguishable in a relationship with Christ Jesus (Gal. 3:28, see also I Thess. 4:17); they were identical olive branches (Rom. 11:13-24). All of these things were adequately fulfilled in the concluding stages of Paul's ministry, and in short time (probably around AD 300-325), charismatic gifts and attesting miracles among the saints faded away.

Jewish-Gentile maturity and completeness is further exemplified in the great mid-first century contribution which was gathered by poverty-stricken Gentiles in Christ to benefit equally poor Jewish saints in Jerusalem (I Cor. 16:1-4, II Cor. 8-9, Rom. 15:25, Acts 24:17). In a year-long campaign, Gentiles built a bridge to Messianic Jews by giving materially to those who had spiritually benefited the Gentiles.

Ever since Pentecost they had potentially been partaking of the fatness of the cultivated olive tree, whose root and trunk were the Jews. Truly, Gentiles were greatly enriched by Jewish spiritual things (Rom. 15:27). Thus, they gladly offered physical goods to their Judean brethren. Such interaction constituted a closure of Paul's ministry in the eastern Mediterranean, enabling him to minister to Rome late in his life.

The successful completion of this contribution campaign (Rom. 15:25) significantly indicated that *to teleion* had indeed arrived, that Gentiles were now firmly included with the sons of Israel in covenant with God as equal branches on the salvation olive tree. The long sought after end, the unity and maturity of faith of both Jew and Gentile, had come to pass.

God's covenant people throughout the nations would be forever together enjoying a common salvation and life, continually nurtured in relationship with Christ. All of these godly people followed the eternal principles of the moral law and embraced truth as they had opportunity to learn it and follow it, never conscientiously rejecting it. Truly, just people increase their love for God as they live by faith; they strive to please Him by doing His will, never denying His name.

The Heavenly Woman of Revelation 12

The symbol-laden book of Revelation, written late in the first century to inform God's people of things "shortly to come to pass" (1:1), is filled with metaphors and dramatic figurative language. As the flow of events as recorded in Chapters 4 through 19 unfold, the author in Chapter 12, interjects a magnificent celestial figure: a "great mysterious sight," a pure, light-bearing woman dressed with the radiance of the sun. The moon was her footstool and atop her head of flowing hair was a garland of twelve stars, a victory crown symbolic of the twelve tribes of Israel.

This high metaphor stands for a lofty spiritual concept, one which transcends time and space. Since the woman was in labor with the man-child, Jesus (v. 2), she had to exist before the time Jesus was born. Evidently, the woman in travail represents the totality of Jewish believers of many centuries ardently longing for the promised Redeemer. She is Israel, of whom "according to the flesh Christ came, who is over all, God blessed forever" (Rom. 9:5).

These Old Testament believers are the very people who were pregnant with messianic hope and anticipation, as reflected in their moral living and teaching. The woman is God's body of the Jewish faithful, bearing light to a sin-darkened Jewish nation caught up in religious parties, tradition (Matt. 15:9), and priestly institutional corruption (see Chapter Four).

This gloriously arrayed, majestic woman in pain signifies a visible manifestation of a spiritual reality, namely the existence of innumerable covenant people of God throughout the Old Testament era. John's powerful celestial figure adequately represents this body of faithful Jewish saints, Zion. Attempts to single out specific meanings of the various symbols embodied in the figure of the heavenly woman only detracts from the magnificent historical and spiritual concept that John is trying to portray.

Throughout Revelation 12, the author introduced imagery and symbolism very familiar to readers of their ancient scrolls. In 600 B.C., Jeremiah characterized contemporary Judah as a woman (2:32); Hosea spoke likewise of Israel (2:2-23), as did Micah (4:10, 5:2-3) and Isaiah (50:1, 54:1-3, 66:7). To describe

God's Jewish spiritual covenant remnant, the apostle John borrowed this prophetic imagery which delivered to the world the man-child, the Christ, in about 4 B.C.(Rev. 12:5).

After His earthly mission ended, the heavenly woman through spiritual metamorphosis soon came to represent baptized Jew and Gentile believers following the resurrected Christ, the renewed people of God (vv. 13-17). Even after flying away to a place of God's protection (vv. 6, 14), the woman bore other offspring, those who followed the commandments of Christ (v. 17),

In historical context, the redeemed woman therefore stands for true-to-God covenant people of Israel extending back to Abraham, Isaac, and Jacob (see Ezek. 37:15-28, Jer. 33:14-18, Mic. 7:18-19, Luke 1:67-73, etc.). In her are a "cloud of witnesses" (Heb. 12:1) – Moses, Joshua, David, Isaiah, Jeremiah, Hosea, other faithful mentioned in Hebrews 11, as well as numerous other saints of previous centuries.

After the prophets had finished their work in about 400 B.C., the covenant woman continued to be a light and truth bearer to the world. She embodied the faithful of God, especially in the House (family) of David during the late Jewish period after the Babylonian captivity and living before the birth of Christ. God-loving, pious Jews who served Him faithfully lived throughout the Roman Empire and in Judea, although rank legalism was very well entrenched in the visible law-conscious parties bound by structure and tradition.

Against this backdrop of spiritual decadence of Roman immorality and corrupt institutional Jewish religion, the messianic community, in the fullness of time, appeared at the dawn of the first century at center stage of history as a radiant woman in travail, pregnant with the One who would rule the nations with a rod of iron (Rev. 12:5, Psa. 2:9). Through various discourses, parables, and repentance-centered teaching, Jesus the Christ prepared the Jewish covenant remnant for life under His kingship.

On the morning of that great and memorable Pentecost of

Acts 2, the glorious heavenly woman – the people and Israel of God – consisted of righteous, devout (v. 5), faithful covenant Jews from scattered localities throughout the Mediterranean (vv. 8-11). They had come to Jerusalem on an extended sojourn to worship the best they knew how, pleasing God by celebrating the days of the unleavened bread and the festival of Pentecost.

These active God-seekers kept the moral law and, to the best of their ability, adhered to the sacrifices and precepts of Moses' teaching. This body of sanctified ones, as expressed metaphorically in the apocalyptic woman, had for centuries earnestly sought the Messiah, whose blood, as part of His perfect sacrifice, would once for all blot out their transgressions. But all the while as justified saints, they had been declared by God as legally righteous ones, and thus freed from their sins, even though they could only offer up as a remembrance of their imperfect "IOU's," various animal sacrifices (Heb. 10:3-4, 9:19-25). Such expressions of worship demonstrate that those faith-filled Jews of good heart only wished to love and serve their Lord with reverence and awe. Clearly, then, God had a saved body of people in place on that Pentecost morning, and Peter positively called them the "house of Israel" (Acts 2:36).

Significantly, on that day of beginning (Acts 11:15), the Holy Spirit manifested Himself, fulfilling marvelous prophetic utterances. Joel 2:28-32 foretold a time of tumultuous change when God's spirit would go far beyond the temple and the children of Israel – in fact to "all flesh" which finally included the Gentiles. Isaiah predicted that instruction would flow from Jerusalem, and people from all nations would be drawn to the Lord (2:2-5), while Daniel promised that in the days of the worldwide [Roman] empire the God of Heaven would set up an everlasting kingdom (2:44, 7:14).

On Pentecost day, Peter preached for the first time to his audience of Jews and proselytes the exceedingly good news of a resurrected Christ, climaxing with the admonition to "repent and be baptized" (Acts 2:38). Now the woman of

Revelation 12 would experience significant change as about 3000 of those Jewish faithful readily accepted the truth that Jesus was the Christ of God, by responding affirmatively to Peter's command. They would be the first fruit of the new (renewed) people of God now under Jesus as the Messiah-King, in accordance with what the prophets had said (Zech. 6:12-13; Daniel 2:44, 7:14). Within the next generation, tens of thousands of individual Jews, embodied in the heavenly woman, would pass from being the faithful under Moses to being renewed believers under Christ.

As that Pentecost day ended, the salvation woman of Revelation 12 consisted of the same people as in the morning, only now about 3000 of those Jews had renewed their covenant pledge to God by being baptized into Christ. Thereafter, day by day, the composition of the heavenly woman continued to change, as God added others to those first fruits – "those who were being saved" (Acts 2:47) – a continuous process.

By the time of Acts 4:4, another 5000 believers among Moses' called out ones had entered the reign of Christ as subjects in God's renewed kingdom. Acts 5:14 records that multitudes of "believers in the Lord" were continually being added to the number already in submission to Christ. As God's people were thus being perfected, the covenant woman continued to experience internal change.

The spiritual advance of God's righteous woman continued when Jesus' disciples scattered far beyond Jerusalem (Acts 8:1-4). In Samaria many Jews still following Moses' law experienced renewal by responding to Christ's good news (vv. 12-13). The Ethiopian treasurer and Saul of Tarsus each underwent a spiritual renewal which culminated in baptism (Acts 8:30-39, 9:10-18). Though these events took place about three years after Pentecost, the heavenly woman consisted of essentially the same saved believers in God.

Now thousands of them were also joined to Christ (Rom. 7:1-7) and enjoying His blessings, yet untold numbers of pious Jews from throughout the Mediterranean, who knew only

Moses and the prophets and were faithfully living in covenant, were still part of the heavenly woman. They likewise continually enjoyed God's protection and salvation in their present truth, despite never being exposed to the teaching of Christ, much less being obedient to it.

Even into Acts 13-19, during the time of Paul's missionary journeys into the Grecian world, the radiant woman continued in spiritual transformation as each Jew looked beyond his respective local synagogue to the universal assembly (synagogue) of Christ. Within that same generation the metamorphosis of the woman had run its course; the gospel had been preached to Jews throughout the known world (Col. 1:23).

Those righteous ones, accepted of God and loyal to the prophets, had become the faithful covenant people of Christ under the apostles. Only such a powerful metaphor as the heavenly woman could forcefully and adequately express this continual renewal of God-fearing covenant Jews over nearly two score years of dynamic change. After all, the woman was not an institution apart from people, nor was she a mere moral force. What a marvelous concept!

This advance of the Jews, from a moral people steadfastly following Moses and the ceremonies of the law to a renewed people under Jesus Christ, essentially had been completed by the time fleshly Judaism, with its institutions and priesthood, was shaken by the destruction of Jerusalem in AD 70. During the previous generation, there had been a continuity of salvation enjoyed by God's faithful Jews on earth.

In fact, it makes mockery of God as a gracious, loving father to conclude that, on the day of Pentecost of Acts 2, all practicing, God-fearing Jews throughout the Roman Empire suddenly had their covenant status voided, their peace treaty with Heaven abrogated. Such a foolish contention kills the woman of Revelation 12, and demolishes the olive tree of Romans 11, rendering these figures meaningless. At no time has the Father treated devout, God-pleasing children like that!

The figure of the victorious woman confirms that all loyal, pious Jews (Acts 2:5, 8:2, 13:50, etc.) contemporary with the apostles and their preaching (Acts 2-20) continually remained in a positive relationship with God in His *ekklesia* as people who did not dwell in spiritual darkness. As they accepted the gospel of Christ, they enhanced their right standing as God's people, renewing their peace treaty with God through a greater understanding of Heaven's redemptive work than ever before. Now they had the fullness of God's revelation and will through the good news of Christ, as displayed in the apostles' teaching.

Countless faithful Jews living throughout the Roman world readily accepted additional truths when they were exposed to them. They never denied the gospel or anything virtuous. Most important of all, as they moved from Moses to embrace Christ, they firmly remained the *ekklesia* basking in God's world of light. None mystically experienced instant spiritual death after Peter had completed the first gospel sermon in Jerusalem in Acts 2. Nor did the woman in Revelation 12 ever die, for she escaped to a prepared place, a promise God made to His disciples (John 14:1-6). In Galatians 4:26, Paul described these very faithful ones as " . . . Jerusalem, which is above, which is the mother of us all."

An untold number of Jews throughout the Roman Empire were represented by this covenant woman, and were protected by God, continuing in good faith as best they knew, given their honest understanding of God's will and purposes. Further, the "certain disciples" at Ephesus of Acts 19:1, who knew only the baptism of John, also were part of the woman, enjoying salvation and God's assurances. No evidence exists to remotely suggest that any of these sincere, virtuous truth-seekers ever experienced spiritual peril. The God of equity and justice safeguards His own and never asks for the impossible of anyone who truly trusts and loves Him and tries to serve Him with the whole heart.

But the imagery of the first century heavenly woman ultimately embraced more than descendants of Israel. Formerly despised Gentiles would now join the renewed Jews in the woman figure, in a marvelous display of unity of all of God's elect in every nation. After Pentecost, the woman's offspring also included those who "keep the commandments of God and hold to the testimony of Jesus" (Rev. 12:17). Here was the fulfillment of the prophets' long-desired goal. God kept His promise to unite all people who seek and serve Him, both then and in all future generations.

God's plan of redeeming man was now perfected. Faithful Jews before and after the cross were embodied in the heavenly woman; Paul's olive tree illustration referred to these same people as the tree's parent stem and its natural branches. God has protected His woman and olive tree, His covenant redeemed, throughout time and regardless of national residence. The woman also had other seed (Rev. 12:17); Paul described them in Romans 11:12-13, 22-24 as obedient Gentiles, branches grafted into the trunk where they became equal partakers of the fat root of the tree of Israel. They are the "remnant according the election of grace" (11:15). John's and Paul's scriptural figures denoting God's faithful coincide perfectly.

The God of grace safeguards His own. In steadfast love He prunes the tree and cultivates it, constantly nourishing it (see John 15:1-8). He is always mindful of the covenant woman, goodness and faithfulness personified. But evil soon appeared in the moral arena. When a huge fiery-red dragon tried to devour the man-child (see Matt. 2:lf, 4:lf, 16:21) and actively persecuted the celestial woman and her seed (Rev. 12:4), God furnished immediate protection (vv. 5-6). These redeemed ones, both Jew and Gentile in one body, were united and spiritually secure, not only in the imagery of the revelator's woman and in Paul's olive tree but also in the word *teleios* (I Cor. 13:10, Eph. 4:13). This term stands for the mature or complete man in Christ in marvelous unity and fullness.

Other Scripture Concepts Showing
Continuity of Covenant

The above material shows that the one olive tree of Romans 11 symbolizes the people of Christ grafted into messianic Israel, and that the apocalyptic woman of Revelation 12 also bridges all of God's elect, before and after the cross. Several other concepts also show the continuity of God's everlasting covenant, among them the New Jerusalem, the temple of God, the remnant people, and the flock of God.

John the revelator described in great detail the one city of New Jerusalem, wherein all of God's elect would dwell in covenant unity, a promise that awaits future fulfillment (Rev. 21:3f). The gates to the heavenly community are inscribed with the names of the twelve tribes of the sons of Israel, and its foundations bear the twelve names of the apostles of the Lamb (vv. 12-14), indicating amalgamation of the apostles and the prophets. Verse three repeats the oft-stated ancient covenantal promise that God will dwell with man and they shall be His people.

Paul spoke of God's spiritual temple as including all people of faith. Jewish and Gentile children of God are in this holy building (Eph. 2:19-21), whose interior contains the Spirit of God (v. 22). Here all of God's saints throughout the Christian era are united under one head, Jesus Christ (1:10), brought together as fellow heirs through His cross (2:16, 3:6).

Throughout the biblical eras, there is one common remnant concept. In the first century, disciples of Christ are called the faithful remnant of Israel (Rom. 11:5), a people of God spiritually united with the Jewish covenant remnant frequently mentioned by several of the prophets of old (Ezra 9:13-15; Neh. 1:3, 8-10; Hag. 1:12-2:2, etc.). These teachers refer to the returnees from Babylonian exile as the remnant, as does Isaiah, who prophesied that the faithful of Israel and Judah would return from captivity (10:21). In Chapter 11 Isaiah goes even further, bridging these covenant Jews with people from all the nations, the "second time remnant" in the era of Christ, as confirmed by Paul in Romans 15:12.

All of these godly Jews and Gentiles, whether living before or after the time of Christ, constitute one sheepfold. It was for this purpose that Christ came into the world, namely, to bring all of the sheep together in one location. They all listen to His voice, and there is one flock and one shepherd (John 10:16, see also 11:51-52).

In this marvelous figure of unity, Gentiles of faith are not a different or a separate entity from the covenant remnant of Israel. As Paul forcefully taught, they are engrafted with messianic Israel (Rom. 11:13-24). The Master's last utterances to God focused on this long-desired oneness: "My prayer is . . . that all of them may be one, Father, just as you are in me and I am in you. May they also be in us so that the world may believe that you have sent me" (John 17:20-21).

Summary

The first century people of God, Jews and Gentiles alike, consistently defined themselves as a continuation of the Old Testament faithful and an extension of the Israel of Romans 11:13f. After all, they shared the same spiritual and ethical goals, as they centered their devotion upon Christ.

Gentiles after the cross were wild olive branches grafted into the long existent trunk of firmly established covenant Israel, not a separate tree or people apart from and independent of Moses and the prophets. And messianic Jews after the cross were similarly in renewal, as the woman figure of Revelation 12 dramatically shows, not some separate figure unattached from the saints in their own past. Believing Gentiles became part of the heavenly woman's family as well (Rev. 12:17), joining faithful Jews to make up "all Israel" which will finally be saved (Rom. 11:26).

These two figures, coupled with the *teleios* of Ephesians 4:12 and I Corinthians 13:10, show that the unity which God had always desired for His elect had come to pass. Nevertheless, Jewish followers of Christ freely practiced their Torah with its long-established ceremonial law and held to traditional teachings, the subject of Chapter Eight. However, they were not permitted to demand of the Gentiles any of their distinctive practices. Despite doctrinal differences, the two groups assimilated well into one body. Evidently, unity did not mean that all held to precisely the same teachings and practices, a lesson that every generation dearly needs to learn.

Chapter Seven

〜

From Torah to Christ: The Continuity of Covenantal Concepts

T HE THEOLOGY of the eternal covenant stresses the continuity of God's revelations from Abraham (and even
before) to the time of the apostles and their contemporaries.
Similarly, the consistent development of such vital concepts as
grace, the necessity of heart-obedience, justification, remission of sins, and the covenant meal, show continuity rather
than contrast between the revelations contained in the books
of the Old Testament and the New Testament.

In opposition, all manner of dispensationalists, seeing two,
three, and as many as seven covenants, tend to stress discontinuity of these biblical themes, distinguishing sharply between
the way of the gospel of the present age and other approaches
toward serving God in the time of Abraham, Moses, David,
and the prophets of Israel.

For people of any time and place, a relationship with God
is the basis for acceptability. God was King of the nations (Jer.
10:7) and provided the way of salvation for His covenanted
ones. His son, Jesus, is the current ruling King and Priest.

During the time of the prophets, covenant Israel consisted of a congregation of royal priests under God (Ex. 19:5), while this same Israel in the apostolic era, was an *ekklesia* of royal priests (I Pet. 2:9), an obvious continuity. Israel always consisted of children of God saved by grace through faith.

All of these God-fearers are similarly justified through the righteousness of Christ. They essentially share the same motive for obeying God, for Israel throughout the ages was elected by God, *not* chosen because of personal merit or a claim of heredity (possessing Abraham for a father, John 8:33-42). Throughout its pages the Bible contains systematic statements which describe the process by which covenant Israel continues to be God's elect.

Grace

The traditional belief that a rigid wrath-filled God of Israel became somehow in New Testament times a graceful, loving Father does not hold up under scrutiny. Like the unchangeable Son, the Father is the "same yesterday, today, and forever" (see Heb. 13:8). Indeed, "He changeth not" (Mal. 3:6; see also Psa. 102:27). Similarly, the concept of unmerited divine favor, given for man's benefit, has been the same throughout time.

The word grace (*chen*) appears more than three-score times in the Hebrew scriptures. Additionally, the related attributes of mercy and lovingkindness (*chesed*) are mentioned in more than a few hundred other places. Though lacking a precise English counterpart, *chesed* encompasses God's extension of kindness, mercy, and steadfast love toward His people, resulting in forgiveness (Ex. 20:6). Therefore, the supposedly monopolistic New Testament grace concept is abundantly manifested in the law and the prophets.

In Exodus 34:6, God is described as compassionate and gracious, patient, and abundant in constant, reliable love and fidelity (see also Num. 14:18). These attributes are also variously mentioned in Psalms 86:15, 103:8-11; Joel 2:13; and Nehemiah 9:17b. God will never forget to be gracious (Psa. 77:9-10). The oft-spoken phrase, "May the Lord make His face shine upon you" (Num. 6:25), is followed by "and may He be gracious to you . . ."

References to *chesed* abound in the Psalms. In 69:16, God is described as abundant in great mercy and redeeming love, *chesed* (see also 23:6, 36:5, 57:3, 86:15, and 89:1-2). Divine favor upon faithful people is abundantly shown, as God directly acted in the lives of His own, saving and comforting them, and abundantly filling the needs of the helpless. Therefore, *chesed* is heavily enmeshed in covenant Israelite thought.

The law itself was revealed in grace and truth to God's chosen, even as the Psalmist prayed, "Grant me thy law graciously; I have chosen the way of truth" (119:29-30). Through God's spirit of grace, salvation came upon the faithful of the house of David (Zech. 12:10). As undeserving Old Testament people were delivered and forgiven, divine grace in love was demonstrated. Such abounding favor is ever present for the needy who humbly approach God for help (Prov. 3:34; Matt. 18:4; Eph. 4:2; I Pet. 3:8, 5:5-6).

God extends this lovingkindness (*chesed*) to everyone who respects the covenant, loves him, and keeps His commandments (Deut. 7:9; see also John 14:23). This principle, deeply embedded in Moses' Ten Commandments (see Ex. 20:6), amply demonstrates that God never intended that the covenant relationship with His people in ancient times be a legal one devoid of grace and mercy. Throughout the book of Romans, Paul reiterated those marvelous concepts, declaring that God had "passed over the sins done aforetime, so that He might show His righteousness at the present time . . . There is, therefore, now no condemnation to them that are in Christ Jesus . . . He who loves his neighbor has fulfilled the law . . ." (3:25, 8:1, 13:8). Evidently, the apostle taught the same thing about lovingkindness as did Moses.

God's supreme act of undeserved favor was evident in the

offering of His Son as the redeemer of man (Rom. 3:24) and provider of saving grace (Acts 15:11; see also 18:27b, 20:24b). As shown by the example of Abraham (Rom. 4:1-16), man enters this domain of grace by faith (Rom. 5:1-2), not by perfection. Because of God's favor, Abraham was counted as obedient in advance of the command to circumcise, and before the opportunity to sacrifice his son, Isaac.

Continually, the ancient patriarch's faith was reckoned as righteousness (Gen. 12, 15; Rom. 4:5), and on this same principle God supplies salvation today to every faith-filled person (Eph. 2:8-9). As good hearts throughout the ages accepted this truth, they were assured that past transgressions were forgiven and forgotten, present sins are removed by the continually efficacious blood of Christ, and all future sins will similarly be blotted out. Great is God's goodness and grace!

Heart-Obedience

Various expressions of obedience, in response to God's commands and guidance, offer visible evidence that the man of covenant believes in God. Indeed, works strengthen a loving faith, but do not generate authentic faith. Disobedience is nothing other than faithlessness, an unthinkable alternative. Obedience responds directly to the very essence of a trusting covenantal relationship; it is wholly compatible with Paul's salvation formula: "By grace you are saved through faith . . ." (Eph. 2:8-9).

God-pleasers have had sin cut from their hearts, even as Jeremiah admonished the people of old to "circumcise yourselves to the Lord, and take away the foreskin of your heart . . ." (4:4). This statement echoes Moses' admonition to Israel to "circumcise your hearts . . .and do not be stiffnecked" (Deut. 10:16; see also 30:6). According to Genesis 17:10, physical circumcision was God's appointed sign of the covenant, signifying a commitment to God. It is the Lord's work to "cut around" hearts, or, as stated in covenantal terms, "a new heart I will give you . . ." (Ezek. 36:26). See also Chapter Two.

The apostle Paul explained this circumcision as the doing of the law (Rom. 2:25-29; see Deut. 30:14). Physical circumcision indeed had value to law observers, but when they willfully broke commandments, the people became as if uncircumcised in heart (Rom. 2:25), endangering their covenant status and acceptability before God. Before creation week God knew that man would ultimately break the covenant, so His eternal plan was to send His Son to remove through blood all transgressions, and spare His covenant ones eternal destruction (see Chapter Three).

Thus, if external works are not accompanied by and have not originated in true heart submission, they are not acceptable before the Father (Lev. 26:31b, Jer. 14:12, Amos 5:21). Obedience must originate and consummate in the heart or mind (Deut. 6:5-6, 10:12-13, 11:13, 30:20). Similarly, Paul's use of faith in Romans was equivalent to a respect for law (Rom. 6:17, 1:5); this principle was extended to winning Gentiles to the Lord (16:26).

Whether expressed in Deuteronomy or Romans, obedience embraces trusting faith and love. It is neither meritorious (deserved by performance) nor free from sin. Moses said that God shows lovingkindness (mercy, KJV) to those that love Him and keep His commandments (Deut. 5:10); Jesus repeated the statement to His disciples (John 14:15, 15:10). In Leviticus 18:1-5, God said, "I am Yahweh," and related the giving of the Ten Commandments (Ex. 20:1f). This statement affirms that it was God who saved Israel, delivering them from Egyptian bondage, an event thoroughly associated with grace.

Since the lives of both Abraham and David (as expressed in Rom. 4) were accepted by Heaven despite imperfection, "living by the law," as proclaimed by either Moses or Paul, never required flawless performance. Thus, the Jewish/Christian *ekklesia,* the called-out ones under God, consisted of good-hearted people who fell short of following God's will.

Through the ages, saints trusted in and obeyed a merciful God, who accounted them righteous. Moses said, "and it shall be righteousness unto us, if we observe to do all this commandment before Jehovah our God, as He hath commanded us" (Deut. 6:25). In Romans 10:5, Paul elaborated upon that statement, saying, "For Moses wrote that the man that does righteousness which is of the law shall live thereby" (see also Deut. 30:6-10). Clearly, it is not the keeping of commandments which brings righteousness, but the God who commands. Further, proper love for God is demonstrated through obedience, insofar as commandments are understood, for the covenanter wholeheartedly accepts God's light as it breaks into his life. Such sincere God-seekers hunger and thirst for all of the light they can find, never rejecting truth.

Justification

In response to man's sins and a desire to provide a way of escape from them, God extended to man the eternal covenant, wherein His people are justified, pronounced as righteous (Gen. 15:6). Such a declaration was ultimately made possible by Jesus' "one act of righteousness" on the cross (Rom. 5:18b). Through His blood, sins are forgiven (Rom. 4:6-8); this cleansing of all sin is continually acting upon the people of Christ (I John 1:7). Continued righteousness is made available by God's grace, expressed in Jesus Christ, who "ever makes intercession" for the faithful (Heb. 7:25).

All of the covenanter's hope rests securely upon this rich measure of grace, which discourages a loose attitude toward transgression or laxity in following God's will. Pleasing God never consisted of structuring biblical commandments into a legal code and conforming to it as the *means* of justification. In contrast, the way of the covenant, by grace through faith (Eph. 2:8-9), continually blots out all sin and simultaneously declares that covenanted ones are justified – acquitted and forgiven.

Therefore, God's covenantal plan is diametrically opposed to a right standing before Him on the basis of a works system (Rom. 11:6), for obedience to such structure ultimately breaks down. Not even to Israel of old did God issue laws and declare that the keeping of them was the means of salvation, for in His grace He had *already* blessed them and made them His people. Nevertheless, the law was useful to show genuine believers how to respond to Heaven's grace. Righteous deeds are the *fruit* of salvation and justification, rather then their *cause*.

God's simple declaration that good hearts are justified eliminates the bartering of ritual performance and works to maintain a proper standing before Him. Instead, deeds done in righteousness are loving responses of faithful hearts to Heaven's saving work. Paul clearly taught that God grants the blessing of justification on the basis of faith, "that it may be according to grace" (Rom. 4:15-16). In this way, God's promise to Abraham of a spiritual nation, a body of called-out ones, could be fulfilled (Gen. 15:1-6).

In response, covenanters approach the Father humbly and in full confidence, pleading guilty to sin and throwing themselves upon a merciful God, while asking for pardon. Such an attitude of mind showed godly intent and is inconsistent with ritualistic prayer and deed. Persistence in disobedience violates God's constant demand for holiness on the part of the created. Throughout the ages God has recognized a quality of life in hearts motivated through perfect *intent* to keep His commandments. They have the law and not sin on the heart (comp. Jeremiah 31:33 with 17:1).

Therefore, attempts at self-justification are futile delusory quests, as demonstrated in the vain works of the institutional Jews whom Jesus and Paul frequently encountered (see Chapter Four). On the other hand, proper motivation demonstrates a love of God through a constant desire to put Him first to serve and please Him, denying self (Matt. 16:24). Such an attitude respects the relationship with the covenant-giver, serving Him out of love from a pure heart (I Tim. 1:5). This means addressing the law in the heart, which is the delight of covenant people throughout the ages.

In contrast is the mindset of people such as the rich young ruler, who came before Jesus seeking justification before God on the basis of responding to a structured law system (Matt. 19:16-22). Focusing on performance with a view to earning holiness, or any demonstrative boasting of having no sin (I John 1:8), are characteristics of people who have no realization of their *need* of God's mercy or of being accounted justified before God.

Righteousness

The righteousness of God is another way to express the salvation which God has authored for man, pointing to Heaven's purpose to "put things right" for man, forgiving him. The "righteousness of God," a concept fully in view of the law and the prophets, is available as a free gift to all who genuinely believe in Jesus Christ, regardless of time and place (Rom. 3:21-22).

Righteousness – as justification – derives its meaning from the same Greek root word, *dikaiosis (-une)*, and both are simultaneous in the mind of God, implying a forgiven state. Such a good standing is reckoned to all covenanters in the same sense that sins are not credited. Thus, as God forgives sin (Rom. 4:7), He establishes righteousness in man at the same time. This free gift (Rom. 5:17) is bestowed upon the faithful who trust in Christ's finished work, rather than their own ability to do good works and lead faultless lives.

Multitudes of ancient teachers fully recognized the necessity of trusting in God's righteousness, rather than their own. The psalmist knew that salvation had been bestowed on faithful people, saying, "Rescue me and deliver me in your righteousness. Turn your ear and save me" (71:2). The poet again associated righteousness with salvation in verses 15-16, fully knowing that only God's righteousness was deserving of mention. Thus, he avoided talking about how he might contribute personally to his salvation. See also Psalm 31:1 and Isaiah 42:6.

All New Testament authors also taught that a right relationship with God was not attained by routine obedience to known law or by personal merit; it was by faith in Christ. Paul's statement, "the righteousness out of faith" (Rom. 10:6), harmonizes perfectly with the teaching of Moses about living by the law (v.5), in that the Forgiving One continues to maintain fellowship with imperfect people who follow the law to the best of their ability. The "doing" of the law (v. 5) coincides with the fulfilling of it, as expressed in Romans 2:25-27, wherein righteous acts validated the covenant relationship through the grace of God (see Lev. 18:5, Ex. 34:5-7).

Therefore, authentic righteousness consists of Christ's obedience unto death (Rom. 5:18-19). In fact, we are saved through His life, for He is constantly interceding for us (Rom. 5:10, Heb. 7:25). Christ's voluntary submission as a sacrifice made remission of sins a reality (see Chapter Three). The life of God's appointed Representative made possible a heaven-originated righteousness for every covenanter as a free gift; it is attained by faith through the mercy of God.

This union with Christ is a present, continuous relationship, something not based on personal righteousness or performance (Phil. 3:9), but that which is through faith in Christ (Rom. 1:17, 3:21-22). Through Him who knew no personal sin, but was "made to be sin" (II Cor. 5:21) – treated as a sinner and punished in man's place – covenanters now clothed in the righteousness of God enjoy every spiritual blessing, especially the comfort of realized salvation. How good is our righteous God!

Remission of Sins

Central to the covenant with God is the promise of remission of sins. Such a comforting benefit is a restatement of salvation, a present favorable status before God, and an obvious connection with divine righteousness. The psalmists of old realized that their good standing before God came because of divine love (6:4, 109:26, 119:41), as did Isaiah (47:17-18). Such teaching was continued by the apostles and evangelists of Christ (John 3:16, I John 4:9-10, Rom. 5:8, etc.).

God has always spoken plainly of the full reality of the covering of sin. David confidently knew that God forgave him of his iniquities (Psa. 103:3, Psa. 51:4-10; II Sam. 12:13). Isaiah promised the penitent that, though their sins were as scarlet, they would be washed whiter than snow (1:18), a·statement that compares with Ananias' admonition to Paul to "arise and be baptized and wash away your sins" (Acts 22:16).

Indeed, the law of Moses created an understanding of the need for forgiveness: "through the commandment, sin might become exceedingly sinful" (Rom. 7:13). The law was like a servant which brought man to a consciousness of the necessity of maintaining a relationship with Him. Though God-fearers of old recognized the inadequacy of animal sacrifices to remove sin (Heb. 9:13), these worshipers confidently knew that God was working in and among them to remove the guilt of transgression, and that, indeed, a purifying was continually taking place in response to unfailing divine promises (v. 14).

Forgiveness was realized by thoughtful covenanters who made the sacrifices according to the law, "sin-offerings" (Lev. 4:13-20), a promise which extended to both rulers and common Jews (vv. 22f, 27f). Such remission, cleansing, and pardon was available to trespassers (Lev. 6:7), certain vow-breakers (Num. 30:1-12), shedders of innocent blood (Deut. 21:8-9), and to all guilty of general wickedness (Jer. 36:3, Isa. 55:6-7) and unintentional sins (Num. 15:22-28).

Thus promised absolute forgiveness under proper appeal, saints in Old Testament times were assured that they stood right with God when their sins were covered (Psa. 32:1-5). By trusting in the Lord, the man of covenant would be encompassed by lovingkindness or *chesed* (v. 10). That a remembrance of sin was made year by year (Heb. 10:3) certainly never implied that sins were "rolled forward" annually, accumulating unforgiven over the centuries until Christ would come. This traditional belief runs counter to Moses' express words (after an offering was made), "it shall be forgiven him" (Lev. 4:20, 26, 35; 5:10, 13, 16, 18; 16: 29-30; 19:22, etc.). The word "remembered" likely refers to a general consciousness of sins, comparable to Paul's phrase, "Pray without ceasing" (I Thess. 5:17), which manifests itself in a humble dependence upon God for continual confession and remission of sin (I John 1:9).

Since forgiveness of sin among the Jews took place in the mind of God, He could account them removed as an accomplished fact at any time, in the same way that a merchant might mark an account as settled even before the check covering payment clears the bank. Nevertheless, the cost for all sin had to be paid by the Son of God at the cross. The transgressions of those beforehand were indeed fully covered, with the ultimate sin-payment penalty still in prospect, that is, looking to the perfect sacrifice of Christ (Rom. 25-26, Heb. 9:15, 11:39-40). In this way, sins were "remembered no more" among faithful covenant Jews prior to Christ's sacrifice.

The Covenant Meal

As individuals of faith of any age came to terms with God by receiving the eternal covenant, the eating of a simple meal made the agreement functional (see Chapter One). As they walked with God, they continued to receive the benefits of the covenant. Participation in the divinely appointed meal, first the Passover, and later the Lord's Supper, proclaimed to one and all their faith in God and His mighty acts, and the triumph of Christ for all believers (I Cor. 11:26).

Throughout the Bible, eating and drinking together expressed social solidarity, whether it was in common familial situations while entertaining friends or at weddings and funerals. Kings hosted parties for various reasons, and partook of bread and wine with other statesmen to bring into effect peace and trade agreements. Through such eating and drinking together, political leaders swore oaths to perfect covenantal arrangements.

In a famous parable, the return of the prodigal son was celebrated with banqueting and feasting (Luke 15:11-32). Other stories show the importance of fellowship in eating and drinking (Mark 2:15-17, 6:35-44, 14:3; Luke 7:36, 9:13-17, 11:37-38, 14:8-24, 15:1-2, 27-32 etc.). When a penitent one returns to Jesus by opening the door (Rev. 3:20), He comes in and sups with him.

When God initiated the everlasting covenant with Abraham (Gen. 15:7-18), the parties ultimately sealed it with a simple meal (Gen. 18:1-8). In Exodus 24:9-11, after the revelation of the Ten Commandments, Moses (with Aaron and seventy priests) ascended a mountain, and ate and drank in the presence of God. The meal was not a postscript to the revelation of the law, but was integral to it, signifying that the eternal agreement was reaffirmed and sealed by both God and man.

The first enduring covenant meal, the Passover, celebrated God's mighty acts toward Israel and against the Egyptian gods. In response to persecuted people, God sent them Moses, who left Egypt's courts and joined himself with the children of the covenant. After God plagued the oppressors with death, Moses led God's people out of Egypt. To mark that event, families prepared lambs, which they ate with unleavened bread and bitter herbs, according to the Lord's instruction (Ex. 12:1-27).

Once out of Egypt, God wanted His people to remember His gracious acts annually in the celebration of the Passover. Its observance persisted throughout the period of the judges, the time of the kingdom, and past its division after Solomon. Even afterward up to the time of Christ, faithful covenanters well understood that, as they remembered the Passover, they walked with God; its non-observance meant disobedience.

Throughout their lives, Jesus and the disciples observed the feast annually. On the night He was betrayed, Jesus in the face of His death used the meal as the occasion to explain the sacrificial service of His life (Matt. 26:17-27). While taking a cup after supper, Jesus said, "This cup is the new covenant in my blood . . ." (Luke 22:20). The next afternoon as the priests and Levites prepared for the ritual slaughtering of lambs in the temple area, Jesus (as the Lamb of God) voluntarily yielded His spirit on Calvary, declaring, "It is finished" (John 19:30).

For the people of Christ, Jesus had now established the covenant supper. As the first and second centuries unfolded, its observance on resurrection day in Christian communities pointed to well-attested historical realities, especially the great teaching and miracles of Jesus of Nazareth. A very early document, the *Didache*, relates that the Lord's Supper was celebrated with many prayers (Chs. 9-10, 14:1). To Ignatius in about AD 110, the Physician's meal was closely tied to sacrifice and ecclesiastical office (*To Smyrna*, Ch. 7). In his *Apology*, 65-67 (issued about AD 160), Justin described in detail the eating of the Lord's Supper, stressing the fellowship and unity within the spiritual family.

While eating this simple meal, Christians through the centuries are an extension of the Old Testament faithful of God, who observed the Passover, thus displaying a continuity among all of God's saints. In fact, the supper of Jesus was established in the very midst of a Passover feast. Now, as God's people remember the Lord Jesus Christ by breaking the bread and drinking the wine, they reaffirm the terms of the eternal covenant: that sins are remembered no more, and that the spirit of God is within them. Renewed hearts have the law written upon them. In an intimate relationship with Heaven, Christians rightly say, "You are our God, for we are your people."

Summary

Both the Hebrew and Greek scriptures contain many concepts which show continuity. The people of the kingdom of the Jewish age – Abraham, Isaac, and Jacob among them (Matt. 8:11) – are in spiritual continuity with the saints of Christ, who have been translated into that very kingdom (Col. 1:13). Though God ruled over hearts during the Jewish regime, He transferred everything to the Son (Psa. 2:8, Acts 2:36); now this kingdom, founded before the creation of the world (Eph. 1:3), has its brightest and fullest expression, with Christ as King.

Similarly, God has always had a body of people. Christ was the Rock of Israel upon which His *ekklesia* (or called-out congregation), was built. In the Christian era, covenant people, the *ekklesia* (or church) stand upon Jesus Christ, an obvious continuity, as expressed in two dramatic figures, the olive tree of Romans 11, and the covenant woman of Revelation 12 (see Chapter Six).

All of these people have been guided by the same moral precepts. Moses embodied them in the law of Moses, but other prophets frequently spoke of them, even as New Testament authors committed them to writings. Further, the covenanted ones knew that they were first loved by God (Deut. 7:6-9, Rom. 5:8), and that their Father always required repentance (Deut. 30:2, Rom. 2:4). Saints on both sides of the cross lived with assurance that, as they maintained God's will (plan) in their hearts, they would not experience everlasting death (John 8:51; see also 3:36, 14:23-24).

Paul understood the confidence of obedience, as he instructed the runaway slave, Philemon, "I know you will do more than what I say" (v. 21). Thus, works are accomplished out of gratitude for a present salvation and God's declaration of righteousness. The God who loves people forgives out of respect for the covenantal relationship. Such a right-standing before God rests squarely upon the surety that faith is built upon the Eternal One, who has continually delivered His people, and can and does call non-existent things as though they were already in place.

The salvation of covenant people through faith-obedience allows for personal defects, while the human-devised formula (faith *plus* obedience) necessitates flawlessness. Guided by moral law and principles for daily living, the people of God – ancient Jews and Christians alike – are not governed by a human-devised legal *system* of rules, which only regulate the outward man and cannot address the heart. No law was ever given as a way of salvation, but for those who, by God's grace, have been made His people, the law instructs them as to how to respond properly to saving grace, pointing man to Jesus.

The words "forgiveness" and "forgiving" have always been part of God's vocabulary, as He has related to people throughout the ages. Righteous Jews of the remote past are our present day covenant brothers, even as the author of Hebrews stated that they, without the Christian community, should not be made perfect (Heb. 11:40). The righteousness of God has been extended to a multitude of believers throughout time (comp. Rom. 3:21 with Rev. 5:9).

Covenant Jews, both in the days of Abraham (Rom. 4:1f) and of the prophet Habakkuk, lived by faith and were wholly dependent upon His righteousness (2:4), in the same way that the people of Christ go about their lives day by day by depending upon the faithfulness of God as expressed in Romans 3:21f (see also Rom. 1:17, Gal. 3:11, Heb. 11:28). God has consistently remembered the promise originally given to Abraham, "and through your seed all nations will be blessed" (Gen. 15:6). Truly, the just shall live by faith, for its foundation ground is the Lord Jesus Christ and His blood shed in the sacrifice of the ages at Calvary.

It's Jewish

When we present our Creator's holy law,
And arguments from scripture draw,   Romans 7:12-14
Objectors say, to pick a flaw . . .
"It's Jewish!"

Though at the beginning our Father blest   Genesis 2:3
And sanctified His day of rest,   Hebrews 4:4
The same belief is still expressed . . .
"It's Jewish!"

And so at creation this rest began,   Genesis 2:2
And then through all the scriptures ran,   Isaiah 56:6
His Son explained: "twas made for man,"   Mark 2:27
"it's Jewish!"

If from the Bible we present,
The Sabbath meaning and intent,   Hebrews 4:9
What answers every argument . . .
"It's Jewish!"

Though the desciples, Luke and Paul,
Continue still this rest to call   Acts 16:13
The "Sabbath day" . . . this answers all,
"It's Jewish!"

The apostle John's plain expression,
That sin is of the law, transgression,   I John 3:4
Seems not to make the least impression . . .
"It's Jewish!"

O ye, who thus His law abuse,
Simply because it was kept by Jews,
The Saviour, too, you must refuse . . .   Hebrews 7:14
He's Jewish!

The scriptures, then we may expect,   Romans 3:1-2
For the same reason you'll reject;   Acts 7:38
For if you will but recollect . . .   Deut. 5:24-26
They're Jewish!

Thus the apostles, too, must fall;
For Andrew, Peter, James, and Paul   John 1:47
Nathanael and Matthew, John and all   Romans 11:1
Were Jewish!

Chapter Eight

⤳

The Messianic Jews and Continuity of Covenant

E VIDENCE OUTLINED in Chapters Five and Six shows that throughout the three premillennial religious "dispensations" – Patriarchal, Mosaic and Christian – God has interacted with his elect essentially through one eternal covenant of peace. Upon His own initiative, but on man's behalf, God set forth this everlasting agreement first with the patriarch Abraham in about 2100 B.C., promising him and his progeny various blessings and confirming them by an oath sworn by Himself (Gen. 15-17).

This compact with Abraham contained every essential term of covenant (see Chapters Two and Eleven). As God continued to interact with His people Israel through the time of Moses, David, and the divided kingdom, this peace treaty with the Almighty One became better defined, as further revelations of God's mind and will came through Israel's prophets and other holy men. Throughout this Old Testament period there existed an uninterrupted line of loyal Jewish saints in agreement with the God of Heaven, all enjoying innumerable blessings because of His gracious covenantal arrangements.

Afterwards, God's spiritual ones in the divine covenant continued to advance in historical development, moving forward into the era when Jesus came into the world (Matt. 1:18-25) to live His earthly life, experience the cross, and overcome death through His resurrection. This spiritual assembly of sanctified, devout, covenant Jews and proselytes remained intact up to the day of Pentecost of Acts 2 and beyond. The gates of hell did not restrain these faithful as they continued their conscientious walk as subjects in the kingdom of heaven throughout the first century, glorifying God and preserving His good name by witnessing before the nations, first in Judea, then in Samaria, and ultimately to the uttermost parts of the earth (Acts 1:8). In time, untold numbers of Gentiles also joined these Jews as covenanted people, continually bathing in God's blessings and favor.

Countering these notions is the teaching that God has given to man two distinct covenants - an old one and a new one - each of which applies to *separate* people of God: the first for Jews before the cross, the second for Christians since then. The theory sees contrast rather than continuity between God's faithful ones throughout the ages.

It is further contended that these two groups, each within separate covenants, are subject to distinctly indexed laws. Some teach that a new law came into existence at the cross, though all certainly see it in place by the time of Pentecost (Acts 2:1). It is further assumed that everyone, whether in or out of covenant, is accountable to this new law.

The two-covenant doctrine suffers because of many scriptural statements, detailed in Chapter Five, which inextricably bind God's people from Abraham through the prophets to the faithful of the Christian era into one everlasting covenant, which was ultimately and gloriously perfected in Jesus. This evidence was followed up by the presentation in Chapter Six of two lofty metaphors - Paul's olive tree in Romans 11 and John's heavenly woman in Revelation 12 - each of which represents God's covenanted ones from Abraham through every "dispensation" to the present. These strong figures and scriptural statements are rendered meaningless by the notion of two or more "everlasting" covenants (a contradiction in terms) - old and new - with two laws governing separate people of God, a violation of the "one's" constantly stressed by Paul in his epistles, as in Ephesians 1:22-23, 4:4-5 (see Chapter Five).

The First Century Covenant Jews

The continuity of God's one everlasting covenant is further shown historically in the religious development of the first century Jewish people of God, as these faithful ones subject to Moses and the prophets also embraced the gospel of the Perfecter of the heavenly agreement (Heb. 13:20). In accepting Jesus as the anticipated Christ of long-time hope and promise, the Jewish community of God in no way had to forsake Moses' Torah or repudiate any longstanding practices in order to please God this side of the cross.

When about 3000 devout, repentant Jews were immersed on Pentecost, no evidence shows that they abandoned any cherished customs or the God-centered teaching of Moses so that they might enter *another* religious system, a new and different covenant with a structured law. Rather, in accepting the gospel of Christ, these Pentecostians renewed their pledge to God and took a vital step in covenantal development within the course of Jewish history and religious thought.

With Jesus Christ as their King, their relationship with God was made better in every way, as explained in the epistle to the Hebrews. Each of these Jews, now buried and raised with Christ (Rom. 6:3-8), was now also married to Him who perfected their justification and righteousness (7:1-7). All the while, those people faithful to Moses experienced no change in covenant status and, assuredly, their secure relationship with the God of heaven was never in peril (see Chapter Six).

Simply stated, no "Christian religion" was initiated on that Pentecost day or at any other time; in fact, no Bible statement shows that Jesus ever started a new religion. No new law replaced the moral precepts associated with Moses and the prophets. No "New Testament church" upstaged ancient Israel of Old Testament times, for Israel *was* the "church," the people of God.

This same body of faithful saints coincided precisely with God's called out people of Christ in the first generation after the cross, except for all the faithless Jews who knowingly rejected the gospel of the Messiah or otherwise fell away in unbelief (Rom. 11:17, 24). Ultimately, obedient Gentiles joined these messianic Jews in a display of the long-awaited unity of all God's faithful throughout time (see Chapter Six). Now the called out, the Israel of God, are no longer confined or separated racially or geographically as they were before Christ came, and Jesus of Nazareth is accepted as the long-awaited Christ of Jewish hope and promise.

Messianic Jews as Obedient to Torah

The Acts historical narrative clearly shows, beginning with the second chapter, that the many thousands of Jews who looked to Jesus Christ as their Head and King carried on acceptable worship (service) which differed only very slightly from what faithful Jews had been practicing for centuries before the cross, at which point it is alleged that the old covenant with its law ended. None of these newly baptized Jews, whether citizens of Jerusalem or sojourners from Rome or 14 other places across the eastern Roman Empire (2:5f), cast aside as obsolete their ancient heritage of the Torah, the Sabbath, synagogue worship, and/or various ceremonial rituals associated with Moses. To the contrary, they honored them all, as well as any refinement of Moses' teaching by Christ and the apostles (2:42).

These believers, now under Christ, regularly met in various places (2:46), "finding favor with all the people" - the rest of the Jewish populace in Jerusalem (v. 47). Each baptized Jew enjoyed such positive acceptance because whatever he did in the name of Christ did not undermine the traditions of the fathers of Israel. In fact, any explanations of the law by Jesus Christ and the apostles were fully in continuity and in absolute harmony with the long existent Jewish prophets and teachers.

Messianic Jews regularly met (often daily) in the temple courts (2:46; 5:21, 42) or in Solomon's porch (5:12) and day after day from house to house (2:46, 5:42). They observed the traditional Jewish afternoon hour of prayer (3:1). When a "large number" of priests became obedient to the faith (6:7), nothing is mentioned that even one of them forsook the priesthood.

It is evident that these Jews continued to circumcise their children and observe Sabbaths like other pious Jews. They participated in both the festival of Pentecost (18:21 KJV, 20:16) and the Lord's Supper (I Cor. 11:20-28), even adhering to Levitical dietary laws. Ten years after Pentecost, Peter continued to respect Mosaic food restrictions, openly boasting that he had never eaten the "unclean" food of Gentiles. In this, he disobeyed God's specific command three times (10:9-16).

Ananias, a "disciple" (Acts 9:10) whose hands baptized Paul, was known throughout Damascus as a "devout man according to the law, who was highly respected by all of the Jews living there" (22:12). Such a description does not undermine Christ's authority at all (18:25). When Paul was a prisoner in Rome thirty years after Pentecost, he boasted before his kinsmen that he himself was a Jew trained in the law, declaring that he had done nothing against his people or the customs of his ancestral fathers (28:17; see also 25:8). Evidently, the apostle did not disapprove of Jews continuing in their inherited ways of religious life - and apparently neither did God.

In about AD 49 at the Jerusalem Conference, the great local leader of God's people, James the Just, discussed the rebuilding and restoring (renewing) process which the Lord had been working out among God-fearing people for centuries among both Jews and Gentiles (15:14-21). This great work had been taking place in the Jewish synagogues even as the Torah was being taught, as expressed in verse 21: "For Moses . . . in every city . . . is read in the synagogues every Sabbath."

The connecting word "for" explains the preceding material in verses 16 and 20, joining the preaching of Moses with the guidance in verse 20 which would soon be promulgated to Gentiles in Christ. Where this instruction was taking place is clearly stated in verse 21 - in the synagogues where Moses' Torah was being taught each Sabbath, just as it had been for many generations past. Thus, nearly two decades after the death of Christ, both Jews and Gentiles were subjecting themselves to Moses' moral teaching. Otherwise, why were they hearing the reading of the Torah "in every city . . . every Sabbath."?

James and others of the Christian sect knew firsthand that the law of Moses instructed the people of Christ in the synagogue, for they were there themselves. Thus they understood that there was a continuity of covenant and moral belief among all of these people of God. Further, anyone who declares that the Torah was rendered obsolete at the cross also must explain why James, the rest of the apostles, and the elders and the whole church were "pleased" to send a letter to various Gentile *ekklesiai*, knowing that they could hear "Moses" preached "in the synagogues every Sabbath day" (v. 21).

About eight years after the Jerusalem Conference, when Paul was in Jerusalem, he was told that in that city alone, there were many thousands of Jews who had believed, and all of them were "zealous for the law [Torah]" (21:20). While these faithful Jews in Christ were keeping the "old law," they were continually in the "way of salvation" (16:17), enjoying a personal relationship and in covenant with Christ.

The conclusion is self-evident: adhering to the moral precepts of the law of Moses was not an obstacle to serving God acceptably even after the cross, and it most certainly was never a part of the false religion confined to a fleshly Judaism enmeshed in legalism. Evidently, these Christians in the syna-gogue were not in a corner engaging in special worship; they were part and parcel of the regular Jewish assembly.

Messianic Jews as Worshipers in Synagogues

For more than two decades after the Pentecost of Acts 2, God-fearing Jews who had been baptized into Christ regularly met in synagogues for collective worship and edification, in accordance with the law and the prophets. In about AD 35, when Saul of Tarsus was aggressively persecuting the "sect of the way" (22:4-5), he knew of no separate assemblies for Chris-tians in Judea and Syria, but in various localities he would enter "one synagogue after another" to flush out followers of the way (9:2).

Late in his life Saul, now Paul the apostle, recalled that he had punished Christ's followers often in all the synagogues (26:11). But, during the time under consideration, Paul also stated that he was "zealously persecuting the church," Christ's *ekklesia* (Phil. 3:6, Gal. 1:13)!

These facts show that the people of Christ, the "New Tes-tament church" of modern terminology, acceptably worshiped God together with Jews in the synagogues during those many years after Pentecost, while no evidence shows that they formed their own distinctive assemblies. There was intimate contact and continuity between members of "the way" and other Jew-ish believers in various synagogues, for according to Acts Christian evangelism tended to begin in Diaspora houses of worship in a given locality (13:5, 14; 14:1; 17:2, 10, 17:1-2; 18:4, 19; 19:8).

Not until well past mid-first century, about AD 55 when Paul resided for two years in Ephesus (Acts 19:1f), is there a hint of Gentiles and Jews in Christ withdrawing themselves from their longstanding mutual synagogue attendance, where they had served God acceptably.

Significantly, Paul and the Ephesian disciples of Christ held out for three months before breaking away from certain "hardened and disobedient" Jews who repeatedly rejected the teachings about Jesus (v. 9). Until then, Paul worshiped in the synagogues, speaking boldly and reasoning with one and all about Jesus as Christ, a state of affairs that would hardly be possible if the sect of the way were fundamentally repugnant to the centuries-old synagogue religion of Israel and Moses (see pages 175–178).

Thus, for most of a generation throughout the Roman Empire, faithful Jews and Gentiles in Christ gathered for public edification on Saturday, attending the synagogue to hear the reading and discussion of Moses' Torah, and to engage in singing hymns and choruses. No apostle or other evangelist discouraged worship at Jewish synagogues on the Sabbath in favor of a Christian church assembly on another day. Evidently, for a significant time – about a quarter of a century past the Pentecost of AD 33 – there was in most localities probably no separate meetings. Years after mid-first century, when the people of Christ began to separate themselves from the synagogue, vocal music in the Christian assembly served as an emotional and didactic aid (Eph. 5:19, Col. 3:16), an obvious adaptation from the a capella music in which they participated in synagogue worship.

After AD 33, messianic Jews who worshiped in the Jerusalem temple (Acts 2:46; 3:1; 5:21, 42; see also 2:42), very likely praised God and prophesied (taught) with lyres, harps, and cymbals (I Chron. 25:1, 6; 6:31f), as people "zealous for the law" (Acts 21:20). More than their employment in homes or other non-corporate settings, faithful Jews in Christ thus used various mechanical instruments in accordance with a direct commandment of God (II Chron. 29:25-29), while reciting a psalm in praise of God in common temple assemblies.

It is not known precisely when the "sect of the way" began to regularly meet on Sunday to edify and encourage one another and commemorate the resurrection of Christ in the Lord's

Supper. The practice was probably introduced in each locality at various times, just as the coexistence of the orthodox and messianic Jews in the synagogue began to disintegrate in various cities at different times during AD 55-65 (the first *recorded* break was at Ephesus in about the year 55). The earliest of church fathers, writing from 95 to 160, unanimously attest to the practice of Christians meeting on the eighth day for collective worship.

Ignatius around AD 110 said that this "eighth day" was the first day of the week, the Lord's day (*To the Magnesians*, Ch. 9). Pliny, writing to Trajan in about the year 117, said that Christians met on a stated day for singing and exhortation. The *Epistle of Barnabas*, Chapter 15 states that "Wherefore we keep the eighth day with joyfulness, the day also in which Jesus rose again from the dead." The *Didache*, issued late in the first century, concurs.

Justin Martyr in about AD 160 stated clearly that Sunday was the time at the common assembly, the day in which the Saviour rose from the dead. It was also the day in which God made the world (*First Apology*, Ch. 67). This solid testimony for the first day's status is joined by statements in the later writings of Clement of Alexandria, Tertullian, and Cyprian.

In the mid 60's, the break between orthodox, institutional Jews, generally in charge of the synagogues, and covenant Messianic Jews, was well underway in most localities, disrupting a longstanding harmonious relationship, even as Christ Himself had foretold that such would occur before the destruction of Jerusalem in AD 70.

Only during those turbulent years between the "beginning of birth pangs" (Mark 13:8), which was the start of the tribulation upon Jerusalem (Matt. 24:21), and "the end" (Mark 13:13), five years later in AD 70, did Jews in Christ experience civil judgments and floggings by institutional synagogue officials (Matt. 10:17, Mark 13:9). John 16:2 reports that "they will make you outcasts from the synagogues" at this very time, certainly implying that *previous* to then, before the trouble of the mid 60's, messianic Jews were not outsiders but indeed functioned as a vital part of the synagogue.

But the enmity for the sect of the Nazarene among the fossilized institutional Jewish orthodoxy thereafter quickly intensified, and before the end of the first century, the hatred was full-blown. By then, the 12th Benediction of the synagogue service would contain a special curse upon all followers of Jesus: "May the Nazarenes and heretics perish in a moment, be blotted out of the book of life, and not be written with the just."

Messianic Jews as Sabbath Worshipers

More than 25 years after the cross, when the law of Moses allegedly had been superseded by a new Christian law, the apostle Paul sent to the saints at Rome an epistle in which he neither encouraged nor prohibited celebration of the Sabbath as binding upon the conscience (Rom. 14:2-21). Significantly, the apostle clearly commended Rome's Jewish community, which kept a Sabbath to the Lord (vv. 5-6) as a congregational activity. On the other hand, their Gentile counterparts had no such obligation, freely gathering together as brothers for edification and fellowship at various times when opportunities arose.

Even past the mid-first century, it was possible for a Sabbath keeper to function in Christ's kingdom and possess the hope of eternal life. Such expressions of worship indeed had religious significance (not merely national or cultural character), in that "he who regards the day regards it for the Lord" (Rom. 14:6). Even second century church fathers, including Justin Martyr and Epiphaneus, wrote that Jews who had turned to Christ were still Sabbatarians, with no references to their regularly observing Sunday as an *exclusive* time of assembly. In about AD 325, the renowned historian Eusebius reported that, in his day, he knew of Jews baptized into Christ who kept both days.

The persistent belief that the primitive first century Jewish saints abandoned the long-practiced Sabbath in favor of the Lord's Day obviously does not stand up in light of either historical or scriptural evidence. For anyone to desert the Sabbath or change it from the seventh to the first day would have brought the Jewish followers of the way undue controversy and a falling out of favor among the rest of their kinsmen (see Acts 2:47). These believers saw Jesus Christ as the *fulfillment* of the prophets, not the negation of them. In short, they still wished to be regarded as good Jews among their fleshly brothers.

And so, the Hebrew-speaking followers of Christ regularly employed the venerable institutions, making offerings in the temple (Matt. 5:23) where they paid the temple tax (Matt. 17:24-27), even as the Christ Himself commanded. They regarded themselves as the Israel of the latter days and the prophets. God's people living in Palestine faithfully observed the traditions of the elders, including the Sabbath (James Dunn, *Unity and Diversity in the New Testament*, p. 127). Nothing that the sect of the way did was hostile to Moses while they kept the seventh day, after the fashion of other Jews.

The called-out of God, the *ekklesia* led by the apostles, never instituted a *new* religion beside existing Israel, but comprised instead *renewed* or restored Israel (Acts 1:6, 3:21). God's promises to holy men of old were being fulfilled among these first century people of Christ. Such continuity of covenantal development is epitomized in one man of God, James the Just, a prominent leader in the sect of the way, who enjoyed a reputation for great piety among the rest of the Jews as well. The contemporary historian, Josephus, reported that the death of James deeply affected both the sect of Christ and also the Jews' religious society. According to Eusebius, James was noted for his extensive temple service.

As the first century progressed, God's called-out among Jews and Gentiles continued to be built "on the foundation of the apostles and prophets," denoting religious continuity (Eph. 2:20; see also 3:5, 4:11). These two groups are again together in Revelation 18:20 and 21:12-14. Thus, the first century people of Christ were in a real sense an extension of moral Jewish religion now internationalized, centering upon a direct relationship with God, through His Son.

The Apostle Paul as Obedient to Torah

Though a minister and apostle in the sect of the way, Paul lived and died a faithful orthodox Jew, loyal to the law of Moses. Agreeing that embracing Christ was not to "forsake Moses" (Acts 21:22), Paul evidently saw continuity and not a contrast of laws and covenants, and old one of Moses and a new one of Christ.

Throughout his life Paul was faithful to the law and the prophets (22:3, 23:1-6, 24:14, 26:4-5, 28:17). More than 25 years after the cross, Paul is called to a Gentile mission by a temple vision (22:17-21). To Timothy he administered circumcision as both a religious and a national rite (16:3). In Cenchrea, Paul had his hair cut in keeping with a Nazarite vow (18:18). He willingly observed various Jewish distinctions in saying, "If food causes my brother to stumble, I will never eat meat again . . ." (I Cor. 8:13; see also Rom. 14:2-3, 6, 14-16, 20-21).

In Jerusalem he recognized the law's validity, in respect to the Jewish high priest, to whom he openly boasted "Brethren, *I am* a Pharisee . . ." (23:6). Note Paul's present tense usage, not I *was*. Addressing the Jewish council as "brethren," Paul intended more than their identification as Abraham's fleshly descendants.

After his second missionary tour, the apostle returned to Jerusalem to bear alms for poor Jewish saints and to make offerings (24:17), and to worship God (24:11). He gave heed to the feast of Pentecost at Jerusalem (20:16). As Paul bade the brethren at Ephesus farewell, he declared, "I *must* by all means keep this feast [Pentecost] that cometh in Jerusalem" (18:21, KJV). He also joined "in sincerity and truth" in the Festival of

Unleavened Bread, which followed the Passover (I Cor. 5:7-8). In such efforts Paul was not merely taking opportunities to preach the gospel; in fact, he took a visible part in honoring the Jewish feasts, continuing in his lifetime worship to God in familiar ways.

Paul regarded such participation in the law of Moses as incumbent not only upon himself but also for all Jews in Christ. It is a concept of the status quo from I Corinthians 7:17 which requires that he who believes as a Jew must continue to live as a Jew (A. Schweitzer, *The Mysticism of Paul the Apostle*, pp. 194-195). Apparently no inconsistency existed (nor was it considered thus) if a disciple in the sect of the way adhered to Moses' precepts in faithful and acceptable worship to God.

Acts 21:21-27 contains the remarkable account of Paul coming before James and the elders at Jerusalem, relating to them the progress of his ministry among the Gentiles. These elders were probably orthodox Jews, though surely some of them must have been baptized into Christ. That all of them were under Moses is plain. If these elders headed up a distinct Christian church, would they require an apostle to serve another religion, the one long practiced by faithful Jews, and observe its rites? Thus, there was likely no separate Christian church in Jerusalem, a city with more than 100 synagogues, according to archaeological findings. All of these elders, even those baptized into Christ, still functioned within Jewish thought and practice.

The Jerusalem elders praised God on behalf of Paul's success in converting the Gentiles to the Spirit God of Israel. But a split was occurring among those Jews, centering on this very work. Everyone wished to avoid trouble by closing the impending breach. The elders reminded Paul that there were thousands of the sect of the way, men of faith in Christ, all "zealous for the law" - the Torah (v. 20) - and that some influential brothers among this great number erroneously believed that Paul had been teaching others "to forsake Moses . . . and not to live according to the [Jewish] customs" (v. 21). If the Law of Moses were not still useful and appropriate for Jews in Christ to follow, why were these elders so eager to label this accusation against Paul as false?

To avoid a confrontation, the elders devised a plan (vv. 22-24). They ordered Paul to accompany four believers, currently under a Nazarite vow (Num. 6:2f), and purify himself along with those men, thus helping them to fulfill their vow. Paul did as he was told. By his actions, all parties would surely see that the rumors about Paul contradicted his living in obedience (and not contrary) to Moses - that he indeed was also "zealous for the law."

This Paul did by participating in the week-long temple rites (v. 26), purifying himself by offering to God eight pigeons and four lambs as sacrifice (Num. 6:9-12), through the ordained priesthood. Further, Paul paid most if not all expenses, amply demonstrating that he was walking orderly, according to Moses' Torah (v. 24b), the law. But if the ancient precepts had been abolished and nailed to the cross of Christ, as often alleged, *why* did Paul offer worship to God in accordance with the law? Was he a partaker of an evil deed (see II John 10-11)? Through all of this experience, this God-accepted Pharisee led a life for Christ in all good conscience (23:1).

What about Gentiles and Moses? Acts 21:25 specifies that these distinctive Jewish ceremonies were not to be bound upon the non-Jewish converts to Christ: "As touching the Gentiles which believe, we have written and concluded that they observe no such thing." Jewish members of the sect could reserve for their worship the ceremonies of the law of Moses, but these things were not to extend affirmatively into the Greco-Roman world. Earlier, the issue at the Jerusalem Conference (Acts 15) had been whether or not the Gentiles needed to convert to orthodox Judaism in order to be a faithful followers of Christ. The answer was "no" (vv. 19-21).

Evidently the apostle Paul lived and died a member of two religious sects: a Jewish Pharisee under the long-established law, and simultaneously a follower of Christ in "the way." He never told anyone that the law of Moses had been abolished at the cross or that it had been otherwise rendered useless. Surely, if God's will was to the contrary, the Lord would have revealed it to Paul. Instead, the apostle continued to keep the Sabbath and other holy days, participating in ritual and religious celebrations long after he embraced Jesus as the Christ in Damascus. He saw the risen Lord as a fulfillment of Moses and the prophets, all of whom taught that when Messiah should come, a relationship must be established with Him.

The Apostle Paul, as Worshiper in Synagogues

During his missionary journeys into the Grecian world, Paul customarily proceeded to the Jewish synagogue upon his arrival in a city (Acts 13:14 and 43-44, 16:13, 17:2, 18:4f, 19:8; see also 9:20). He would first preach to his brothers in the flesh (Rom. 1:16b, 2:9-10), while, simultaneously to Gentiles, he proclaimed the gospel of Christ on Jewish Sabbaths. In Pisidian Antioch according to custom (see 17:2), Paul proclaimed Jesus as Christ to "men of Israel and Gentiles who worship God . . ." (v. 16). They invited Paul back the next Sabbath, and all came to hear the word of the Lord (13:44), the preaching of the grace of God (v. 43).

At Iconium, Paul and Barnabas as usual entered the synagogue on the Sabbath, speaking so forcefully that a "great number of Jews and Gentiles believed" (14:1). Again and again they spoke boldly (v. 3) before moving on to Lystra and Derbe, winning a large number of disciples (v. 21). Thereafter, Paul and Barnabas retraced their steps, and while revisiting the brethren, "appointed elders in every church" (v. 23).

The *ekklesia* or called-out "in every city" (Tit. 1:5), was mostly made up of Jews and proselytes, and these Christians, for many years after Pentecost, could essentially be identified with the Jewish synagogues "in every city" (15:21). These spiritual leaders of Acts 14:23, whose faith was worthy of being imitated (Heb. 13:7, 17), had long served as elders among

God's Jewish saints. As these guardians of the flock embraced Jesus as the resurrected Christ in their lives, they kept intact their ancient beliefs and practices dating from Moses.

On his second missionary journey, Paul found on the Sabbath a place of worship at Philippi, where he taught Lydia and others about Christ (16:13-15). In Thessalonica (17:1f), Paul proclaimed the risen Christ on three successive Sabbaths, "as was his custom" (v. 2), resulting in some Jews and Gentiles joining him. Next, Paul's party reached the synagogue in Berea, where some members of Moses' called-out assembly and other Gentiles became believers in Christ.

In the synagogues at Berea (17:10), Athens (v. 17), and Corinth (18:4), Paul reasoned "every Sabbath" with both Jews and Greeks, trying to persuade them that Jesus was Christ. Seeking to convert people to a new religion was never His stated mission. The pattern continued at Ephesus (18:19). Interestingly, a Jew named Apollos lived in that city. He was thoroughly versed in scripture, and "had been instructed in the way of the Lord . . . teaching about Jesus accurately, knowing only the baptism of John" (18:25).

Apollos' scriptures were those issued by Moses and the prophets, yet he faithfully taught about Jesus without specific knowledge of how the apostles may have amplified the long-established teaching. Luke called it "the apostles' doctrine" (2:42). Such glowing approval of Apollos could not be possible unless such covenant Jews were God-approved, even as they advanced from Moses' teachings to the universalized religion which centered upon the good news of the resurrected Christ.

The same could be said of the twelve "disciples" (a term identifying the God-approved) who had not experienced baptism into Christ (19:1-7). Yet, all of these stood firmly as olive branches on Paul's salvation tree of Romans 11 and as part of John's heavenly woman in Revelation 12 (see Chapter Six). Moreover, Paul's audiences of believers had as "fathers" the patriarchs of Israel, a fact which displays additional continuity among all of God's elect.

On his third missionary journey, Paul spoke boldly in the Ephesian synagogue for three months (19:8). None of his tours gives evidence that Paul ever preached or "worshiped" on Sunday in a Christian church (but see 20:7). He never encouraged any group to start a new assembly or to gather together regularly on another day. Paul's custom was to explain and amplify the scriptures and worship on the Jewish Sabbath in a synagogue as the Christ Himself did (Luke 4:16). For decades after the cross, Jews who had been baptized into Christ in every locality still served God acceptably by adhering to the many precepts and duties introduced by Moses which, over time, had become firmly entrenched in their worship culture.

Gracefully, Paul took these right-standing moral Jews where they were in their religious development, worshipers of the Creator on the Sabbath, and built upon this good measure of faith the testimony of the resurrected Jesus as the long-awaited Christ. Paul never regarded any Jewish audience he faced as unusual or unsound, since, all the while, Paul knew that each hearer was harmoniously in covenant with God and in fellowship with contemporary saints and other faithful ones throughout the ages since Abraham.

The first century apostolic sect, today commonly called the "New Testament church," was therefore *not* a "new Israel," governed by another "law of Christ" mandating a new organization, one which would meet exclusively on a specific day for collective worship. Instead, the spiritual thousands in this messianic Jewish sect, the way, came forth directly out of God's faithful remnant guided by the Jewish prophets. Together with the Gentiles, all of these faithful throughout time make up the covenant Israel of God.

Chapter Nine

꙳

The Messianic Jews and Continuity of Covenant – Continued

C HAPTER EIGHT discussed the concept of continuity of covenant through Abraham, Moses, and Christ in the spiritual development of the first century faithful Jewish remnant. As these people of God responded to the gospel of Christ after the Pentecost of Acts 2, these covenant elect did not have to abandon centuries-old ways of worship under Moses' Torah. Rather, they kept the "old law," while faithfully devoting themselves to God day by day and ultimately assimilating with the Gentiles in the renewed body of Christ.

Various two-covenant proponents have registered strong objections to this teaching, maintaining that God's old covenant arrangements with the people of Moses and the prophets are to be sharply distinguished from the community of Christians which Christ allegedly established on Pentecost. They maintain that members of the first century Jewish sect, the way, could not possibly have remained true to Christ while keeping any part of the law of Moses, though Christ Himself did so. Many say that Paul visited synagogues *only* because of their ready-made audiences for preaching the unique gospel of Christ. But this assertion is wide of the mark, in that nothing in Acts actually expresses this modern notion, nor can it be legitimately inferred from any text.

Some have stated that Paul did not understand the full significance of a "law of Christ," or that he participated in Jewish ceremonies in ignorance or in moments of weakness. Such arrogance implies that they understand better about what was involved than did the personally trained apostles of Jesus. A few have written that the apostle complied with Jewish customs *solely* because of the principle of "to the Jews I became a Jew . . ." (I Cor. 9:20), but such has no biblical foundation for support.

The two-covenant doctrine often see the period from the Pentecost of Acts 2 in AD 33 to the destruction of Jerusalem in AD 70 as a "transition period" when God overlooked the Jews' keeping of the law of Moses. According to this theory, explained in a section below, Jews in Christ during this time were really not worshiping God "in spirit and in truth" while celebrating Jewish holidays, the Sabbath or participating in temple sacrifices, etc. – they were merely observing social customs and well-established Jewish practices.

A belief that Messianic Jews kept Moses' commandments strictly because of custom during the first century fails to consider many hard hitting realities. The very fact that Paul, as a believer in and apostle of Jesus Christ, could repeatedly visit the same Jewish synagogues and participate publicly in them, shows the virtual identity of religious thought and corporate worship between the synagogue of the Jews and the new sect of the way, the people of Christ.

This harmonious state of affairs would not even begin to be possible if Paul's discourses and words of exhortation in the Jewish assemblies were offensive or otherwise radically unacceptable to the God-fearing Jews whom Paul met on every stop of his missionary journeys, faithful people as yet unbaptized into Christ. Indeed, to reason differently is to accuse Paul of compromise and a denial of the Christ, an implication which gives some people no trouble.

Similarly, the sect of the Pharisees which contended for the necessity of circumcision at the Jerusalem Conference in Acts 15, must have held essentially the same beliefs as those of the sect of the way, the baptized into Christ. Otherwise, these Pharisees would not have gained even the slightest standing at the conference, but would have been quickly dismissed, and never invited back.

These first century Jewish covenant people of God differed from their fellow countrymen's age-old worship according to Moses by their acceptance of Jesus as the anticipated Christ spoken of by David, Jeremiah, Ezekiel, and other prophets. To non-religious people across the 3000-mile expanse of the Roman Empire, followers of the way must certainly have appeared as a mainline sect within the diversity of Jewish religious parties which believed in monotheism with Yahweh as God, ministering angels, spirits, and a future resurrection (see 23:8). Secular history records that the Roman government constantly identified Christianity as bound up with the Jewish faith (Tacitus, *Annals* 15:44).

Was the 'Old Law' Nailed to the Cross?

The biggest objection to the conclusion that Jews in Christ could worship acceptably and still adhere to their ancient practices from the prophets is that the law of Moses was "nailed to the cross," thus ending it forever. The proof text is Colossians 2:13-14: "And you, who were dead in trespasses and the uncircumcision of your flesh, God made alive together with Him, having forgiven all of our trespasses, having canceled the bond which stood against us, with its legal demands, this He set aside, nailing it to the cross."

First of all, these verses do not say that the *law* itself was nailed to the cross; it was rather the *bond*, which is the curse or the debt it placed upon the Jews. It is the "damning evidence of broken laws and commandments which always hung over our heads" (Phillips Translation). Thus, Christ paid this debt on the cross for everybody, and the debt created by sin was nailed there with Him. A parallel passage, Galatians 3:13, declares that "Christ redeemed us from the *curse* of the law" – not the law itself.

By example, if a friend's house appeared on the delinquent tax roll list on the bulletin board at the courthouse, and you redeemed his property for him, you have only removed the bond (debt) which the tax created, not the law of taxation itself. The tax bill can now be nailed to the courthouse door, marked paid in full. The popular Jewish custom was to nail the proof of a paid debt in a public place, to show its redemption. Such an act obviously signified the removal of the *bondage* to the debt, not the law which defined it.

Similarly, Jesus did not blot out any law on the cross but removed its damning evidence – the curse and debt it created because of sin. Jesus died, ". . . in order that the just requirement of law might be fulfilled in us" (Rom. 8:4). Since He kept the law perfectly, His faithful followers are entirely free from its curse, the condemnation. Through Him we also have met law's demands and stand righteous before God because Christ's fulfillment of law is imputed to us as a free gift. But nothing ever happened to the law itself at the cross.

Both Jesus and Paul summarized the law as the Golden Rule (Matt. 7:12, Gal. 5:14), which is precisely the same thing as the law of Christ (Gal. 6:2). Everyone throughout time is responsible to that standard. It was not nailed to anything as an ending. Further, Jesus did not come to earth to annul the law of Moses in order to bring His people "Christian law." Instead, He exemplified God's existing law as He fulfilled all of its demands and purposes. He emphatically personified the kingdom (rule) of God, something anticipated by the law and the prophets. This did not pass away.

Any destruction of the law of Moses at the cross runs counter to Christ's expressed words in Matthew 5:17-18: "Think not that I have come to abolish the law and the prophets. I have come . . .to fulfill them . . .Till heaven and earth pass away, not an iota, not a dot, will pass from the law until all is accomplished" (see Chapter Thirteen). Tradition would have Jesus teaching, "I came to disannul the law by fulfilling it," the very opposite of the Lord's meaning which was to confirm and restore the full intent and purpose of the law of Moses.

If the law were nailed to the cross, then all of its prophecies had to be fulfilled and blessings dispensed by that time. But much of what was said by Moses, Jeremiah, David, and other prophets applied to events after the cross: Christ's death (Isa. 53:7-9), His resurrection (v. 10), the subsequent ascension into heaven, where He assumed His kingship (Dan. 2:44, 7:14), the entrance of the Gentiles (Amos 9:11-12, Isa. 11:12), the era of apostolic teaching (Joel 2:28-32), and the passing of the Jewish economy with the destruction of Jerusalem in AD 70 (Deut. 28:15, Isa. 29:3-7, Mal. 4:1-4, etc.). Yet is insisted that "*till* heaven and earth shall cease" means that the Jewish law would end at the cross, precluding any further application of Old Testament prophecies past AD 70 as well.

But "till" does not mean "to cease" in Matthew 5:18, any more than in several other passages (Acts 3:21, 23:12; Matt. 24:38; Eph. 4:13, etc.). In Acts 8:40, Philip is described as traveling and preaching until he reached Caeserea. But thereafter Philip did not stop evangelizing, for he was still doing so years later in the same city (Acts 21:8). The law continued past AD 70 because its moral principles have timeless application; similarly, the prophets also spoke of some events to be carried out to consummation after AD 70 concerning Jerusalem and Rome (Zech. 14:1f, Dan. 2:44, 7:14, 9:27b; see also the book of Revelation).

In no sense, then, did the death of Christ destroy the law and the prophets. If it had, Jesus did something which He did not intend to do. Furthermore, the attitude expressed by contemporary Jewish authors such as Josephus, Baruch, Esdras, and others was that many people practiced the law for decades long after the death of Jesus. Philo, for instance, declared that the law would have no end (*Life of Moses* II.136).

Nor can two-covenant advocates find the law dying at the cross, and another for Christians emerging thereafter, based on Romans 7:1-4. They appeal to that passage as proof that any believer in Christ this side of the cross is guilty of spiritual adultery if he keeps the law of Moses and a "law of Christ" at the same time. But Paul clearly stated that one man in this account is "the law," and the other is not a "New Testament law," but Christ Himself. Romans 7 presents the problem of a woman bound to the law, but wishes to be free from it to marry Christ.

But she could not be bound to both the law and to Christ at the same time (v. 3). Since the law could not die, and Christ is eternal, there is but one alternative to this dilemma: she herself must die (v. 4)! The woman accomplished this end by being buried with Christ in the grave of baptism, to be raised united with Him (Rom. 6:3-8). Nowhere in Romans 7 does it say that the law itself had to end at the cross in order for anyone to embrace Christ. The woman, and by extension anyone else, had to die (7:4).

Moreover, God's ordained law of Moses is "holy, just and good . . .spiritual" (7:12, 14). It can convert and revive the soul (Psa. 19:7). Loving God and loving neighbor is the law's sum and substance, and on these hang the law and the prophets (Matt. 7:12). The law magnifies our sinfulness (Rom. 5:20), something not possible if it ended at the cross. Rather than nailing the law to the cross, let it continue to point out the full measure of transgression.

Is AD 33-70 a 'Transition Period' for Old and New Covenants?

Some supporters of the two-covenant doctrine see in the nearly forty year period between the Pentecost of Acts 2 in AD

33 and the destruction of Jerusalem in AD 70 a generation-long period of transition (often called the "latter days") when God allegedly allowed the old and the new covenants, each with their respective laws, to exist simultaneously. God supposedly gave the Jews of that era sufficient time to abandon the old covenant in favor of Christ's "better way" in the new covenant as an act of grace, so that they might ultimately leave one religion in favor of another.

But the Bible nowhere mentions this so-called "transition period," nor is that term ever used in scripture to describe any coexistence of eternal (everlasting) covenants – the old (first) one with its law of Moses "becoming obsolete and growing old and ready to disappear," (Heb. 8:13) and a new covenant and law under Christ. The author of Hebrews never stated that two covenants were simultaneously in force, and that there was a final doing away of Moses' law in connection with the fall of Jerusalem in AD 70.

Historically, the quelling of Judea in the year 70 did not even end the longstanding Jewish sacrificial system, much less their religion. Animals thereafter were regularly offered in a Jerusalem suburb and Jews still flourished in numerous synagogues throughout the Roman Empire. In fact, in more than a few score instances, contemporary Jewish authors even spoke of the temple as still in existence. Apparently it was in their hearts.

Other scriptures thought to show the AD 33-70 interval are Romans 13:11-12, "now is salvation nearer . . ." and I John 2:8, "the darkness is passing away . . ." but each of these, in context, fails to mention any transitional process nearing a completion in AD 70. Rather, the two passages refer to lofty themes of salvation, the casting off of sin, and walking in the light of Christ.

It is easy to overstate the effect of the destruction of Jerusalem upon the "sect of the way," the people of Christ. The AD 70 event had little impact on the furtherance of Christ's gospel or the extension of His kingdom. Even among the Jews themselves, "much of Jewish life was not seriously interrupted [by the fall of Jerusalem] . . . Indeed, large parts of the Jewish people were unaffected or marginally affected . . ." (Hershel Shanks, Ed., *Christianity and Rabbinic Judaism*, pp. 126-127). Many religious historians see it just as much a political event as a religious event.

Since both the Mosaic old covenant and the new covenant, (as well as other covenants which are mentioned in the Old Testament), are spoken of as "eternal" and "everlasting," how can two such covenants (and possibly others) be operable at the same time among the same people and, more importantly, from the same God? Assuredly, He is not the author of such inconsistency. Further, in heaven, which "everlasting covenant" will be operative, or will there be simultaneous eternal covenants there also? (see Chapter Fourteen). This kind of confusion results when trying to maintain the two covenant doctrine's transition period.

Christianity's Jewish Roots

If it is difficult to appreciate American history without giving proper place to its European heritage, trying to understand the *ekklesia* or the called-out of Christ while ignoring its Jewish origins and early development will result in serious distortions of the very nature of the faith. The sect of Messianic believers originated in Jerusalem of Judea. Its leaders were all Jewish apostles, with Jews comprising the bulk of the brethren in every locality. They served the same God and adhered to identical moral precepts as Israel had for centuries.

Incomplete collections of New Testament scriptures assembled in the second and third centuries are responses to the Jews and their rival canons of scriptures. To answer "the law and the prophets," various leaders in the rapidly developing institutional church of God around the year 200 began to assemble Paul's letters and gospel histories and other writings into counterpart sub-canons, all of which (except possibly Luke) were similarly written by members of the Jewish messianic sect.

Most significant of all, the 27 books in the ultimate New Testament canon, a reality in Egypt by the year 367 and about 30 years later in the Carthage district of North Africa, are extensions of spiritual teachings promulgated by the prophets, fully in continuity and in absolute harmony with God's earlier revelations, for the same moral law undergirds it all. In fact, the New Testament collection can never be understood properly apart from the backdrop of ancient Israel's prophets and teachers. For instance, every major idea of Romans 1-7 – the universality of sin, God's wrath and faithfulness, and the nature of justification – are expounded upon in Jeremiah, Isaiah, and other Jewish writings.

The object of believers' worship is Jesus Christ, the Lamb of God (an allusion to Jewish sacrifice), who sprang from Judah (Heb. 7:14, Rev. 5:5). He was born of Jewish parents (Matt. 1:16) who circumcised him on the eighth day, according to Jewish law (Luke 2:21). He attended the catechumenal synagogue school, celebrated the Passover, and discussed doctrinal matters with Jewish scribes in the temple.

His ministry, which started in the synagogues (Luke 4:16-28), freely drew material not only from the Old Testament scriptures but also from mainstream contemporary rabbinic writings which were circulating in Israel during the generations immediately before His birth. His God-centered teaching was altogether within Jewish tradition. Christ's vicarious removing of sin is rooted in Moses' sacrificial system, and the Lord's Supper which commemorates Christ as the sacrificial Lamb is an extension of Jewish Passover traditions. The rite of baptism [into Christ] is based upon a Jewish practice, even unto remission of sins.

The disciples of Christ all behaved and thought like Jews. Jesus taught them from Jewish tradition and from the prophets and other literature, using simple natural beauty and Judea's agricultural setting for most of His illustrations and parables. Initially the Master's mission was aimed exclusively at Jews, "the lost sheep of the house of Israel" (Matt. 15:24). During the generation after the Pentecost of Acts 2, the evolving religious community of God overwhelmingly consisted of Hebrew-speaking believers who regarded Jesus of Nazareth as the Christ of God whom covenant Jewish people had long been awaiting. When Peter preached, he addressed his kinsmen as "men of Israel," "brethren," etc. (Acts 2:22, 29, 36; 3:12, 17; 5:35).

Stephen, Paul, and other believers in Christ in the first century Jewish society continually referred to various heroes of the Jewish past, such as "our father Abraham," thus further demonstrating continuity between the Jewish people over the centuries and all saints in Christ after the cross. Thus, the Acts narrative is an extension of God's mighty deeds, recorded by Hebrew prophets, and further exhibited in Jesus' ministry. At the Jerusalem Conference in Acts 15, Jewish religious leaders, all believers in Christ, decided that their rituals did not have to be followed by the Gentiles, but determined that the emerging faith should never depart even slightly from precepts concerning the ethics and morality found in Moses' law – concepts also long adhered to by faithful Gentiles and ancient patriarchs, all of whom were subject to natural law.

Thus, Jesus' statement to the Samaritan woman that "salvation is of the Jews" (John 4:22) is indeed among the most profound of religious truths. For centuries on end they had been entrusted with the oral and written oracles of God (Rom. 3:2), so that they might uphold His good name among the nations. The Jews, in the form of the covenant Old Testament woman (Rev. 12:1f), faithfully preserved proper service toward the true spirit God, maintaining the unblemished lineage of Christ through the tribe of Judah.

Though institutional Judaism with its rival parties was essentially corrupt by the time of the Christ, the faithful remnant, pictured in the heavenly woman of Revelation 12 and the olive tree of Romans 11, stood above all law-works regimentation. The remnant of covenant believers held true to God's ways of adoring the Shepherd of Israel by emphasizing brother-to-brother relationships.

The people of Christ are but a continuation of ancient Israel through extension and renewal of the everlasting covenant. Thus, the community of believers, the called-out or body of Christ this side of the cross, is rightfully called the Israel of God (Gal. 6:16); other imagery carried over from the law and the prophets describes God's followers after Pentecost as the city of God (Psa. 46:4, Rev. 3:14), the temple of God (I Cor. 3:16-17, Eph. 3:21), the twelve tribes (Acts 26:7, Jas. 1:1), and Jerusalem (Gal. 4:26, Heb. 12:12). In Revelation 7:4-8, 14:1-7, and 21:12, believers in Christ are the true Jews and the fullness of the 12 tribes of Israel, the common designation of the Jewish race throughout Numbers, Joshua, and the books of the Kings and the Chronicles.

For many centuries, God's covenant Israel had been composed solely of Jews and proselytes. Now after the cross, those covenant ones through the apostles' preaching could renew their pledge to God by embracing the gospel of Christ. These faithful would soon be joined by the Gentiles in the long-desired oneness of spirit proclaimed by Isaiah, Jeremiah, and other Jewish prophets. Jesus Himself foretold this positive Gentile response and their fusion with covenant Jews into one body, declaring that "men shall come from the east and the west, and shall sit down with Abraham and Isaac and Jacob in the kingdom of heaven" (Matt. 8:11).

Significantly, the book of James addressed scattered believers in Christ as "the twelve tribes dispersed abroad" (1:1), warning them not to engage in respect of persons among those coming to their synagogue (2:2, A.V.). The "assembling together" of Hebrews 10:25 is *episunagoge*, a gathering of baptized believers, but the language is Jewish. As a safeguard against apostasy, the writer of Hebrews was admonishing his readers not to forsake the "synagogue," whether it was a corporate setting of believers in Jewish places of worship, or in various house and family gatherings wherein saints in Christ met together to "stimulate and encourage one another unto love and good works" (v. 24).

In about AD 60, Paul spoke before King Agrippa of God's called out as "our twelve tribes earnestly serving God (present tense) night and day" (Acts 26:7). Evidently, the term "twelve tribes" refers to the sum total of Jewish believers who possessed "the faith of our Lord Jesus Christ" (Jas. 2:1). According to the author of Hebrews, these very people, as well as Gentiles, had come to "Mount Zion, to the heavenly Jerusalem, the city of the living God . . . the assembly of the first born" (12:22-23) – all long-established Jewish imagery.

Other biblical language suggesting continuity between God's people, before and after the cross, occurs in the Book of Revelation where believers in Christ are associated with temple or sanctuary worship (11:1-5) and ministering to Jerusalem. The real Jews are further contrasted with false worshipers, representing themselves as being in covenant, who "claim to be Jews but are not" (2:9, 3:9). In the New Jerusalem, the city of perfected saints, the 12 apostles and the 12 patriarchs of the tribes of Israel are present, further bonding more than four millennia of God's elect (21:12,14). In 4:4, 19:4, and elsewhere, the 24 elders before God's throne are probably these same spiritual leaders of covenant people through the ages (but see also I Chron. 24:4-18).

The apostle Paul designated the called out in Christ as the "Israel of God" and the "seed of Abraham" (Gal. 6:16, 3:29). They were also "the circumcision" (Phil. 3:13). In Matthew 19:16-22, Jesus encountered the rich young ruler, telling him to keep the Ten Commandments, quoting six of them, in order to be His disciple. Jesus was essentially saying, "Follow me and become part of renewed Israel." Those who continued with Him will sit upon twelve thrones, judging the "twelve tribes of Israel" (see above). Again, the people of God after the cross were described in terms of popular Jewish scriptural motifs, further pointing to continuity and commonality among God's covenant ones throughout time.

The second and third century church fathers taught that such Christ-followers were the true Israel. Justin Martyr wrote, "As, therefore, Christ is the Israel and the Jacob, even so we, who have been quarried out from the bowels of Christ, are the true Israelic race" (*Dialogue with Trypho*, Ch. 135). Irenaeus taught that the church is the seed of Abraham (*Against Heresies*, IV.8.2). Later, Hippolytus said, "For it is not of the Jews that he spake this word of old, nor of the city of Zion, but of the Church. For all the prophets have declared Zion to be the bride brought from the nations" (*Discourses* III).

Throughout the first century, Jewish saints in Christ did not believe that apostolic teaching required a full break from their longstanding religious heritage and practice. In the gospel of Christ they did not see a blanket release from their many obligations in the law of Moses. Believing in Jesus as the Christ was to them simply a renewal of firmly established prophetical teaching, an extension of faithful service to God and a presently possessed right-standing with God before those Jews had come in contact with the gospel of Christ.

Salvation indeed originated from among the Jews (John 4:22). How God interacted with His covenant Israel for centuries before the cross provides the vital background for understanding the apostolic message about Christ, as recorded in the scriptures of the New Testament. God's covenantal promise to the ancient fathers, together with the law's types and shadows and prophetic statements, lies at the very heart of understanding Christ's life and mission (Gen. 15:7-19, Luke 1:72, Rom. 15:8). The good news for those people of Israel, then, is that there is peace with God through accepting Jesus, who is the Lord of all creation.

This God-centered teaching is the substance of the one hope of Israel (Eph. 4:4, Acts 26:6-7, Gal. 6:16), which finds renewal in the gospel of Christ – His good deeds among men, His death, burial, resurrection, ascension, and His yet future second appearing (Heb. 9:28). All books from Matthew to Revelation must be understood against the backdrop of Israel's hope and history and the present realities in Christ, all of which correlate with the blessings of Abraham (Gen. 15-17, Gal. 3:14) and encompass all nations (v. 8).

Summary

To faithful first century Jews who became part of the sect of the way, commonly called Christianity, the teaching of Moses remained an integral part of their lives, just as the constitution is vital to Americans throughout the various generations. More than that, this law also guided their political and social lives. Since Jewish believers saw in Jesus of Nazareth the fulfillment of the prophets from Moses to Malachi, embracing Him as Christ was fully in continuity with their age-old Jewish identity. Thus, the rapidly emerging sect of the way after Acts 2, initially consisting entirely of messianic Jews, did not function apart from the visible religion of Moses. Rather, it proved to be a natural development within a long-established covenantal tradition, one dating from the time of Abraham.

By the middle of the first century, the mission of preaching the gospel of Christ to the Gentile world was well underway. This significant extension of God's kingdom – the royal rule over hearts – was never a break from prophet-led Israel, but a reaffirmation of God's promises made for centuries to holy men among the Jews. Amid all of these historical developments, no new-in-kind covenant supplanted the everlasting one given to Abraham, David, Jeremiah, and the contemporary prophets. No new law of Christ superseded the law of Moses. Assuredly, God never gave *a separate* "everlasting covenant" to Abraham, another to Moses, another to David, then still another to God's people of the late Jewish period, only to replace them with a new eternal covenant for Christians this side of the cross.

Instead, God's saints throughout time enjoy through the everlasting covenant a relationship in continuity and in harmony with each other. They will equally share the same reward in heaven. Just as initially the celestial woman of Revelation 12 (see Chapter Six) stood exclusively for right-standing Jewish people living before the cross, they were after that time still the same covenant body of the redeemed, even as many first century individual Jews joined themselves to Christ, day by day and year by year. They functioned with other saints in the sect of the way, including Gentiles. Such a glorious transformation (see Rom. 12:2) as depicted by the figure of the heavenly woman is the very essence of covenant renewal. It perfected the ancient eternal agreement (as explained in the book of Hebrews, especially 9:15-18), fulfilling it more than at any time in the entire Old Testament era (Acts 3:18-25).

In the present age there is therefore no "new Israel," or "spiritual Israel," concepts which two-covenant proponents employ to distance the allegedly superior Christians from the Jewish faithful. According to the imagery of the longstanding olive tree in Romans 11, the body of Christ in the first century and thereafter, consisted of restored individual Jews and ingrafted Gentiles harmoniously existing together (a unity explained in Chapter Six). This new (renewed) assembly under Christ exists in continuity with God's covenant Jews before the cross, and thus the faith of all saints since the first century in a special sense is legitimately the Jewish faith.

The amalgamation God's faithful people throughout time is further reflected in the life and preaching of the apostle Paul. As the youthful Saul of Tarsus, God even then considered him faithful (I Tim. 1:12-13), albeit with incomplete understanding. After he was convinced that Jesus was indeed the long-awaited Christ, he did not leave the "Jewish faith" to become a member of the "Christian faith." Instead, the apostle saw in Christ the fulfillment and renewal of the Jewish Torah (see Rom. 10:4).

He remained a faithful Jew, adhering to the law and the prophets, long after he embraced Christ. In Acts 23:6, nearly thirty years after the cross, Paul plainly boasted that he was *presently* a Pharisee – a practicing Jew without God condemning him for remaining such – and in Acts 21:21f he willingly participated in a week-long Jewish ritual in expression of worship to God (see Chapter Eight). These actions are strange indeed if the law of Moses had been nailed to the cross, as the two-covenant doctrine has concluded.

Therefore, to speak of the "conversion of Paul," as if he changed religions from Judaism to Christianity, does not match biblical facts. Similarly, no scripture supports a concept of the "conversion of the Ethiopian Eunuch," the near-3000 on Pentecost, or any of the Jews who accepted the gospel of Christ on Paul's missionary journeys (Acts 13-19). None of these learned that some new religion had displaced the proper covenantal religion of the Jews. More than that, these people did not run counter to Jewish law or sin against the temple (Acts 25:8) by embracing Christ.

How these first century saints in Christ employed available religious writings further demonstrated continuity among God's people from the earliest times. More than a generation after the Pentecost of Acts 2, Timothy was told that the "scriptures" would make him "wise unto salvation" (II Tim. 3:15). At issue cannot be apostolic writings, for none of them had yet begun to be assembled into a closed canon or collection. So those scriptures were various Old Testament documents read in the synagogues, where hopeful God-conscious people gathered together to hear men read and comment publicly from the scrolls.

From these writings of Moses and the prophets, Christ's apostles and evangelists could obtain the sound doctrine (II Tim. 4:3), and preach salvation through faith which is in Jesus Christ (II Tim. 3:15). Further, these very scriptures were useful for teaching, rebuking, correcting sin and error, and training in righteousness (v. 16), thus equipping first century baptized believers for every good work. Jeremiah, Isaiah, Ezekiel, the Proverbs, the Psalms, and other Jewish writings brought every man of God complete spiritual teaching and moral discipline, even in the first century, and can do so today for all of His covenanted ones. These things show a common religious thought and practice in the preaching and writing of the Israel's prophets and that of the Christian apostles and other holy men after the cross.

Chapter Ten

❦

The New Covenant of Jeremiah 31:31-34

A NY STUDY OF THE COVENANT must consider the key
prophecy of Jeremiah 31:31-34 concerning a new
covenant, quoted by the author of Hebrews (8:8-12) after the
mid-first century and unmistakably applied to the apostolic
era. Jeremiah's famous passage clearly promises a relationship
which God would enter with Judah and Israel as yet future:

> (31) Behold, the time is coming, declares the Lord,
> when I will make a new covenant with the house of
> Israel and with the house of Judah. (32) It will not be
> like the covenant I made with their forefathers, when
> I took them by the hand to lead them out of Egypt,
> because they broke my covenant, though I was a hus-
> band to them, declares the Lord. (33) This is the
> covenant I will make with the house of Israel after that
> time, declares the Lord. I will put my law in their
> minds and write it on their hearts. I will be their God
> and they will be my people. (34) No longer will a man

teach his neighbor, or a man his brother, saying, "know the Lord," because they will all know me, from the least of them to the greatest, declares the Lord. For I will forgive their wickedness and will remember their sins no more.

In this passage, two-covenant advocates distinctly contrast an alleged "fleshly" old covenant made with Israel's fathers after Egyptian deliverance with a "spiritual" first century new covenant, the "better way" under Christ, presuming a superior experience with God. The reasoning is that the author of Hebrews is making a "God-inspired, infallible interpretation" of Jeremiah's text, exclusively fulfilling the ancient prophet's announcement of a new-in-kind covenant for the first century people of God (see also Chapter Eleven). To them, such use of Old Testament material is the ultimate in scripture interpretation, allegedly allowing the Bible to interpret itself. But the Bible nowhere specifies a proper interpretive method, the correct hermeneutic.

Such insistence upon an *exclusive* fulfillment runs counter to the manner in which the apostles frequently employed the prophetic writings. Instead, the manner in which the author of Hebrews used Jeremiah 31:31-34 was a common first-century Rabbinic hermeneutic known as *rez pesher*, wherein a writer freely lifted material from the prophets irrespective of its original context, and applied it to his on-going argument to communicate a particular contemporary truth to his audience, revealing the "hidden meaning."

Far from being an unethical, reckless use of Old Testament passages, such "misquotations" by modern standards were quite acceptable in both first-century preaching and writing. Some obvious examples are:

Matthew 2:15 quotes from Hosea 11:1, "Out of Egypt I called my son," and applies it *forward* to the time when the child Jesus was brought back from Egypt after Herod had died. But the prophet of 725 B.C. referred those words *backward* to the time when God delivered the Hebrews from Egyptian bondage.

Matthew 2:18 uses the words of Jeremiah 31:15, "A voice is heard in Ramah, lamentations and bitter weeping, Rachel is weeping for her children," while referencing the slaughter of innocent Bethlehem infants at the time of Christ – a passage of *doom*. In the original context God told Jeremiah that Rachel is weeping from her grave, because her children will be taken into Babylonian captivity. God is saying to stop weeping, for the children will return – a passage of *hope*.

Matthew 27:9 borrows from Zechariah 11:12-13 and his story of the thirty pieces of silver. The apostle applied it to the betrayal by Judas, while Zechariah, in the original setting, told how he had flung to the potter the unworthy reward he received. As with dozens of other examples throughout the apostles' writings, here is a clear difference which can be accounted for only because of *rez pesher*.

Even Jesus Himself employed this common first century hermeneutic. "Is it not written, Ye are gods?'" was the Son of God's response to the Pharisees in a debate about His relationship with His Father (John 10:34). But the source of the quotation, Psalm 82:6, discussed a wholly different subject, the judgment of unjust rulers.

Early in His ministry Jesus quoted Isaiah 6:9-10, which in its original context, was God's call of the prophet in 730 B.C., and applied it to the Jews of His day and their lack of understanding of His parables (Matt. 15:9). Jesus later altered the application of this *identical* text before *another* audience (John 12:37-41), and Paul used Isaiah 6:9-10 in yet a *third way* thirty years later to describe the Jews in Rome who rejected Christ (Acts 28:23-28).

Other interesting examples of *rez pesher* are in Acts 1:20, where Luke applied Psalms 69:25 and 109:8 wholly out of their original settings while discussing the apostleship of Matthias; Jude's use in verses 14-15 of the apocryphal work I Enoch 1:9 (see also 60:8); the application of Psalm 95:7-11 by the author of Hebrews in an appeal for faithfulness

(3:7); and Paul's tendency to favor the altered Septuagint Greek texts of 250 B.C. over older Hebrew texts when he quoted the Old Testament several times in Romans 9, 10:18, etc.

Evidently, the writer of Hebrews also adopted that very common first century hermeneutic by "fetching" Jeremiah 31:31-34 from its immediate historic "habitat" and applying it to his thematic argument that Christ is "better" in every way, especially in His mediatorship of a "new covenant," His perfect one-time sacrifice, and His satisfying Old Testament types and shadows.

And so, it is foreign to the Bible and contrary to the common usage of Jewish writings by first century writers to designate a quotation of an Old Testament passage as an "inspired Holy Spirit interpretation" to give "God's real meaning and intent," when such a reference actually pointed to their well established interpretive system, *rez pesher*.

Jeremiah's New Covenant Realized in the Jews' Return from Exile

Evidently, a New Testament writer's recall of a Jewish prophet's writings to current events never precluded an earlier historical fulfillment in Israel's history. Indeed, Jeremiah's famous new (renewed) covenant of 31:31-34, first prophesied in about 593 B.C., was realized about 60 years later, when God's people in the houses of Judah and Israel – to whom the covenant oracle was specifically addressed – returned from Babylonian exile. After all, Jeremiah did not address the Gentiles in his new covenant prophecy, but certainly some individuals in the groups named – Judah and Israel – would still be living at the time when Cyrus would allow the Jews to resettle the holy land in 536 B.C.

That the fulfillment of Jeremiah's landmark covenantal promise (31:31-34) took place five centuries before Christ is made particularly apparent when it is compared with another passage written by the prophet's younger disciple, Ezekiel (36:24-28):

> (24) For I will take you out of the nations; I will gather you from all the countries and bring you back into your own land. (25) I will sprinkle clean water on you, and you will be clean; I will cleanse you from all your impurities and from all your idols. (26) I will give you a new heart and put a new spirit in you; I will remove from you your heart of stone and give you a heart of flesh. (27) And I will put my spirit in you and move you to follow my decrees and be careful to keep my laws. (28) You will live in the land I gave your forefathers; you will be my people, and I will be your God.

What beautiful, comforting promises! God would show His holiness, which had been profaned among the nations (see v. 23). As the Lord God cleansed the house of Israel/Judah from idols, the people glorified the good name of God among the nations where they had heretofore dishonored His name. Indeed, God would keep His promises to save His people from all uncleanness and all evil ways (v. 29).

And so, amid the atmosphere of Jerusalem's doom, Jeremiah promised glorious future hope and blessings, while Ezekiel, already in captivity in Babylon, continually preached that God would lead His people back to their own land after their experience in exile. Both prophets thus spoke of a renewed covenant people, not a new class or kind of covenant people under a future Messiah who would define another type of relationship with God, to be made more than five hundred years later. Note this stunning parallel:

The Revival of Israel and Judah Foretold
Two Prophets Announcing the Everlasting Covenant
A Renewal of the Covenant given to Abraham, David, Israel-Judah

Jeremiah 31:31-34	Terms of the Covenant	**Ezekiel 36:25-28**
For I will forgive their iniquity, and their sin I will remember no more (34b).	[1]*	I will sprinkle clean water on you . . . Wash you with pure lather. You shall be clean from the inside (25).

* This is the foundation of the entire covenant
upon which the other terms below are built.

I will put my law within them . . . write the law in their hearts (33).	[2]	A new heart . . . a new spirit I will put within you (26). See also 11:19-20, 18:31. I will . . . cause you to walk in my statutes (27). I will take away your stony heart (26).
I will be their God, and they will be my people (33b).	[3]	You shall be my people, and I will be your God (28b).
They shall not teach, know Yahweh, for they shall know me (34).	[4]	From all your idols I will cleanse I will put my spirit within you ... ye shall keep my ordinances (27) See also 37:23, 39:29

Follow up discourses by both prophets reinforce the above:

Jeremiah 32:36-40		**Ezekiel 37:24-27**
I will gather them out of the countries where I have driven them . . . I will bring them to this place (37). See also 44b.	[5]	They shall dwell in the land . . . where your fathers dwelt . . . (25). See also 36:24, 28; 37:1-23.
I will give them one heart and one way . . . (39).	[2]	They shall also walk in my ordinances, and observe my statutes, and do them (24b).
They shall be my people, and I will be their God.	[3]	I will be their God, and they shall be my people (27b).
I will make an *everlasting covenant* with them . . . (40).	[x]	I will make a covenant of peace with them; it shall be an *everlasting covenant* with them . . . (26).

Term number five (at left) shows that all of the other four comforting promises would take place when Judah and Israel would return from Babylonian captivity, which is unmistakably the greater context of Jeremiah 30 - 34 and Ezekiel 36 - 39. Most significantly, *every* point above is within the scope of the everlasting covenant (Jer. 32:40, Ezek. 37:26). Once safe again in the land of the fathers, the renewed people of God would be showered with blessings: God's law would be in their hearts, they would possess a new spirit, God would dwell in the midst of them, and – most especially – He would cleanse them and forgive them of their sins. What exceedingly great assurances!

In response to such good news, the happy covenant remnant of Israel at the time of Jeremiah could – even before the foretold restoration – sing with gladness and shout the great name of Jehovah (Jer. 31:7). More than seventy years later, God would gather a great company of His people and bring them back (v. 8). They would be delivered from oppression and captivity, returning to Zion in a renewed spiritual relationship, and not to Bethel's carnal worship. They would cling to the Father of blessings, weeping for joy (v. 9), and not to their former idols in a life of spiritual decadency.

And so, the faithful in Jerusalem's public places listening to Jeremiah addressing the "house of Israel and the house of Judah" (31:31) about the promise of a new covenant would be greatly comforted by the prophet's consoling words of the nation's renewal, uttered amid the harsh reality of impending Babylonian captivity and the destruction of Jerusalem. The Jewish community would not be thinking of the Gentiles, for the prophet did not mention them at all. Since most commentators agree that Jeremiah 30 - 34 is the Book of Consolation and hope for Israel and Judah, it should follow that the new covenant passage (31:31-34), deeply embedded within this five-chapter section, indeed addressed the Jews' return from Babylon and the promised blessings to the faithful remnant once they returned to the land of the fathers.

Note also the appearance of key words and phrases through-out Jeremiah 30–31. Repeatedly the prophet spoke of a restoration and a rebuilding of the Jewish economy after the exilic experience (30:3, 17, 18; 31:4, 8, 38). The weary, scat-tered covenanted faithful would return to their own land (31:16-18), refreshed (v. 25), and with new hearts and a knowl-edge of forgiveness of sin (vv. 33-34). Even more significant is the recurrence of the phrase "the days (or time) are coming . . ." in 30:3; 31:1, 27, 31, 38), further bonding 31:31-34 with *all* of the events of Chapters 30–32.

Thus, any assertion that the new covenant passage 31:31-34 does not have primary reference to the Jews and their return, but must be fulfilled principally (if not *exclusively*) in the era of Christ (see Heb. 8:6f), makes Jeremiah's new covenant con-textually awkward. It is an unwarranted intrusion – a proverbial "bolt out of the blue" – into a greater context that thoroughly describes the rebirth of Judah in about 536 B.C. in their former land.

Over and over, the prophet describes the restoration of Judah in terms of rebuilding cities and palaces, and replanting of vineyards and gardens. At that time – when Israel and Judah shall return into their own country – the people would sing aloud of the goodness of the Lord and adorn themselves with timbrels, so that they may go forth in the dance of the merrymakers (31:4). Indeed, Yahweh would "make them walk by brooks of water, in a straight path from which they will not stumble" (31:9).

Such reinterpretation by the author of Hebrews of Jeremiah 31:31-34 to make it fit into a new context more than 600 years later is the reverse of the normal procedure of looking for the nearest possible fulfillment, a practice that premillennial theo-rists frequently violate (see Chapter Fourteen). However, in the first century, such employment of an ancient text was legitimate because of the prevailing hermeneutic, *rez pesher.*

Jeremiah's New Covenant and Ancient Treaty Arrangements

Covenants in ancient times, including the one God made with Israel, were not dated by a year-number, but by a significant event, such as "when I took you out of Egypt . . ." And so, as a king delivered a lesser nation from another, or conquered it outright, a treaty was made, capped by ceremonial arrangements. The ability of the greater king to fulfill the covenant is stated in the various terms of the covenant (see Chapter One).

From the perspective of Judah and scattered Israel in about 593 B.C., the new covenant of 31:31-34 would now be distinguished from the *former* arrangement God had made with His people when Egypt released them. Jeremiah taught that the eternal covenant would in the future possess a new frame of reference. As the Divine Warrior and King of the covenant, the God of heaven who had already led His people out of Egyptian captivity would deliver the Jews from the impending Babylonian capture with equal force (see 16:14-5, 23:7-8).

This release, fifty years into the future and after the fall of the nation in 586 B.C., would distinctively demonstrate to one and all God's power and absolute faithfulness to the covenant – that He would staunchly fulfill it and keep it. Because of idolatry and disobedience, Judah had broken the longstanding agreement (Jer. 3:6-14), and (as with the northern ten tribes previously) the covenant technically was no longer in force to them. It had to be renewed. Thus, the touchstone for covenant dating the release from Egypt's grip – no longer applied.

Therefore, the Jews in Jeremiah's day should begin to think of God not primarily as the One who brought their ancestors out of Egypt, but as the future Deliverer who would bring His people back from Babylon and other countries where He had banished them, as reported by Jeremiah. "The days are coming, declares the Lord, when men will no longer say 'as surely as the Lord lives, who brought the Israelites up out of Egypt,' but they will say, 'as surely as the Lord lives, who brought the Israelites up out of the land to the north and out of all the countries where He had banished them.' For I will restore them to the land I gave their forefathers." (Jer. 16:14–15, 23:7).

The 'Heart' in the New Covenant

Evidently, the new covenant of Jeremiah 31:31–34 does not involve the establishment of a new-in-kind agreement to be fulfilled exclusively among Christians who would be governed by a new law. Instead, the prophets words found expression in changed natures, as the faithful Jewish community, no longer under Babylon's yoke, forsook their idols and once again resolved to walk in God's ways. They would reclaim their ancestral land with God's commandments in their hearts, as did their fathers (Deut. 6:6). They would return with a new resolve and a heart liberated from sin's bondage, knowing God's will and having the power to do it as expressed in Ezekiel 11:19-20. In response to this measure of covenant faithfulness, God would blot out their sins (Ezek. 36:25; see also Ex. 34:6). They would truly know God, from the greatest to the least (Jer. 31:34).

To participate in this intimate covenantal experience, the law in the heart was essential (Psa. 37:31, 40:8, 119:11). The acceptable doing of God's will is related to the state of the mind. Knowing righteousness meant that the law in the heart was the spiritual standard for these exiles (Isa. 51:7). The concept of creation of a clean heart and mind was an exercise for all Old Testament faithful (Prov. 22:11; Psa. 51:10, 17, 73:1, 13; Deut. 6:5-6, 11:18).

Individuals would insure that the law was in their minds by returning to God with circumcised hearts (Lev. 26:41, Jer. 4:4, 9:25-26; Ezek. 44:7,9). This personalized religion and God's acceptance of it was made possible by a good heart, rather than mere outward obedience to structured commandments. The latter mindset externalizes law and behavior, with little attention to the *personal* state of individuals, that is, the condition of their hearts. Covenant people are assuredly not laboring under a law-works system, but look to continual inward renewal while glorifying God to the best of their ability.

Covenant Renewal in Isaiah 40-66

In harmony with the same grace-centered preaching of Jeremiah and Ezekiel, the prophet Isaiah's writings in Chapters 40-66 contain a repository of covenant traditions of Israel's recreation after returning from Babylonian captivity. The ultimate aim of such teaching is the furtherance of individual inward renewal in the "everlasting covenant" (55:3, 61:8b), a concept that coincides nicely with the comforting teachings of both Jeremiah (32:40) and Ezekiel (37:26).

The prophet prepared the people for judgment and captivity (40:1-11) by promising that ultimately God would redeem them in a "second exodus" (40:3-5, 42:16, 43:16f, etc.), thus renewing the ancient covenant conveyed to Abraham and Moses. This return was effected by God's divine plan, His word (40:8, 55:11). The nation, the offspring of Abraham, would eventually become great; the people would again work in their own land, rebuilding farms and cities (49:8-13, 18-24). The covenant faithful among the nation would thus be benefited as they sought the Lord and anticipated their deliverance from oppression with unwavering faith (48:1, 51:1).

Amid these splendid promises, God's righteousness and faithfulness would constantly be evident. He would continually bathe Jacob/Israel (48:1b, 58:2) in lovingkindness, with the constancy of waves lapping up on the rocks of the sea shore (48:18). Such words of consolation and compassion would cheer the captives (49:13b) – relief would come! More than to the Jews, the promise of blessings to the Gentiles is woven in (49:6), ultimately extending the sphere of covenantal salvation to every nation.

Once unburdened by captivity's yoke, sorrow would flee, to be replaced by gladness and joy (51:11). But the unfaithful who forsook the covenant by rejecting God's ways are depicted as a drunken woman wallowing in the dust of her own desolation (51:17). God's wrath would pour forth upon them and they would suffer desolation and destruction, famine and the sword (v. 19). As Isaiah cried "Awake, awake!" he urged reliance upon God's strength.

In this context, the prophet Isaiah introduced the servant (52:13), specifically identified in 49:3 as the nation Israel, called in righteousness into a covenant to be a light to the Gentiles (49:6, 43:6; see also the book of Jonah). Especially, the servant also typifies the ideal vivacious servant, Jesus Christ, who would also minister to the Gentiles (42:1, Matt. 4:16, Luke 2:32). In truth and righteousness, He would bring forth justice for all in the everlasting covenant by perpetuating it not only for Israel but also for the Gentiles. Thus, Isaiah 52:13-53:12 discusses the servant's role among the nations, first as the corporate *nation* Israel and, ultimately and more gloriously, to all the world in the *person* of Jesus.

As the people of God returned from Babylon to Zion, there would be great joy amid singing, because of a loving God's salvation and deliverance (52:7-10, 55:10-12). New relationships would arise, and a fostering God would extend mercy to all (54:2-3, 13-14; 55:1, 10-12). Isaiah echoed the Abrahamic promise that descendants would possess the nations and reinhabit the desolated cities (54:1-3). The prophet then appealed to the "everlasting covenant of peace" (v. 10), which pointed to the renewed agreement which would emerge from the exilic experience. It squarely rested upon the fidelity and veracity of God. The phrase "My lovingkindness shall not depart from thee" (v. 10a; see also v. 8) attests to "divine covenant constancy" (William J. Dumbrell, *Covenant and Creation*, p. 195).

In absolute righteousness, God would build a splendid new city (vv. 11-12). This heritage of God's faithful servants was sought by godly people as early as Abraham (see Heb. 11:10-12), by David, by the restored Israel after Babylon, as well as by the saints of the messianic era. All would equally participate in the new life with God, where water, milk, and wine would all flow abundantly in the city.

All promised blessings are within the context of the everlasting covenant, further defined as the "sure mercies of David" (55:3). Other comforting pictures of assurance and prosperity comprise the rest of chapter 55, climaxing with the scene of joy, peace, and song because the nation Israel would never again be "cut off" (v. 13b). God's promised blessing of Jewish restoration therefore ushered in a renewed age in covenantal history.

In Israel's renewed relationship with God, sin would no longer be remembered and the law would be in the heart. God would forbear His people while vigorously rebuking the idols and every evil ruler. In chapters 60-66, the people of glorified Zion are further described as wearing a new name (62:2), an unmistakable sign that God's faithful were interacting with Him in the "everlasting covenant" (61:8). Through it He would deliver His people by "new heavens and a new earth" (65:17, 66:22) – a renewed order of the Jewish religious economy after the exile.

Isaiah identified the instrument of Israel's restoration and redemption, the servant Jesus Christ, as a "covenant" (42:6) who would ultimately extend light – salvation – to the Gentiles (vv. 1-6; see also Matt. 12:15-21). Since the servant is metonymy for covenant, all of its blessings are authored and dispensed by Christ Himself. He delivered the Jews returning from captivity from spiritual bondage (idolatry), and ultimately set free *all* souls imprisoned in moral darkness (Gal. 4:8, John 8:35-47).

In 49:8 Jesus is again designated as a "covenant," the One who would renew the nation (44:26) by restoring to them Jerusalem and the waste places of Judah. Further, in the messianic era he would "raise up the land" (49:8b) by extending it "from sea to sea" (Psa. 72:8, Zech. 9:10), through the proclamation of the gospel of the kingdom to both Jews and Gentiles.

In short, Isaiah 40-66 paints a glorious picture of post-exilic Israel in a new spiritual order where they are abundantly blessed in the everlasting covenant. They partake of a fountain of blessings where there is neither youth nor age – all are alike (58:11-12; see also 41:18). As God's servant, the nation would be continually protected and supplied with every spiritual provision. This lofty metaphor has further spiritual application to God's covenant people of New Testament times, in the person of the consummate Servant, Jesus Christ, in His earthly ministry and death on the cross.

Clearly, God's call to return His people to the land of the fathers is the essence of covenant renewal. They would rejoice in a city called "Sought out" (62:12). They would be a people returning from Babylonian travail and oppression, born in a day (66:7-9) to worship God once again in the victory circle, while beholding their dead enemies (vv. 23-24). Truly, God's gracious covenant dealings take God-seeking individuals into His counsels to participate in glory and divine favor, wherever they are, regardless of time or location.

Covenant Renewal Among Post-Exilic Prophets

Once the Jewish faithful were again secure in the land of their forefathers in about 536 B.C., various prophets admonished the people to renew their covenant pledge with God, stressing also the necessity of rebuilding the temple. Haggai and Zechariah both appealed to the newly settled to repent and return to God. Haggai had as his theme the defilement of the rebellious Jews through sin and God's implementation of the covenantal curses for disobedience (1:1-6), while Zechariah stressed the necessity of continuing in righteous living, exhorting the people not to be like their idolatrous forefathers, as in the days before Israel, and finally Judah, were carried away into captivity (1:2-6).

When those ancestors refused to hearken to God after the prophets spoke out against their sins, they forsook the "everlasting covenant" spoken of by Ezekiel, Jeremiah, and Isaiah (see Chapter Five). Now Haggai and Zechariah were reminding the faithful not to become covenant breakers. Their choice was clear: strengthen your relationship with God, or His wrath will similarly pour forth upon you.

In chapter 8, Zechariah fired the hopes of faithful Jews by announcing that, in mercy and lovingkindness, God had returned to Zion and would dwell with renewed hearts in what would be called the "Faithful City" (Jerusalem – v. 3). The comforting statement, "They shall be my people and I will be their God in truth and righteousness" (v. 8), is a covenantal term which promises that God would protect and care for His own. Good things would come through hard work with their hands (vv. 9-13) and adhering to moral law. The spiritual blessings God promised to His own throughout the chapter represent both a fulfillment and renewal of God's eternal covenant in love, peace, and truth. The Lord Himself would celebrate with His people with joy and singing, as taught by Zephaniah (3:17).

The message of Malachi, who preached in Jerusalem late in the fourth century B.C., demonstrated an important continuity with the covenant-centered truths uttered by earlier Hebrew prophets. He emphasized the importance of internal attitude and heart over all external displays of ceremonial religion (1:10-13, 2:2-3, 3:16-18). Malachi also explained God's covenantal blessings, which are rooted in personal obedience, and the covenantal cursings which would surely come to arrogant evildoers. He stressed a moral code of behavior which was consistent with the nature of the Covenant Maker (3:5-7; see also Isa. 1:15-20).

Ezra and Nehemiah (about 455-430 B.C.) implemented Malachi's reforms as they addressed the social and religious evils of their day: priestly disorders, problems of mixed marriages, non-payment of tithes, and doctrinal formalism. Ezra had a temple-centered, covenant-orientated mission, as shown in the beautiful Levitical prayer (Neh. 9:5-37) which reviewed God's grace and power and righteous deeds (v. 8) with everyone in the everlasting covenant of love (v. 32). It ended with the people asking for a restoration of Israel's prosperity in their land of promise.

Through the influence of such God-centered covenantal teaching, a spiritual Messiah-seeking remnant did carry on, and Jerusalem flourished as the City of Truth (Zech. 8:3) for an additional five centuries up to the era of Jesus Christ, as depicted in the continued life and vitality of the covenant remnant figures – the celestial woman of Revelation 12 and the longstanding olive tree of Romans 11 (see Chapter Six).

Summary

The new covenant theology of Jeremiah 31:31-34 is properly set within the parameters of chapters 30 through 34, which describe the comforting promise of Israel's and Judah's restoration and renewal after their half-century long Babylonian experience. That Jeremiah 31:31-34 pertains to the era after the exile is confirmed with fuller explanation by two other Jewish prophets of that same era: Ezekiel's blueprint for the returnees from Babylon in chapters 36-39, and Isaiah's elaboration of the same concepts in chapters 40-66.

Each of those three prophets foresaw the removal of the Jewish people from Judea to Babylon and, ultimately, their successful return to their own land. All of these events constituted the vanguard of the new covenant, a gracious relationship with God which is not absolutely new by the time of the post-exilic era, because such things had *already* taken place earlier in the history of God's people. Though both the Hebrew word for new, *hadas*, and its Greek counterpart, *kainos*, can convey the idea of something absolutely new and never previously existent, each also frequently means "to renew" or "to restore," thus further expanding upon or reiterating an existing concept. Several examples of such are given in the first part of Chapter Five.

William Dumbrell reports that in Jeremiah 31:31 the Greek Old Testament (the Septuagint) translates *hadash* as *kainos*, at this point as an adjective referring to a "qualitatively new dimension being added to the covenant experience . . . [It is] not merely or necessarily a totally new divine initiative which has no temporal reference to the past." Evidently, Jeremiah 31:31-34 expanded and creatively renewed the ancient promise that burned in the hearts of God's people from Abraham through the prophets up to that time.

Thus, in both historical and literary contexts, Jeremiah did not at all prophesy of a new-in-kind covenant or agreement, or an entirely *different* order, attached to *another* law under the future Messiah. Rather, the prophet was comforting the beleaguered covenant faithful in Jerusalem during the years 600-586 B.C. by foretelling of the glorious time of renewal and spiritual prosperity among the houses of Israel and Judah, only a few generations after their impending captivity.

Ezekiel, in the vision of the valley of the dry bones, augmented Jeremiah's words by graphically depicting a new age after the period of exile when the two houses of Judah and Ephraim (Israel] would be brought together as one nation in a divine grafting operation (37:15-23). The final chapters in Isaiah and Jeremiah 30-34 (and elsewhere) emphasize this same post-exilic experience wherein, after a period of appropriate discipline, there would be one harmonious people of God in the holy land transcending the old geographical division that had formed after Solomon died in about 950 B.C. This restoration is probably Jeremiah's reference point when he refers to the new covenant, not the messianic era.

Assuredly, as the writer of Hebrews argued after the cross, the ancient agreement would see further renewal in Christ, especially as it would embrace the Gentiles. A covenant which includes the resurrected Christ benefiting all nations is better, hence "new." It is not different, but the eternal covenant now has evolved into its fulfilled consummate state. Though Jeremiah 31:31-34 saw a complete historic fulfillment in the resettlement of Judea after 536 B.C., it has even a more significant meaning in the New Testament era, where the eternal covenant would become "better" (Heb. 8:6-7).

Ever since His crowning upon His ascension into heaven

(Acts 1:11), Jesus as Christ has functioned as God did in Old Testament times, as the divine Deliverer of people from any kind of oppression and the captivity of sin. Historically, the enemies of God's people had been Egypt and Babylon; when God freed Israel from these oppressors He showered them with a multitude of blessings. Now through His resurrection, Jesus the Righteous Warrior has delivered His people from the enemy, Satan, by overcoming and binding him.

If there were no continuity of covenantal arrangements among all of these people, then how were Joshua, Daniel, Ezekiel, Amos and the multitude of other Old Testament era faithful rescued from satan's domain and the grip of sin? How did they gain salvation? Further, why are these and many others cited in Hebrews 11 as supreme of examples of authentic faith, if indeed they are somehow of reduced status compared to us? Through Christ came the better deliverance through the shedding of His blood, bringing about the ultimate guarantee of forgiveness and the present assurance of salvation in the covenant relationship.

Therefore, students of scripture must recognize that the meaning of a biblical text has to stand by itself in its own context, appropriately relating truths to the Jewish audience contemporary with the prophet. An apostolic understanding of any Hebrew scripture, including Jeremiah 31:31-34, is a legitimate *reinterpretation* of the earlier writings. Both the meaning of the ancient passage in its original pre-Christian framework and also its first century application must be respected. (See "Accommodation" in *International Standard Bible Encyclopedia* 1:24-28.)

The eternal new covenant in the Christian era is also "better" because it abolished the well-used Jewish ceremonial and sacrificial orders (Heb. 8:13, 19-22), which were God's types and foreshadows of Christ's one-time unrepeatable sacrifice (see Chapter Three). All earthly high priests have been discharged in favor of the One from heaven. The gold-plated stone temple in Jerusalem crumbles in comparison with the magnificence of Christ's spiritual house of believers. Perhaps in part, God allowed its destruction in AD 70 so that Jews would see past the temple mount to the Christ.

Significantly, the everlasting covenant is no longer dated such as "made when I brought you out of Egypt . . ." As expressed on page 199, the covenant would now be dated from the return the return from Babylon, for God would fulfill his promise never to abandon them (Lev. 26:44). What a comfort! They would reoccupy the lands that their fathers had originally inherited in Joshua's time. All covenantal blessings, especially their cleansing through forgiveness of sin, would be restored, and compliance with God's will would come from the heart. As God promised to re-establish and renew His people, Jeremiah appropriately called this process a new covenant.

So, instead of Jeremiah 31:31-34 proving the existence of two *contrasting* covenants, with a first (old one) forever abolished, and another (entirely new one) in force since Pentecost, the prophet spoke of God's interaction with the covenant faithful among Jeremiah's people, before and after the Babylonian exile, *well before* the cross (as *also* taught by Isaiah and Ezekiel in the prophets' phrase "everlasting covenant"), and also with the people of Christ from *every* nation after the cross (as amplified by the author of Hebrews in 8:8-12 through the contemporary hermeneutic, *rez pesher*).

Jeremiah's famous new covenant teaching amply demonstrates the uninterrupted existence of God's covenant people from the turbulent days prior to Jerusalem's fall in 586 B.C. into the messianic era. Under Jesus Christ, the embryonic covenant which originated with the family of Abraham, and was renewed in Israel through Moses, David, and the prophets, is made complete and mature, reaching its inevitable full development and embracing a worldwide vision.

And so, far from teaching two *contrasting* covenants, Jeremiah 31:31-34 (Hebrews 8:6-13) stunningly confirms the *continuity* of the *one* eternal (everlasting) covenant between God and His chosen people, throughout the ages.

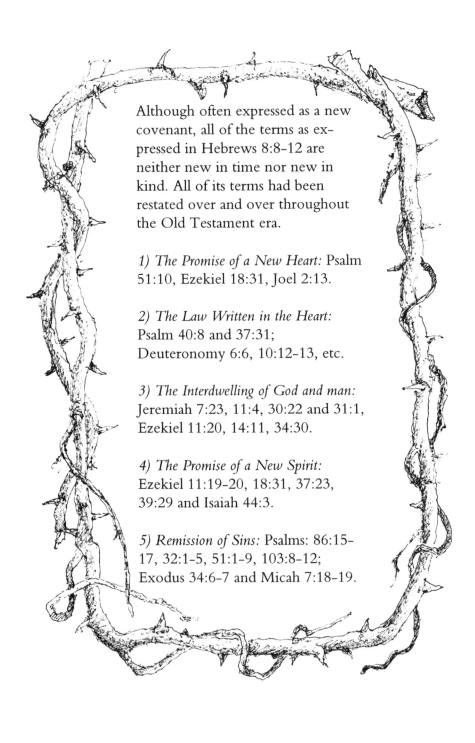

Although often expressed as a new covenant, all of the terms as expressed in Hebrews 8:8-12 are neither new in time nor new in kind. All of its terms had been restated over and over throughout the Old Testament era.

1) The Promise of a New Heart: Psalm 51:10, Ezekiel 18:31, Joel 2:13.

2) The Law Written in the Heart: Psalm 40:8 and 37:31; Deuteronomy 6:6, 10:12-13, etc.

3) The Interdwelling of God and man: Jeremiah 7:23, 11:4, 30:22 and 31:1, Ezekiel 11:20, 14:11, 34:30.

4) The Promise of a New Spirit: Ezekiel 11:19-20, 18:31, 37:23, 39:29 and Isaiah 44:3.

5) Remission of Sins: Psalms: 86:15-17, 32:1-5, 51:1-9, 103:8-12; Exodus 34:6-7 and Micah 7:18-19.

Chapter Eleven

⌒∾

What is 'New' About The New Covenant of Hebrews 8:6-13?

T HE PRECEDING FIVE CHAPTERS develop the far-reaching concept of a new covenant, an expression which uniquely appears in Jeremiah 31:31 in the writings of the Old Testament. But others among the Jewish prophets employed various descriptive words in association with Jeremiah's new agreement.

Ezekiel said that God would remember the everlasting covenant with His people Israel (16:60), not only in the prophet's day but also when David (Jesus Christ) would be over them as prince forever (37:25), in the messianic era. Isaiah invited Israel to incline the ear and partake of the sure mercies of David of old in the everlasting covenant (55:3), wherein their seed shall be known among all the nations in the messianic age (61:8). Jeremiah described Israel as being blessed in "one heart and one way" in the everlasting covenant (32:40), not only when they came back from Babylonian captivity but also when Israel and Judah would come together under Christ (50:5).

In a glorious return from captivity, Ezekiel declared that

God would give His covenant house of Israel "one [new] heart and . . . a new spirit" (11:19, 18:31). In sprinkling clean water upon His people, Yahweh said that He would put into them "a new heart and a new spirit," replacing their stony hearts of flesh (36:26; comp. Jer 17:1, 32:39). Further, God would put His spirit within them (v. 27), described in 39:29 as a "pouring out of His spirit."

Both Isaiah and Ezekiel proclaim God's everlasting agreement with man as a "covenant of peace" (Isa. 54:10, Ezek. 34:25a, 37:26). In connection with this compact, God declared that His lovingkindness would not depart from Zion, a promise so absolutely sure that in fact the mountains and hills of its desert setting would first be removed (Isa. 54:10). Covenanters returning to Zion, as well as God's people under Christ, would enjoy the agreement of peace with showers of blessing and eternal protection from all enemies (Ezek. 34:25b). This peace compact is the everlasting covenant (Ezek. 37:26, Jer. 32:40).

In righteousness and justice, God would execute the covenant (Hos. 2:18-19). Its words would never fail (Isa. 59:21), as Yahweh brings salvation to the people and preserves those who respected Him (Isa. 49:8). God's intimate, personal attachment with His people would ultimately extend beyond the community of the Jews to include the Gentile nations as well, in the covenant of righteousness (Isa. 42:6).

These many words of comfort from the Jewish prophets explain the glorious eternal (everlasting) covenant which God has extended toward man, first with Abraham (Luke 1:55, 72-73; Gen. 17:7-19), then renewed and extended under Moses (I Chron. 16:15-18), and again at the time of King David (II Sam. 23:3-5; see also 7:11-17). Jeremiah 32:40 and Ezekiel 37:26 clearly connect the new covenant theme with the faithful of both Israel and Judah, restored and unified after Babylonian captivity, while the author of Hebrews further extends the eternal covenant to every nation in the era of Christ, from the first century onward (13:20).

Thus, this everlasting covenant, the gospel of Christ, is actually found throughout each phase of the history of God's dealings with man. From Abraham's day (Gal. 3:8, 29) and even before, through the centuries into the messianic era, multitudes of faithful people have enjoyed the blessings of God's eternal covenant, all partaking magnificently in Heaven's grace. Verily, a covenant remnant has always stood before all of the nations as a testimony of God's faithfulness to His promises and oaths to His people.

Besides the many above biblical references to the everlasting covenant, that phrase occurs in two other ancient texts. In Genesis 9:16-17, God established an unconditional "everlasting covenant" with all flesh, specifically promising never to flood the earth again. Much later, Isaiah stated that "the earth" (heathen nations) had broken the "everlasting covenant" (24:5) by transgressing various laws and statutes, all of which likely refer to moral prohibitions set forth by various patriarchs under natural law (Gen. 26:5, 3:22, 4:3-7, 17:1, 20:3-7; Ex. 18:7; Job 23:11-12, etc.).

The righteous of Isaiah 24:5 enjoy God's gracious, saving commitment to man, and His promise and oath first given to Abraham, for the everlasting covenant is God's commitment to bless people from *all* nations (Gen. 12:3), saving them. Since Abraham is the father of a "multitude of nations" (Gen. 17:5-6), people other than the Jews had the privilege and obligation to respond to God's everlasting covenant. Evidently, God always looked with favor upon those among "the earth" who persevered in doing good (Rom. 2:5) and kept the positive requirements of moral law (vv. 14-15, 26-29).

In contrast, the immoral of "the earth" of 24:5 possess no spiritual relationship with God and are strangers to the eternal covenant of peace (Eph. 2:12, Heb. 13:20). They are as the spiritually uncircumcised of Romans 2:26-29, for physical circumcision was a sign of covenant indwelling with God (Gen. 17:13). Perhaps Isaiah stated that the earth had broken the "everlasting covenant" to remind Israel's faithful that the violation of moral precepts would result in pollution of the people, always bringing curses upon them.

The New Covenant of Jeremiah 31:31-34— Hebrews 8:8-12 Restates Existing Concepts

A review of each term of covenant in Jeremiah 31:31-34 (and the corresponding passage in Ezekiel 36:25-28) shows that the famous new covenant passage does not introduce anything entirely new but restates time-honored aspects of salvation found in older Jewish writings, in Jeremiah, Ezekiel, Isaiah, the Psalms, and in the books of Moses.

(1) The Promise of a New Heart. Ezekiel 36:26 emphatically promises that God will place a new heart within each of His covenanted ones. Such a blessing had already been stated by Ezekiel in 11:19, where new hearts would replace stony hearts. As people cast aside their transgressions and enter in covenantal union with God, they gain a new heart (Ezek. 18:31). A pure heart or clean heart is the very thing for which king David prayed (Psa. 51:10).

A new heart is a rent heart (Joel 2:13), filled with respect for God (Jer. 32:40). It is a circumcised heart (Deut. 10:16, 30:6), a merry heart, one which loves God wholeheartedly (Deut. 6:5). Therefore, Ezekiel's "new heart" is not "new in kind," but one which exhibits a changed nature, a renewal, derived from a concept centuries old.

(2) The Law Written in the Heart. Jeremiah 31:33 promises that God would write His law in the heart, but this feature of the new covenant was sung centuries before by the poet David: "The law is within my heart" (Psa. 40:8, see also 37:31). Moses also urged that the law resides in the heart of God's covenanted ones (Deut. 6:6, 10:12-13, 30:14; see also 32:46, Psa. 111:10). Thus this promise and reality have been around a long time.

(3) God and Man Bound Together in Love. Jeremiah 31:33 contains the famous phrase, "I will be your God and you will be my people," a spiritual blessing that dates from the very time of the initiation of the everlasting covenant, in Abraham's day (Gen. 17:7). From then onward, and in many contexts by several prophets before Jeremiah proclaimed his new covenant prophecy, this comforting interdwelling of God and His people was oft- stated, as earlier in the book of Jeremiah, at 7:23, 11:4, 30:22, 31:1, and later at 32:38.

Ezekiel also reaffirmed this promise of divine strength and consolation in 11:20, 14:11, 34:30, 36:28, and also in 37:27, a passage Paul later quoted (II Cor. 6:16). Other significant usages are in Exodus 6:7 and 29:45, Leviticus 26:12, Hosea 2:23 and Zechariah 13:9. So Jeremiah's words obviously reach back to ancient times; they were also restated after Jeremiah's day in the post-exilic period, as well as in the New Testament era.

(4) The Promise of a New Spirit. Ezekiel 37:23 gracefully declares that God gives to each covenanter a new spirit, but earlier the prophet had uttered this very promise (11:19-20, 18:31). Therefore it is nothing new (comp. 39:29). Isaiah reassured his audience that after they would return from Babylon, God would pour His Spirit upon His seed (44:3; comp. 59:21). Joel 2:28-32 foresaw the pouring out of God's Spirit in the "last days," a promise that extended from the late Jewish period into the Christian age (Acts 2:17-21). Therefore all covenanters, before and after the time of Ezekiel, would be blessed with a new spirit. But it is a treasured concept which obviously had been introduced long ago.

(5) Remission of Sins. Jeremiah 31:34 expresses God's greatest gift to His people: "For I will forgive their iniquities and remember their sins no more." Again, this new covenant concept is nothing new, for Old Testament people over the centuries had received the forgiveness of their transgressions and sins by a gracious, merciful God. When the redeemed of

Israel experienced the blotting out of sins, those deeds were thereafter no longer regarded by God as existing and were not imputed to His people, for in forgiving transgressions God had paid the price for them (Isa. 44:22).

King Hezekiah assured his people that after God cast their sins behind His back, He never turned and looked at them again, completely separating Himself from them (Isa. 38:17). The psalmist of old joyfully sang, "As far as the east is from the west, so far hath He removed our transgressions from us" (103:8-12; see also 86:15-17, 32:1-5, 51:1-9). Micah taught that God pardons iniquity, and delights in lovingkindness, in casting Israel's sins into the depths of the sea (7:18-19). See also Joel 2:13.

This climactic feature of Jeremiah's new covenant – the remission of sins – is as old as Moses. Exodus 34:6-7 emphatically declares that "Yahweh [is] a God merciful and gracious . . . keeping lovingkindness for thousands, forgiving iniquity and transgression of sin . . .", a promise reaffirmed in Numbers 14:18 and Deuteronomy 5:9-10.

Even before Moses, Abraham experienced remission of sins, since God accounted him righteous, justifying him by faith (Rom. 4:1-15). Therefore, to "know the Lord" (Jer. 31:34a) means to experience God's forgiveness and attendant blessings: a new spirit and heart, the law written on that heart, and the comforting fellowship where covenant people who have the remission of sins are intimately bound to God.

Truly, nothing new is introduced in the terms of the new covenant in Jeremiah 31:31-34 (Heb. 8:8-12).

Irony and the Promise of a New Covenant

Whenever a writer wishes to place special emphasis upon the specific concept at hand, he might employ a rhetorical device such as irony. While doing so, there is no revelation of a hidden meaning or suggestion of allegory; rather, the irony itself focuses attention directly upon a certain word or phrase, legitimately expressing the very opposite of the common meaning of the words actually used. Thus, irony purposely conveys an other-than-literal meaning for a particular thought and its phrasing to add greater force to it.

The previous section of this chapter shows that the components of the new covenant of Jeremiah 31:31-34 are not at all innovative, for each of them is not only found in earlier sections of Jeremiah, but also in the writings of many past Jewish prophets. Perforce, the author of Hebrews, quoting Jeremiah 31 after the cross, cannot be arguing for anything entirely new as well (8:6-12).

Further, Chapter Five demonstrates that biblical words using the word "new" – such as new commandment to love, new creation, new creature in Christ, etc. – often do not carry the idea that these concepts had never before been in existence. This conclusion is confirmed by Paul's use of the term "new covenant" in Galatians 4:21-31 and in II Corinthians 3:4-18, as well as by the author of Hebrews in 8:6-12.

Galatians 4:21-31

In a plain, straightforward discussion of the nature of two women – Hagar (Mt. Sinai, earthly Jerusalem) and [Sarah] (Jerusalem from above) – Paul called each of them a "covenant" (v. 24). The apostle employed allegory and perhaps also irony as he contrasted the two women: the system of slavery in the "Jerusalem *that is now*," [i.e., in mid-first-century], as demonstrated in the powerful man-devised Jewish religion in his day, associated with Mount Sinai, and the freedom issuing from the "Jerusalem *above*," as embodied in a grace-faith relationship with God, something Paul outlined in Galatians 3. A description of this freedom found in the longstanding covenant is supplemented by a quotation from Isaiah 54:1f (Gal. 4:27-28). It led people along the way of promise and liberty to covenantal intimacy with the living God.

In sharp contrast, the first-century Hagar/Mt. Sinai woman is not a covenant at all, for Paul equated her with Christ-rejecting, Talmudic Judaism with which the evangelist had to contend at times on each of his missionary journeys. Referring to this human-devised system as a "covenant" is surely ironical, for it actually points to a "broken" agreement with God (Jer. 31:32) In Galatians 4:30, Paul emphatically climaxed his total rejection of the tradition-bound Jews embodied in Hagar: "Cast out the bondwoman and her son, for the son of the bondwoman *shall not* be an heir with the son of the free woman."

All party-centered religious systems had no association with God's everlasting covenant, for each of them was founded and perpetuated by human authority. The pitiful bondage which Judaism's rabbis and scribes imposed upon the people is the very opposite of the wholesome freedom which Christ offers in the eternal covenant of peace (Heb. 13:19-20).

II Corinthians 3:6-18

Paul's second letter to Corinth clearly contrasts a "new covenant" with a veiled, condemning, mind-hardening "old covenant," which as in Galatians 4 is not at all God's authentic, glorious everlasting covenant of the spirit but is the very antithesis of it. This seemingly ironical "old covenant" stands for unbelieving, party-minded Jews' improper reading of Moses with legalistic, veiled minds (vv. 6-7, 14). It is not of the spirit, for it does not have Christ in view. In the same manner, the "new covenant" of verse six is also not any kind of God-originated agreement either, but is merely Paul's term to refer to a perverted rendering (reading) of Moses' writings.

The backdrop of II Corinthians 3 is the far-reaching conflict between Paul and his Christ-rejecting opponents, legalistic Judaizers whom Paul had introduced in 2:17 "as the many, corrupting the word of God . . ." Among other things, they sought to impose circumcision and other Mosaic ceremonial law upon Paul's Grecian converts (see also Acts 15:1-14). The apostle emphatically objected to such interference with his primary life charge, namely, to extend to the Gentiles the good news about Christ.

Entrusted with the gospel to the "uncircumcision," Paul labored among Jews as a secondary mission (Gal. 1:16; 2:2,7). The book of Acts records how Paul, upon entering a city, first met with his kinsmen and afterwards moved on to make known Christ among the Gentiles (Acts 13:46, 18:6). His letter to Galatia clearly shows that God commissioned Paul to be the apostle to Gentiles (see E.P. Sanders, *Paul, the Law and the Jewish People*, pp. 179-180).

Paul continued to have relationships with synagogues throughout the Roman Empire, because in them Christ's faithful regularly worshiped (see Chapter Eight). He dearly wanted his fellow Jews to share the promises God made with the patriarchs and the prophets of old with the newly converted followers of Christ, and ultimately to see the assimilation of both Jews and the formerly pagan Greeks into one covenantal body, a concept developed in Chapter Five.

Rejection of the gospel by approaching Moses' teachings through the traditions of Judaism, is what Paul appropriately called, ironically, an "old covenant . . . a ministry of death [and] condemnation . . ." (vv. 7, 9, 14). God's agreement itself is not a "covenant that brought death," as often alleged. Rather, Paul is addressing Judaism's perversion of an "old covenant." Further, would God deliberately require His chosen people, Israel, to relate to Him in an everlasting "covenant of death"? (see I Chron. 16:17).

Much to the discredit of these splintered, party-focused Jews, their oppressive rules mixed with the law of Moses as embodied in the Talmud would "kill" newly converted Gentiles, because they pointed out to them God's commandments without furnishing the way to fulfill them. Fortunately, through the gospel of Christ (Rom. 1:17), the "Greeks" were fenced off from the Judaizers' vaunted circumcision and ceremonial law as a basis of religious authority (Acts 15:1-2, Gal. 3-4). Anyone embracing the elders' ceremonial traditions effectually read death into those commandments which God all along had planned to discard as obsolete after Christ had come. He is the Substance of the covenant.

Verses 7 to 18 show that the Judaizers had compared Paul negatively to their hero, Moses, who allegedly had brought them the "true faith" and the law. Such a specious appeal is not in accordance with the longstanding eternal covenant at all, but is actually something far removed from it – a "broken" agreement (Jer. 31:32). It was a condemning ministry, not to be compared with the spiritual covenantal mission, wherein freedom under the Lord resided (3:17; see also Gal. 5:1). If the Judaizers would embrace Christ, the veils over their faces and hearts would disappear. They would then see God's real purpose in His sending of Jesus Christ among men.

These traditionalists also depended on letters of recommendation (vv. 2-3), but had nothing on Paul, whose letter they were (the *ekklesia* at Corinth) was written by God on the tablets of pure hearts and spoke for itself. Thus, in II Corinthians 3 the false teachers were put to rout, even as they had been in Galatia. Legalism, as embodied in cold Talmudic Judaism, was a thorough degeneration of authentic covenantal religion, and actually misrepresented Moses and the prophets, to whom these self-styled custodians of the truth constantly appealed to uphold a man-devised religious system.

Hebrews 8:6-13

Employing the same rhetorical figures as Jeremiah and Paul, the author of Hebrews used the term "new covenant" in 8:8 as a vehicle to distance God's covenanted ones from institutional, legalistic Judaism, which overemphasized the Levitical priesthood and insisted upon the continuance of ceremonial sacrifices as a basis for fellowship in the churches of the author's acquaintance. The issues were the same as in Galatia and Corinth, where various Jewish parties equated salvation with law keeping and circumcision (Gal. 3-4), adhering to traditions which they themselves had authored and handed down (II Cor. 3:1-17, Mark 7:11).

Against this pervasive first century backdrop of Judaism, the author of Hebrews heightens the concept that Jesus in the eternal covenant (Heb. 13:20), makes it better in every way. In 8:6-8, the two-covenant advocates have often stated that God was "finding fault" with the "first covenant," in order to initiate a second one without fault. Indeed, is God capable of making anything with defects? If God made a faulty "old covenant," how can people be assured that a new covenant is without fault?

Most important of all, how could the promise of a "new covenant" be "finding fault" with an *established* God-authored everlasting covenant, which the faithful long possessed since the time of Abraham? Instead, the text of Hebrews 8:8 distinctly states that "God found fault *with the people*," not a covenant.

As the author of Hebrews used the comparative word "better" in verse 6, he employed irony. It was his way of saying that there was and always had been only one covenant of grace, and that any legalistic use of Moses to enforce set-aside laws involving ceremony cannot be substantiated by Christ's teaching and is therefore false. Further, in verse 13, the author speaks of the "first [covenant becoming] obsolete."

Instead of a relationship with Jewish faithful "growing old and ready to disappear" (v. 13b), it was the longestablished Judaic *system* with its sacrifices, temple rituals and the types and shadows that God would no longer require. These were tutors to bring the people of Moses to Christ. In each of these instances, the author used common words such as "new," "better," and "first" as vehicles of irony, forcefully driving home far-reaching truths about the superiority of God's graceful eternal covenant, over and against prevailing Jewish systems which had originated long ago during the "intertestamentary period," 400 B.C. to AD 33.

Thus, the phrase "new covenant" involves the renewal of God's authentic, positive, ancient, well-known, and highly loved plan through which salvation always came by grace, and not through achievement as a debt for works. Entering into the eternal covenant with God by Jews or Greeks meant approaching the gospel and accepting it with an unveiled face and heart (II Cor. 3:7, 14-16), and ultimately experiencing Christ's glorious covenantal spiritual mission, and the writing of His law on the heart.

Through his writing, the author of Hebrews reaffirmed Jeremiah's new covenant promise (31:31-34), which originally had been directed to covenant Jewish people returning from Babylonian exile (see Chapter Ten). After the cross, the writer of Hebrews properly applied the new covenant motif also to the people of Christ to comfort them in their current tribulations and their spiritual struggle against persistent Jewish legalism. In both instances, the affirmation of a new covenant would stimulate God's chosen unto love and good works (Heb. 10:25a) through the use of familiar concepts of salvation, the terms of God's everlasting agreement.

Summary

Jeremiah's new covenant statement, as reintroduced by the author of Hebrews and applied to the Christian era, offers no innovations. Instead, the ironical expressions in Hebrews 8:6-14 properly reaffirm the longstanding everlasting bond between God and man, the one way in the everlasting covenant. The use of the term "new covenant" (in the manner of Paul in II Corinthians 3 and Galatians 4) also pointed to a deeper dynamic of intense, ongoing conflict between the life-strangling institutional Jewish religious society, and "the way," who were always the saints of God.

These people of the way, a general term describing right-eous individuals, are not only mentioned in the book of Acts but also throughout the Old Testament in such varied scrip-tures as Psalms 1:6, 25:9, 67:2; numerous places in the Proverbs; Isaiah 35:8, 40:3, 43:16; Jeremiah 5:4-5, 32:19; Malachi 2:8, 3:1, etc. The narrow way in truth, indeed the only one con-templated (Matt. 7:13-14), is personified in Jesus (John 14:6). Therefore, since there has been but *one* approach or avenue to God through the ages, resulting in *one* body of redeemed ones, who can conclude that the saints in a relationship with God service *two* (or more) distinct covenants?

Though a new covenant was promised by both the Jewish prophet and the author of Hebrews, its terms were as old as Abraham and had been enlarged upon over the centuries for God's covenant people. After all, what could the new cov-enant of Hebrews 8 mean to a body of God-fearers who were *already* being continually blessed with favor in God's everlasting covenant? Hebrews 8 is really not promulgating anything en-tirely new.

The apostle Paul and the writer of Hebrews each em-ployed irony to heighten the seriousness of the battle of authentic faith with formal Judaism, which failed to see that God had deliberately planned the obsolescence of Moses' ceremonies, the many sacrifices and ordinances, and the types and shadows. All of these copies of heavenly realities had to pass away (Heb. 9:23).

The new covenant is therefore "better," not because of its alleged superiority over God's covenantal arrangements with His people from the past, but because of its worldwide appli-cation, the presence of Christ as the reality and substance of the covenant, His one-time pleasing sacrifice (Heb. 10:9), and the passing away of the temporal ordinances and ceremonies, and other ephemeral aspects of Moses' law.

Throughout the ages since Genesis and up to the present time, the terms of the eternal covenant have never changed: (1) God freely giving His people a new heart, (2) His law written on the heart, (3) the experience of divine fellowship where He will be our God and we will be His people, (4) the giving of a new spirit, and (5) the forgiveness of sins. All of these point to a continuity of blessings and promises which the God of covenant freely bestowed equally to faithful Jews of old and saints of Christ. Additionally, God's people would wear a new name (Isa. 62:2). These five oft-repeated terms of covenant, renewed and made better over the centuries, in fact define the essentials of true religion. All of these majestic concepts describe a new covenant, as if there need be *another* eternal agreement beside the one made with Abraham and reiterated with Moses, David, and the prophets.

Unwilling to consider any teaching beyond Moses and ceremonial law and their temple worship in Jerusalem, Talmudic Judaism soundly rejected the gospel of Christ which itself had come through Moses. This good news was touched upon at various times in the Jewish era, something the covenant remnant fully recognized. It centered upon the one hope (Eph. 4:4) in the way of the Lord, as presented through the anointed One (Psa. 2) who is "David" (Ezek. 37:27, Jer. 33:15-17), the Christ and the High Priest ranking with Melchizedek (Heb. 7:1-8:4). Clearly, Jesus is revealed within the Old Testament writings (compare, for instance, Rom. 3:21-22, 10:6 and Deut. 30:11-13, Rom. 15:8 with Isa. 11:1f, etc.). The message of Moses and the writing prophets points to Christ in the eternal covenant.

As various Judaizers who met Jesus failed to see Him as the Christ in the very scriptures they revered and pored over (John 5:39), they would therefore remain veiled (II Cor. 3:7f), and live in darkness, a pitiful spiritual state which the apostle Paul ironically called a "covenant," an inordinate desire to be under law (Gal. 4:21). He admonished those Jews to remove their legalistic veils and allow the comforting rays of Christ to shine on their faces. Indeed, the glories of salvation in the way of grace are disclosed in almost every book in the Jewish and apostolic scriptures, from Moses to Malachi, from Matthew to Revelation, as well as in other non-canonical Jewish books.

Chapter Twelve

༄

Arguments of the Two Covenant Doctrine Answered

A DVOCATES OF THE two-covenant concept go to great lengths to contrast what they call a Jewish old covenant, which was allegedly nailed to the cross of Christ, and a Christian new covenant, supposedly initiated several weeks later, on the Pentecost of Acts 2. In direct opposition to this view, Chapter Six introduced two striking metaphors, the olive tree of Romans 11, and the heavenly woman of Revelation 12, to demonstrate the renewal, advance, and continuity throughout time of all God's faithful covenant Jews and the people of Christ, all bound together in one location, Zion (Heb. 12:22). This eternal agreement experienced spiritual development through the course of history, but it still remained one central covenant, one peace treaty with the God of heaven.

Paul's illustration of the olive tree of Israel (Rom. 11:13-24) adequately developed the principle of covenant in continuity, wherein first century Gentiles and reformed Jews thrived side by side with the faithful Jewish remnant, the people of God contemporary with the cross and others in union with God, extending back many generations to the time of Abraham. In addition to these God-fearers through the ages, the first century, grafted-in Gentiles now were a part of the Israel of God (Gal. 6:16), the *ekklesia* of Christ." Each became a "partaker with them of the rich root of the olive tree" (Rom. 11:17b), which continues to grow to this day.

Accommodation of the two-covenant concept requires that this olive tree of salvation, consisting of Old Testament Jews, was cut down at the time of the cross, uprooted, sawed up, and hauled away, and *another* tree (representing Jewish and finally Gentile believers in Christ) was planted in its place at Pentecost. But the passage is clear, mentioning only one domestic tree. It demonstrates a common salvation in one body for all of the faithful, both in prophetic and apostolic times. Therefore, there is but one covenant for God's people throughout the ages.

The striking imagery of the heavenly woman of Revelation 12 also embraces the entire time period of the popular two-covenant doctrine. As with the olive tree illustration, the woman figure stands for God's saints throughout time. Though initially representing the Jewish covenant remnant before Christ, God's woman, after delivering the man-child Jesus, continued to produce offspring throughout the first century – "those who . . . hold to the testimony of Jesus" (Rev. 12:17). Just as the covenant olive tree still thrives, so does the covenant woman continue to bear children, even to this day.

If God indeed authored two separate covenants, there would have to be *two* women. The one representing Old Testament Jews died at the cross, and was buried in a cold, silent grave of past dispensations, while a new fully mature woman suddenly appeared from nowhere on Pentecost, to represent people in the present "New Testament church." But Revelation 12 speaks of only one heavenly woman. In the same way, the covenant is eternal in duration, representing people of faith from Abraham up to the present, throughout all intervening times.

Admittedly, the woman underwent significant changes as

she first represented the faithful patriarchs, Jews, and ultimately followers of Christ. The book of Acts records the spiritual advance of many thousands of first century God-fearing Jews, who by accepting Christ demonstrated the principle of transformation, in which a body must die in order to put on its new form in baptism. Every seed planted in the ground undergoes the same experience. Such rededication by these Jews shows that the covenant woman of Revelation 12 was in metamorphoses, just as a caterpillar turns into a butterfly.

Throughout the Bible, scriptural concepts describing the people of God, such as the called out, the body, and the kingdom, are always spoken of in the singular, transcending time and religious parties. But the two-covenant doctrine generally requires that there be two or more of each of these concepts. Theology involving more than one covenant is indeed "closet dispensationalism," and it labors under the unwarranted assumption that God terminated an "old law of Moses" and its first covenant at the cross (or fifty days later on Pentecost), and ratified a new law, along with a "second covenant."

New in Kind – New in Time

The two-covenant doctrine attempts to make a case for absolutely distinct old and new covenants by appealing to two Greek words for "new": *kainos* – generally denoting new in quality, to bring on a superior innovation, and *neos* – which refers to new in time, "having recently come into existence" (S.G. Green, *Handbook to the Grammar of the Greek New Testament*). It is argued that these shades of meaning of "new" are critical in understanding various passages wherein that word appears in conjunction with covenant.

Jesus referred to a "new covenant in His blood" at the Last Supper (Luke 22:20), and Paul spoke of his people as being servants of a new covenant (II Cor. 3:6). Hebrews 7:22 mentions a "better" covenant, while 8:7 tells of a "second" or another covenant. Jeremiah 31:31–34 and Hebrews 8:7–12 pointedly declare that "the days are coming, says the Lord, when I will make a new covenant with the house of Israel and Judah . . ." The contention is that the new covenant is *new-in-kind* because it was allegedly a superior innovation, different from the old covenant of Moses, because of a change in priesthood, law, worship, etc. Two-covenant advocates insist that new is *new!*

Actually, the *kainos/neos* distinction does not consistently hold true throughout the New Testament. *Kainos*, used 43 times, denotes the new and better name (five times in Revelation), new Jerusalem and new heavens and new earth (Rev. 21:1–2), new things (Rev. 21:5, Matt. 13:52), new kind of creature or man or self (by Paul in three epistles), the new teaching by Paul to the Athenians (Acts 17:19–21), and newness of spirit and life (Rom 7:6, 6:4). *Neos*, used 26 times, denotes the new- in-time convert (I Tim. 3:6), but especially has reference to youth or the younger, youthfulness, as in I Timothy (five times), Luke 15:12–13, 22:26, 18:21, Acts 5:6 and 26:4, John 21:18, I Peter 5:5, etc. Clearly, a difference between new in kind and new in time is present in Greek usage in each of these instances.

The *kainos/neos* distinction is blurred in many other significant places. In Hebrews 9:15, Jesus is the mediator of a *kainos* covenant, but the same writer in 12:24 described Jesus as the mediator of a *neos* covenant, a usage that stresses the recent mediation of Christ's death as a surety for the everlasting covenant. This shows the essential synonymity of the two terms (compare also *neos* in Col. 3:10 with *kainos* in Eph. 4:22–24). Jesus' *kainos* tomb (Matt. 27:60, John 19:41) was a recent, hence new-in-time tomb because there had never been a body in it.

If a sharp *kainos/neos* distinction were valid, the Greek usage in reference to a new tomb should be *neos*. Matthew and John are not talking about a new type of tomb. Similarly, Mark's (*kainos*) tongues or languages in 16:17 describe the first-time use of tongues before a particular audience, not new or recently invented languages, the very meaning which two-covenanters attach to the new covenant.

Any distinction between *kainos* and *neos* completely disappears in Luke 5:36-39 (and in its parallels in Matt. 9:16-17 and Mark 2:21-22) where each word is used three times interchangeably and synonymously. There are two occurrences of *kainos* garments in verse 36; the four others are to new wine. It is not a new kind of wine; it is a wine of *recent manufacture*, hence relating to time.

The clincher appears in Matthew 9:17, where Jesus suggested the putting of new wine into new wineskins. They are not both *kainos*, new-in-kind, or *neos*, new-in-time. Rather, the instruction is, "Do not place *neos* wine into *kainos* wineskins . . . ." Therefore the new-in-kind/new-in-time Greek word distinction is without merit, and the new-in-kind covenant for Christians this side of the cross cannot be proven by appealing to "the Greek."

Ironically, the two-covenant doctrine might have been better served if the new covenant had been expressed in terms of *neos* (new in time), rather than *kainos* (new in kind), for Paul in I Corinthians 5:7 admonished the saints to "clean out the old leaven, that you may be a (*neos*) lump." Here is an unmistakable contrast, wherein there is something old to be abandoned and something new to be sought.

The apostle clearly identified the Corinthians' old leaven as certain sins (in v. 1), and directed them to become a new lump. Paul seems to be talking about an individual putting on a new self (Eph. 4:24), becoming a new creature (II Cor. 5:17), etc. But all of these instances of new are *kainos*. Since the two Greek words are synonymous, attempts to use *kainos* and *neos* to differentiate between an allegedly superseded Jewish old covenant and a new covenant for saints in Christ obviously meets with insuperable difficulties.

It is doubtful that many Greek grammarians would serve up the clean distinction between *kainos* and *neos* to the two-covenant position. Those two Greek words may be used as the same thing, as even the celebrated W. E. Vine mildly admits (*Dictionary of New Testament Words*, p. 792). Moulton and Milligan in the *Vocabulary of the Greek New Testament* are more emphatic, stating clearly that "Papyrus [ordinary] usage hardly tends to sharpen the distinction between *kainos* and *neos*." They cite an example wherein the words are used interchangeably in one context, in reference to the town of New Ptolemy.

Arndt and Gingrich's Greek-English lexicon comments on the two Greek words for new. They define *kainos* as "unused . . . not previously present . . . fresh start (pp. 394-395). Covenant renewal, therefore, contemplates a new context for an old concept, hence, *kainos*. *Neos* carries the idea of "fresh . . . novice . . . young" (P. 538), as a new blossom on a plant. These scholars do not make the sharp new-in-kind, new-in-time distinction.

Authors and compilers of Greek lexicons and dictionaries merely record what *they* think a given Greek word means, when translated into English. Obviously, they are not God-directed and may succumb to doctrinal biases. Word meanings may vary from document to document; assuredly, there are no extant Greek lexicons and dictionaries from the biblical era for guidance.

Koine Greek

That the New Testament was written in Koine Greek connotes to many people that the Greek language of the New Testament era was essentially static, frozen in time. To them it is a *different* Greek, the "inspired" language, somehow developing as a result of God's providence. Based on these assumptions, Greek word definitions are routinely applied in all doctrinal disputes, and by quoting "the Greek" the implication is that the conclusion is of God. But, is it actually possible to determine all biblical word meanings (even the nature of covenant) with precise consistency, even unto the shades of value of words?

In fact, all of these notions are just plain myths. First century Greek was very much a living language with definitions, usage, and applications constantly evolving, often within very short periods of time, even as English and all other active languages do today. Studies of Greek words and definitions are merely starting points for determining what a particular biblical text might mean.

The Importance of Context

Formulating a belief of the new covenant around fine Greek word distinctions is obviously improper. To be sure, taking a word definition out of a Greek lexicon, and applying it across the New Testament to fit every context, will result in serious distortions of the original intent of the authors. To illustrate, the words "kill" or "beat" on the front page of a modern newspaper refer predominantly to serious crimes, while the same words appearing in the sports section might describe lawful athletic prowess in team situations.

Nor is it proper to study a particular word such as "eternal" (everlasting, forever), "run references" in a concordance, and assume that it conveys the same meaning in the other biblical contexts. Two-covenant theorists maintain that the eternal "old covenant" is age-lasting or age-abiding, in the same sense that the Passover (Ex. 12:14) and the service of Hebrew and foreign slaves (Ex. 21:6) were to last "forever." Since these processes ceased at well-defined times long ago, they say that the *old* covenant similarly ended in the first century, when it was allegedly replaced by an eternal *new* covenant.

Such a conclusion is not justified, in that it fails to consider several passages from the major prophets (cited in Chapter Five) which contextually intertwine the traditional two covenants. The highly significant historical setting or context also must be considered. Throughout history, God's eternal/everlasting covenant is inextricably associated with the tribal covenantal blood sacrifice (see Chapters One and Three) common in biblical times and even operative today among many "third world" nations.

Irrespective of biblical "dispensations," the people of God associated their relationship with the Creator in the blood covenant (Gen. 15-18; Jer. 34:17-20; Heb. 9:15-18). Thus, any study of the nature of old covenant and new covenant must properly be understood in the context of both written documents and in historical setting. Attempts to formulate contrasting covenants often result in prooftexting, a hermeneutic that shows little concern for the flavor of the entire document, and especially the social background in which it was originally written. Obviously, building a doctrine on proof texts seriously distorts the author's original intent, wresting words and phrases from both their historical and literary contexts.

Attempts to contrast covenants are essentially arguments from the silence of scripture. No New Testament personage or even Christ Himself actually expressed the specific notion that a distinct old covenant ceased at the cross or in AD 70 with the destruction of Jerusalem, to be supplanted by a new covenant of Christ. If the apostles thought that there were two distinct covenants, old and new, they surely would have written about them also, delineating them clearly and forcefully as Paul did (in Romans 5) concerning two men – Adam and Christ. In that lengthy context, the apostle unmistakably contrasted the far-reaching effect of their work, intertwining powerful opposites: Adam's trespass and the judgment which followed, and the grace of Christ and the justification which it brought (vv. 15-19).

The point is this: a scripture discussion involving distinct old and new covenants would have *more* importance and potentially *greater* influence, *if* such concepts indeed had been promulgated with full apostolic authority, and also the passing of something equally significant, an entire system of law –

Moses' – in favor of a new law for Christians. However, the apostles were absolutely silent about carving out such distinctions between either covenant or laws, for evidently there were none.

Instead, God revealed to Moses and many other servants moral principles which transcend all man-devised dispensations. Similarly, God's eternal (everlasting) covenant with man is consistently expressed in the singular throughout the ages (Gen. 17, Psa. 105, II Sam. 23, Isa. 55, Ezek. 37, Jer. 32, Luke 1, Heb. 13). Therefore, God's one eternal covenant is more like the earth "abiding forever" (Eccl. 1:4) – that is, as long as the generations of men come and go (v. 3). God's eternal agreement with man will never cease (see Chapter Fourteen).

As with other types of literature, the meaning of a particular scripture becomes evident only by examining both its historical and literary contexts, and not merely by cross-referencing other passages where the same key word appears, nor by prooftexting.

Moral Law and Law Involving Ceremony

Though proponents of the two-covenant doctrine do not differentiate between various aspects of law associated with Moses, a distinction between its moral and ceremonial aspects is well attested in religious history, in the writings of the earliest church fathers such as Ignatius, as well as Irenaeus, who regarded the latter as a way to learn about Christ (*Against Heresies* IV.13.?), and also later thinkers from Thomas Aquinas to Charles Hodge. These men have shown that universally applicable laws defining morals and ethics transcend all man-made dispensations, providing spiritual guidance for *all* men. On the other hand, God also commanded ceremonial law, a system of blood sacrifices and other offerings, as types and shadows of messianic realities, in covenantal evolution through Moses.

The latter duties were a *pedagogues*, a tutor to guide the

people of Israel to the ultimate Teacher who would appear in the fullness of time as the Christ of Jewish hope and promise. Clearly distinct from this schoolmaster is the "holy, just and good" (Rom. 7:12) portion of Moses' law, consisting of long-established moral and ethical guidance, which to the ancient Psalmists brought sweet delight (1:2), causing rejoicing and comfort through heartfelt obedience (119:2, 10, 11, 34, 58, 69). These moral precepts not only applied to the Jews (Deut. 12-13), but also guided disciples of Christ as well (I Tim. 1:8-10, II Tim. 3:15-17). Obeying such laws has never been a burden to God pleasers even among the Gentiles and patriarchs of old (I John 5:3).

In contrast, duties involving ceremony – the Passover, the temple sacrificial system, and dietary restrictions, etc. – had in fact become a wall of separation from the neighboring Gentiles, segregating them from the ante-cross covenant Jews. In fact, the enmity between the Jews and Gentiles existed because of Moses' ceremonial laws, which excluded the nations from an intimate temple experience at Jerusalem. In his famous history, the Roman historian Tacitus noted that "the *rites* [i.e., ceremonial duties] of Moses were contrary to those of all other mortals. These Jews accounted as profane everything held sacred by us [Romans]."

In Galatia, Paul feared that certain Judaizing brethren in Christ were pursuing these "weak and miserable" ceremonial elements (4:3, 9), which included the observance of special days and seasons (v. 10). In another context, certain believers in Jerusalem insisted upon the rite of circumcision as a prerequisite to salvation in Christ (Acts 15:1-2). Paul corrected such misguided Christians by showing that these "rudiments" or beggarly aspects of the faith, with the "ordinances" (Col. 2:16), were merely shadows of the ultimate reality – Christ Himself.

The arrival of the Substance rendered the Jewish types and shadows superfluous, even as a peeled banana skin is merely "rubbish" or garbage (Phil. 3:2-5, 8). Just as the skin has value in protecting the fruit for a specific time, so did the ceremonies and sacrifices of Moses prove to be necessary until Jewish covenanters could directly gain access to the resurrected Christ Himself.

Any foreshadowing of Messiah is confined to law involving ceremony, because these very ordinances were ultimately to be set aside when faith (Christ) came (Gal. 3:19, 25). On the other hand, Moses' *moral* features coincide with timeless natural law; hence they are *not* tutelage to bring Jews to Christ. Indeed, uncircumcised Gentiles were also duty bound to follow such moral expressions of God's justice and standard of acceptable behavior before Him (Rom. 1:18-29, 2:14-15).

In apostolic preaching and worship throughout Acts, the moral/ceremonial distinction is even more apparent. Evidence in Chapter Eight amply shows that, well after the cross, the apostle Paul insisted that his kinsmen submit to regulations pertaining to ceremony – as he did himself – but staunchly refused to impose Mosaic ritual upon Gentile believers. Consistently, Paul upheld Moses' moral precepts among Jewish followers of Christ, as in Romans 7, yet taught that the ceremonial provisions constituted a schoolmaster who would ultimately be dismissed (Gal. 3:24-25; see also I Cor. 9:20-21).

A distinction of law between moral precepts and ceremonial duties, therefore, has always been in use by God's people. It is functionally discernible. Israel of old saw the difference in such statements as "I desire faithful love, not sacrifice" (Hos. 6:6). A failure to separate moral law from the ceremonial would have compromised the purity of first century apostolic preaching. Significantly, a full generation after the cross, the author of Hebrews declared that such ceremonial symbols are "ready to pass away" (8:13), nigh to becoming inoperative (see also Acts 10:11-15). These "tools of the classroom" were historical relics by the second century.

The key phrase "no longer under a tutor" (Gal. 3:24-25) thus would forever elevate God's people from pedagogical ceremonial law, from which originated the types and shadows that looked to the reality of the ultimate Deliverer whose redeeming work would turn people to Him through faith (Gal. 3:19-29). The maturity of the Jews' covenantal development would come then, for Christ as the embodiment of moral law, is "better" in every way, as stated by the author of Hebrews.

God-fearers are still bound to ancient expressions of moral precepts, each of which guides in the ways of right. Though moral law does not specifically embrace justification by faith (Gal. 3:24), it addresses infractions against its great truth. Thus, the ever-present duty of all saints in Christ is to adhere to God's moral laws, as initially expressed orally, then in written form to all Jews and the "Greeks" (Matt. 5:17-19, Rom. 2:9-12). Moral living exalts Christ in ways that obeying "ceremonial" rules about baptism, the Lord's Supper, and other signs of the covenant, through necessary, can never do.

Unconditional and Conditional Covenants

Some proponents of multi-covenant arbitrarily declare that the "Abrahamic" and the "Davidic" covenants were unconditional, while the "Mosaic" covenant was conditional, a distinction that rests solely on a legal basis, since there is no scriptural support. Actually, all of these named covenants have both conditional and unconditional features.

In respect to the prophetic nature of the Old Testament revelation of Christ, every stage of convenantal development was unconditional, in that in the fullness of time Christ would appear on earth to minister, experience the cross and resurrection, and receive His kingship from God. These events were the centerpiece of God's purposeful plan for man's redemption, and all of these promises would eventually be accomplished, regardless of earthly events. No conditions were placed upon God accomplishing this aspect of covenant.

But for people throughout the ages, the eternal covenant has always been conditional upon leading a life of active faith. Anyone living at the time of Abel, Noah, Enoch, Abraham,

Isaac, Moses, the prophets, etc. also enjoyed this standing by faith (Heb. 11:1-5) and could have turned his back on the Lord through ungodly living and forfeited all covenantal blessings and benefits.

Thus, Abraham's covenantal relationship with God was unconditional from the standpoint of the coming of the Messiah, but his personal salvation had to be based upon faith. Abandoning it meant the sinner severed himself from the covenant. Continuing in faith meant uninterrupted justification, a rightstanding before God, and a constant cleansing from sin.

The material aspect of covenant, including the "land promise" to the descendants of Abraham, was essential to maintaining a pure lineage for the coming of Messiah and the setting up of types and antetypes, the shadows and realities, which Messiah would fulfill. All of these vital aspects point to God's desire to have a loving relationship with His people in the eternal death-bond agreement. As an aspect of grace, God would provide in Jesus Christ the sacrifice required for sin, so that transgressing man would not have to die to pay for his wrongdoings (see Chapter Three).

Is the Law of Moses a System of Carnal Law?

Proponents of two covenants labor under numerous unwarranted assumptions and beliefs about the nature of God's covenant relationship with Old Testament Jews. Allegedly, the people of God before Christ had no latitude under Moses' law, because it was made up of strict legal definitions and prohibitions, which eventually brought alienation from God — in short, a carnal system of condemnation, death, and failure.

They regard the old and new testaments as no more alike than Adam and Christ (see Rom. 5). Since the first covenant allegedly demanded complete conformity to an "imperfect" Mosaic law, under that economy spiritual life could not be attained. Few men walked with a God of wrath, while in the second covenant all subjects have continual access to a God of love. To them the old covenant brought bondage, while the newer promoted freedom. Somehow, God's people this side of the cross seemingly are thought to be spiritually superior to the Jewish saints (see Luke 7:28).

Two-covenant advocates teach important biblical themes in apposition: a weak, supposedly unprofitable *earthly* system based upon commandments inscribed upon tables of stone, against a better *heavenly* arrangement, with the law implanted in the mind of man; the blood of animals in the old, versus the blood of Christ; carnal ordinances and spiritual sacrifices; purifying the flesh and purifying the soul; life through a works system and life through believing; codified commandments amid a few promises and New Testament divine commitment overflowing with promises; a temporal inheritance and a heavenly one.

Assuredly, non of these misleading cliches have scriptural support, misrepresenting plain statements of scripture. God, who like Jesus, is the same "yesterday, today and forever" (Heb. 13:8; see also Mal. 3:6), has been continually a merciful, loving, protective Father for all peoples – ancient Jews as well as for the people of Christ today. From the earliest days of Abraham to the generation of Christ, a covenant spiritual remnant has existed. They were a God-seeking, loyal people of faith, an authentic body, a kingdom headed by God. Obviously, any apostolic statements about the law and meritorious justification never applied to these untold number of pious covenant Jews who enjoyed a right relationship with God, full of life and promises.

Spiritual life for God's people in either era resulted from the remission of sins through a life of faith, not by achieving and responding meticulously to commandments culled from available scriptures. The blood of Christ not only flowed forward from the cross, but also backward to an untold number of worthy Jewish saints of old, and even to obedient God-fearing Gentiles with pure hearts. Sin-cleansing never came by adherence to routine, but through a relationship with God, who provided all spiritual blessings, especially continual acceptance and the forgiveness of sin. All of the faithful throughout the ages are reconciled to God in life through the eternal covenant; none was justified on the basis of lawkeeping or flawless service. For these good hearts, it was always by faith, not by rules for all.

Jewish saints such as Moses, David, Hosea, Isaiah, etc., are as much our covenantal brothers in Christ as are Paul, Barnabas, and Mark. All of these kept the moral law, loved their enemies, turned the other cheek, etc.; all were saved by grace in a relationship with God. They were free of guilt, enjoying divine love and full pardon, and experienced joy and peace in the resultant life of faithfulness.

First century Jews and Gentiles were saved in the same manner (Acts 10:34, 15:11). Among these Jews were Jesus' apostles and others whom God accepted while Christ was alive; they were presently saved because they were part of the longstanding Jewish covenant remnant, and not because they submitted to Christian baptism, though required. These first century saints were covenant brothers with the Jewish faithful of old, in God's called-out *ekklesia,* the spiritual the body of the saved throughout time.

Thus, common misconceptions and misrepresentations associated with the system of faith of covenant Jews as being bookkeeping followers of a religion with legal definitions and precisely measurable penalties in a highly formal code, glibly assigned to all Old Testament people, must be permanently dismissed as fundamentally untrue. Neither they nor covenanters in Christ can claim rights and privileges through legal obedience to law. Instead, all of these saints enjoy the love and mercy of God in a relationship with Him in the eternal covenant, by grace through faith.

Is the New/Everlasting Covenant
Exclusively Messianic?

Proponents of the two-covenant doctrine assert that the splendid promises of "new heavens and a new earth" (Isa. 65–66), a new spirit and a new heart (Ezek. 35–36), together with the law written on the heart (Jer. 31:33), did not find fulfillment among the Jews who returned from Babylonian captivity because these blessings were conditioned upon steadfast faithfulness to God. (Jer. 18:7-9).

Further, they say that the prophets of the post-exilic period – Haggai, Zechariah, and Malachi – as well as the historical writers Nehemiah and Ezra paint a picture of spiritual decadence amid hard times, not one of spiritual exultation. The priesthood had been corrupted by Grecian philosophers, while the second temple did not contain God's glory, His spirit. Therefore, there is nothing in Judah's history after 536 B.C. which fulfilled the new covenant of Jeremiah 31:31-34, so its exuberant promises were fulfilled *exclusively* in the messianic era.

In response, though Israel and later Judah entered into captivity because each had broken its covenant with God (Jer. 11:10), God nevertheless would never fully abandon or completely destroy his people (Lev. 26:44). The warrior God would ever be with them (Ex. 3:12). Granted, the returnees who resettled Palestine were constantly in dire straits, but that was insignificant; Israel-Judah had not been a major player politically since the glorious era of David and Solomon, 1000–925 B.C.

Despite the lack of a king and a strong government, there was throughout the late Jewish period a spiritual remnant which constantly drew near to God by preserving the prophets' writings, forsaking idols, and maintaining the sanctity of the Sabbath. While adhering to moral principles the people ardently looked for the spiritual Messiah. As explained in Chapter Six, this group of faithful – the Old Testament church – is embodied in two striking figures: Paul's olive tree and John's heavenly woman, each of which extends backward to the time of Abraham and forward into the Christian era.

The small spiritual remnant among post-exilic Judah was being saved through faith by a God of comfort. Even Ezekiel's promise of a new spirit in 11:9, 36:26, and 37:17 (passages thought by some to be exclusively messianic) is virtually duplicated by Isaiah, who taught that the seed of Jacob received the spirit after the time of Babylonian exile. Isaiah declared in 32:14-15 that upon these very people the spirit would descend from on high, making fertile forests and deserts. "I will pour out my spirit on your offspring, and my blessings to your descendants," promised Isaiah (44:3; see also 59:21). Further, Ezekiel spoke in 39:29 of this spiritual outpouring upon the house of Israel as if the return had already been accomplished. Such a God-granted blessing to Israel's offspring would bring spiritual life and blessings upon the faithful who obeyed God following their resettling in Palestine after 536 B.C.

The canonical post-exilic writings also confirm that God's spirit was among these very people. Zechariah affirmed the restoration of Judah through their cleansing of sin by the high priest Joshua (3:4b, 9). Covenantal interdwelling between God and man as specifically expressed in 8:8 (see also 2:11) is the very essence of covenant renewal. Continuance of God's agreement of life and peace with restored Judah is also assured by Malachi (2:4-5), who saw no reason to deal treacherously with one another because all shared a common Father (v. 10). Malachi chided his kinsmen who might break marital faith, admonishing the people not to do that because they are one with God "in flesh and spirit." Haggai also plainly declared that God was with these covenant ones (1:13, 2:4). "My spirit is abiding in your midst. Do not fear," said God, as he admonished His people to be strong and do His work.

Through a striking image of two sticks becoming one, Ezekiel demonstrated that Israel and Judah would be a united nation under one King (37:15-24). Fulfillment came in the

Jews' restoration after 536 B.C., when they resettled their own land, experiencing salvation and cleansed hearts (v. 23). Israel would once again become holy (v. 28), serving God faithfully through union with Him in the everlasting covenant (v. 26a).

Jeremiah spoke of this very spiritual experience (32:37-41) with *them,* a word which thirteen times contextually refers to the returnees from Babylonian exile. As Ezra succinctly reviewed the history of Israel (Neh. 9:5-37), he recognized recurrent apostasies of the forefathers (vv. 16, 26, 28), even as many in his day were also out of favor with God. Despite the adversity (vv. 32, 36a), Ezra could end his prayer with comforting words: "O our God, the great, mighty and awesome God, who keeps His covenant of love . . . ", offering great encouragement to the people (v. 32).

The covenant-seeking remnant continued to abide in God's agreement during the two centuries before Christ. The books of the Maccabees, *I Enoch, Ecclesiasticus,* and other writings point to the existence of righteous people who abided in the covenant of grace. These and other contemporary non-canonical works discuss many spiritual concepts, including the kingdom of God, the Messiah to come, the end-times, and the resurrection of the dead, as well as moral choices.

As God's everlasting covenant was about to be renewed in the first century messianic era, faithful Jewish covenanters earnestly awaited the kingdom of God and looked for the consolation of Israel (Luke 23:51, 2:25). Simon, Anna, Zechariah, and Mary, among others, stood above visible Jewish partyism (see Chapter Four). The sanctified temple evidently contained God's spirit, for it was His house (Luke 2:49). Thus, it is unwarranted to relegate spiritual post-exilic Jews to an inferior status and deny them participation in the everlasting covenant.

Chapter Thirteen

∽

Scripture Arguments of the Two Covenant Doctrine Examined

T EACHERS OF THE two-covenant concept appeal to several places in the New Testament in order to justify the concept of a new-in-kind covenant with a new law for the people of Christ. Let us examine each of these in context.

Matthew 5:17

Chapters Five through Ten present the case for the continuity of God's eternal covenant throughout the ages. In the covenant prophecy of Jeremiah 31:31-34 (Heb. 8:8-12, 10:16-17), the moral standard of both eras is bridged by the term "law in the heart." All of God's special revelation to the prophets and the apostles shows a continuity of thought and development, culminating with Jesus Christ (Matt. 5:19).

The ethical and moral law of Moses reflects God's character and righteousness, and continually the prophets identified it as the law of God (Psa. 119; Josh. 24:26; II Kings 10:31; Ezra 7:6-

10; Jer. 9:13, 16:11, 31:33, 44:10; Dan. 6:5, etc.). Nehemiah admonished the people to "follow the law of God given through Moses" (10:28-29; see also 8:8, 18-9:3). Hosea said that the people had ignored the law of God (4:6b, 8:1). The chronicler understood that the law of the Lord coincided with what God had given to Moses (I Chron. 22:12, II Chron. 6:16b).

Such a law can convert the soul (Psa. 19:7) and is profitable for teaching and instruction in righteousness to the people of God on both sides of the cross, thoroughly equipping them for *every* good work (II Tim. 3:15-17). Why? Because the ancient moral precepts are universally applicable. This law is holy (Num. 15:40), righteous (Deut. 4:8), just (Zech. 7:9, 12), good (Deut. 12:28), and a delight (Psa. 1:2). In view of God's lofty description of Moses' law, man should not esteem it as common, inferior, or wanting (see Acts 10:15).

The ancient law not only defines sin but it condemns transgression and restrains evil, stating moral precepts regarding blasphemy, bestiality, cruelty to the blind, etc., which are not explicitly forbidden in the text of the New Testament. The ancient precepts teach holiness of God, the origin of sin, and the need to conduct good, pure lives to please Him (Rom. 7:12-14).

Despite this lofty position in which both the prophets and the apostles placed the law of Moses (law of God), it is insisted that as Jesus came to fulfill it, He rendered it obsolete, abolishing it by nailing it to His cross (see Chapter Nine), citing as proof text Matthew 5:17: "Do not think that I have come to destroy the law or the prophets; I have not come to abolish them but to *fulfill* them . . ."

In the word "fulfill" most two-covenant proponents assume that the text concerns itself with the culmination of Jewish prophecies in the life and person of Jesus Christ. Such a notion is absent, but the "law" and the "prophets" are specifically expressed. In Matthew 5:17, Jesus emphasized timeless eternal principles and unswerving commitment to God's law, rather than a superficial acknowledgment of it or a dismantling of it, through substitution of an alleged "new law of Christ."

Principally, Jesus contrasted destroying the law with fulfilling it, juxtaposing the words as opposites, even as He sharply distinguished between the key words in the famous statement, "I came not to bring *peace* to the earth . . . but a *sword*" (Matt. 10:34). And so, far from abolishing the law or thoroughly disposing of it, Jesus came to restore the full meaning and intent of Moses' law, while simultaneously firmly opposing institutional Jewish distortions of the ancient precepts.

Matthew 5:20 further shows the binding significance of even the law's "least commandments." In fact, anyone setting aside these precepts of the ethics and morality of Moses' law is considered "least in the kingdom of heaven" (comp. Matt. 11:11). Evidently, such a one is still part of the body of Christ, hence not lost, but definitely in need of reconsidering the importance of adhering to all of God's commandments. Continuity of law is evident in Matthew 5:17, in that there is nothing about following Jesus that would be obnoxious to Moses.

Matthew 9:14-17

The proverbial expression, "and men do not put new wine into old wineskins . . . but they put new wine into new wineskins" has been applied metaphorically to show a contrast of old and new covenants. The new wine needing new wineskins is said to be part of the inauguration of the "gospel age" and the coming of the messianic bridegroom, Jesus (Mark 2:19). Others think that the old wineskin cloth represents the old law of Moses and that the new cloth is the teaching of Christ, and it would not be safe to mix them.

Actually, in context, Jesus is discussing the subject of fasting, and when His disciples should properly do so. Luke's account of Jesus' statement about wineskins helps bring about its meaning. In 5:39 Jesus says, "and no one after drinking old wine wants the new, for he says, 'The old is better.'" The point of Jesus' expression is that for His disciples to fast while He is with them would be as absurd as to put new wine into old wine-skins. The subjects of covenant and law are obviously not contemplated in Matthew 9:14-17 (Luke 5:36-39).

John 1:17

After declaring that Christ is the fullness of grace in John 1:16, John wrote, "For the law was given through Moses; grace and truth came through Jesus Christ" (v. 17). Two-covenant advocates often inject into this text the notion that Israel of old labored within a law system that brought condemnation and death, a belief based on II Corinthians 3:6-18 (but see Chapter Eleven and section below). In contrast, it is said that Christians function in an era of grace, enjoying a covenant of the spirit that brought life.

It is not necessary to see a sharp contrast in John 1:17 to come to an understanding of the verse. Actually, law existed before Moses (as in Genesis 26:5) as well as afterwards, in Jesus' words about keeping His commandments (John 14:23-15:17). Therefore, the phrase "for the law was given through Moses" has a special, limited use, perhaps pointing to the historical fact that the law was channeled from God to man through the mediatorship of Moses.

Nor was "grace and truth" monopolized by Jesus Christ, who as the embodiment of truth and reality indeed brought grace to its fullest expression. Grace, or God's favor, is a concept fully visible and oft-expressed throughout Old Testament times, especially as embodied in the term *chesed* (see Chapter One). God's favor abounded in the lives of His covenanted ones over and over, both in the time of the patriarchs and the prophets – from Moses to Malachi and beyond. Therefore, the "age of grace" is not confined merely to a New Testament age but if there be one it has to extend many generations back to the time of Genesis.

And so, John 1:17 is not an absolute statement contrasting two concepts, anymore than Romans 6:14-15, where Paul states that Christians "are not under law but under grace." Everyone now is subject to moral law and other command-ments. Otherwise, no Christian would be guilty of sin (see Rom. 4:15, I John 3:4), and there would be no need of the grace spoken of to forgive sin. Perhaps both John's and Paul's statements actually show that we are most especially under grace, yet it is something that is true for covenanters of all ages, as shown in the section on grace in Chapter Seven.

Just as all of God's people throughout the ages have the law in their hearts (see Chapter Eleven), the ancients also had an intense awareness of transgression, as expressed frequently in many Psalms. Their worship was acceptable as they cried to the Lord, every trusting in Him and divine righteousness, jus-tification and remission of sin from the Author of grace who gives covenanters of all ages equal support and comfort. The "age of grace" concept of the two-covenant doctrine actually leads to spiritual elitism, an unthinkable alternative to the no-tion that God has dispensed grace equally to faithful people of all ages (see Acts 10:34).

Acts 2

The Pentecost of Acts 2 is taken as a watershed by all two-covenant theorists, for on that day they insist that the new covenant with an accompanying law was initiated, forever replacing the old covenant governed by the law of Moses, which supposedly had been nailed to the cross of Christ. Re-cent books clearly advance these ideas, with one of them calling the second chapter of Acts the "hub of the Bible."

Significantly, the chief historian among the New Testa-ment authors, Luke the physician, and the careful compiler of the Gospel of Luke and Acts of the Apostles, at *no* time or place suggests that there has been a change in covenant systems or the establishment of a new law, new kingdom, or new *ekklesia*. Since Luke is absolutely silent about these concepts, they cannot be considered as apostolic. Nevertheless, the arrival of the Holy Spirit in Acts 2 has covenantal importance, signifying the "renewal and quickening of the initial bond, rather than the introduction of a new covenant" (Eric Franklin, *Christ the Lord, A Study in the Purpose and Theology of Luke-Acts.* p, 98).

Peter's lengthy quote of Joel's prophecy of the Spirit's outpouring is important for another reason. In *According to the Scriptures*, C. H. Dodd notes that early Christian teachers consistently quoted an Old Testament text bearing significance, for the purpose of bringing to mind the entire plot or context of the original scripture (p. 13). For Peter's audience on Pentecost, the reading of Joel 2:28-32 was meant to recall the greater context, 2:18 - 3:21. The early prophet focused on God's renewal and restoration of Israel (see vv. 2:19, 24-26; 3:1-2, 15-17, 18), not a "new Israel" under a new covenant governed by a "law of Christ." Pentecost is therefore an occasion for covenant renewal, *not* the establishment of anything new.

This restoration motif is evident in the structure of the book of Acts itself. In 1:6 the apostles legitimately ask their risen Lord, "Is this the time you are restoring the kingdom to Israel?" Two-covenant proponents have concluded that such a question arose out of the apostles' continual misunderstanding of the spiritual nature of the kingdom. This can hardly be true, since Christ Himself had spent His last forty days on earth instructing them about the spiritual reign of God (v. 3). After such intense specific teaching, how can anyone presume that the disciples failed to comprehend the spiritual renewal of God's kingdom in the hearts of the covenant people? Earlier, Christ had committed it to the apostles (Luke 22:29-30), by opening up their understanding of scripture concerning Him (Luke 24:25-27, 45).

The response of Jesus to the apostles' pertinent question in verses 7-8 points to covenant renewal, promising them power when the Holy Spirit would come upon them, an event which occurred on the Pentecost of Acts 2. Since Jesus was soon to depart from them and ascend into heaven, the apostles inquired about the *time* of restoring the kingdom. So the kingdom of Luke-Acts is a *renewed* kingdom, fully consummated with the crowning of Jesus as King of kings upon His ascension into heaven. Ultimately the infusion of the Holy Spirit in believers allowed them to speak in tongues (Acts 2:4-6).

If Jesus intended to inaugurate something new on Pentecost, whether a law, a "church," or a covenant, He should have responded to the apostles' question in Acts 1:6 by plainly saying that a new kingdom or covenant would soon be in place. They asked about time and not the founding of anything, and He responded about time. Also, if the two-covenant thesis were valid, Luke would have made a reference somewhere in his massive writings, at least indirectly, to this alleged covenantal "changing of the guard." Every discourse in Luke-Acts is silent about it.

Several weeks later, when Peter was preaching from Solomon's colonnade, he proclaimed the restoration of all things foretold by the Jewish prophets (Acts 3:21), with the promise of covenant renewal actualized at the time of the glorified Jesus (vv. 13-15, 18) and the restored kingdom of Israel. God had announced these things beforehand by the mouths of Samuel and other prophets (vv. 18, 24).

In Peter's Jewish audience were the sons of these very prophets (Acts 3:25), and the recipients of the blessing which God had covenanted with the fathers, when He said to Abraham (and Isaac and Jacob – v.13), "And in your seed all the families of the earth shall be blessed" (v. 25). The events of those days (v. 24) fulfilled this language of covenant, and the foretelling of the restoration of all things (v. 21). Initially, these blessings would come to the Jews (v. 26a), also ultimately to the Gentiles (Rom. 1:1-16, 2:9).

At the Jerusalem Conference several years later (Acts 15), the apostles forcefully made the identical point about a restoration of God's kingdom. James twice mentioned the rebuilding and the ultimate refashioning of David's tabernacle, renewing the broken contract which God's Israel had neglected, so that all – Jew and Gentile alike – might be a people of the Lord in the eternal kingdom (vv. 13-18).

In quoting Amos 9:11-12, James declared that other prophets also had been preaching renewal (v.15). Therefore, God would first rebuild fallen Israel, and then the mission to the Gentiles would commence, as it did in Acts 10 in the household of Cornelius. Subsequent preaching by Peter and Paul was not a break with Israel of old, but a reaffirmation of their place in God's plan of redemption.

All preaching and witnessing throughout Acts builds upon the restoration foundation established in Acts 2-3, when God's people embodied in Israel again became a light to the nations. Pentecost, therefore, did not mark the birth of the church; instead, it occasioned the renewal of God's on-going Jewish elect, so that the apostles could witness the resurrected Christ "in Jerusalem, in all of Judea and Samaria, and even to the remotest parts of the earth" (Acts 1:8).

This preaching would start prior to the influx of the Gentiles, the "residue of men" (Acts 15:17), into the body of the covenant redeemed, in response to Jewish prophecy (Isa. 42:6, 49:6; II Sam. 7, etc.). Also compare Isaiah 11:10 with Romans 15:12. Indeed, the concept of covenant renewal resides deeply in both Jewish prophetic promises and apostolic teaching and preaching.

Hebrews 10:1-10

Hebrews 10:9 declares that "He takes away the first in order to establish the second." The two-covenant view assumes that the writer is discussing the subject of *covenants*, first (Moses) and second (Christ), an old one and a new one. But the word "covenant" does not once appear anywhere in Hebrews 10:1-10! The subject under consideration is *sacrifice*, contrasting their frequency during the time of the Jewish nation with the once-for-all-time, all-fulfilling sacrifice of Jesus Christ.

Therefore, the meaning of the passage is that God took away the first set of sacrifices (vv. 1, 3, 5, 6, 8, 11, 12, 14) in order to establish the pleasing sacrifice of Christ. It was Christ coming to do God's will (v. 9a) which is being discussed. In this, the writer of Hebrews delivered the final blow to the legalistic temple cult, the self-styled true believers among the party-oriented Jews. Since their sacrificial system could not permanently satisfy, God had to be pleased with a sufficient sacrifice, His own Son. The notion of covenant should not be carelessly injected into this context. The author clearly is discussing sacrifice.

Hebrews 8:7-13 – The New Covenant

As a vital part of the ongoing argument of the author of Hebrews that Christ is "better" than the angels, Moses, or the Levite priestly system, etc., proponents of two covenants see Christ in Hebrews 8:7-13 as the superior mediator of a new-in-kind agreement between God and man, one radically different from similar arrangements made with Abraham, Moses, David, etc. In this Christian "dispensation" they see God inaugurating an absolutely unprecedented new covenant with His people, different from anything He had given in the past.

The two-covenant doctrine maintains a clear demarcation between contrasting Mosaic and Christian covenants. Their second (new) covenant has been in effect since the Pentecost of Acts two, when it supposedly annulled the former (old) covenant that was allegedly "faulty" (a misreading of verse 7) and ready to "disappear," since it was "becoming obsolete and growing old" (v. 13). They see the old as a mere figure of the true (9:24), with carnal ordinances (9:10), which cannot be approached with a clear conscience (9:8-9). The old is regarded as inferior (see 8:7), while the new is the "true covenant" (8:2), the one approachable with a clear conscience (9:8-9).

This traditional covenant view builds its case on the use of certain words such as "first," "another," "better," and "superior," all of which are found in Hebrews 8:6-7. Significantly, none of these words appears in the writing of the originating prophet, Jeremiah, who in 31:31-34 foretold the "new covenant" about 675 years before the author of Hebrews cited it in 8:8-12. But, in what sense does the author of Hebrews at 8:13 regard Jeremiah's covenant as "new," rendering the "first" one obsolete?

How the word "new" is used in the context of Hebrews 8 is critical to a proper understanding of the term "new covenant." First, what is described as old and new by the author of Hebrews does not in any way alter the nature of the everlasting covenant God gave to Abraham (Gen. 17:7), and also Moses (Psa. 105:10), David (II Sam. 23:5), and the prophets (Jer. 32:40). Second, evidence presented in Chapter Twelve shows that new-in-time and new-in-kind distinction among the Greek words for "new" is absolutely untenable, neutralizing the notion that the covenant in the Christian era is new-in-kind.

Third, several other biblical concepts and words are said to be at once "old" and "new," especially love, the heart, creature, body, the eternal moon in its various phases, etc. As explained at length in Chapter Five, all of these concepts either refer to an ongoing process of renewal or express a continuity of an existing object or emotion, not necessarily the creation of something which never had existed. God's admonition of love, for instance, is simultaneously an "old" and a "new" commandment (I John 2:7-8, II John 5). Only accommodatively does Hebrews speak of more than one covenant.

And so, as the author of Hebrews discusses old covenant and new covenant, he is not referring to two *different* agreements between God and man. Instead, he is describing two historical time periods of covenantal development with respect to such things as sacrifices, offices, priesthood, and tabernacles. The covenant itself is the same eternal one which Abraham enjoyed as described in Hebrews 6:13-20; God's promises to the ancient patriarch are part and parcel of the covenant throughout the generations of man.

To this covenant, active in the days of Israel and the prophets, the law of Moses was added (Gal. 3:17-19). It consisted of transitory laws of diet and ceremony which became superfluous after Christ had come, and totally fell into disuse by the second century. Evidently, Christ's mission was not to bring to man *another* covenant to replace the "old" one, but rather, with His teaching and life, to establish a new set of circumstances and responses with regard to the eternal covenant long enjoyed by the ancient faithful.

Equally relevant to defining the nature of new covenant are the concepts expressed in Hebrews 8:9, which states that "It [the new covenant] will not be like the covenant I made with their forefathers when I took them by the hand to lead them out of Egypt . . ." In this verse, two-covenant proponents see a new covenant clearly contrasted and plainly distinguished from the covenant made with Israel after Egyptian deliverance. But God's arrangements with Moses after the Israelites had been freed from bondage, were never intended to be a distinct old covenant, for such language as "when I took them . . . out of Egypt" served a date setting function which pointed to broken covenant that needed to be renewed with Israel and Judah (see Chapter Ten).

The words "new covenant" first found their way into scripture in Jeremiah 31:31-34. At that time the prophet foretold the renewal of the ancient agreement and expanded its benefits for God's generations of faithful returning from Babylonian exile, in about 536 B.C. Such application was the next installment of the ongoing revelation of His gracious plan for man, as embodied in the eternal covenant (Ezek. 37:26, Jer. 32:40).

Now in the first century, the author of Hebrews taught that God once again under Christ has renewed the ancient pledge to His people, making it better, fuller and fleshed out as never before. Thus, the application of Jeremiah 31:31-34 by the author of Hebrews in 8:8-12 to the present era of Christ actually demonstrates the *continuity* of God's oaths and promises made with man, not a bifurcation of them into contrasting agreements.

Besides the author of Hebrews among New Testament writers, only Luke and Paul use the words "new covenant," and then not to establish a contrast with an old covenant (see below). The New Testament authors did not develop the now-traditional concept of a new covenant, for Matthew and Mark simply say "covenant," nor did any of the early church fathers from 95 to 175 – Clement of Rome, Ignatius, Papias, Justin, and more than a dozen others. The popular two-covenant concept first emerged in Christian thought around AD 180 in the teaching of Irenaeus (see Chapter Five).

The significance of the historical record is that the use of the terms "old covenant" and "new covenant" upon the text of Hebrews (and Paul's letters) is imposed prematurely – in fact, 150 years too soon! The relevant question, then, is this: why was not the two-covenant concept employed by *any* of these many authors and church leaders of the *ekklesia* for more than 150 years after the "new covenant" had been supposedly established on Pentecost of Acts 2, in AD 33? Further, why was it not until Eusebius, early in the *fourth* century, that any writer applied the term "new covenant" to a body of writings, a New Testament canon, distinct from the writings of the Jewish prophets?

No apostle or early orthodox church father taught that Jesus instituted a new *kind* of covenant in the way modern two-covenant proponents define it. In fact, *all* major doctrinal themes and promises (such as the remission of sin, justification, grace, kingdom, repentance, and the necessity of a heart relationship between God and man), shine forth just as brightly in Old Testament writings as they do anywhere in the New Testament collection (see Chapter Seven). Through the ages, as God renewed and reinforced the ancient contract over the years until the time of Christ, He did not delete or replace any of the essential terms of the beloved covenant (see Chapter Eleven), and it is described as eternal and everlasting on both sides of the cross.

Throughout the ages, all of God's faithful are sons of God (Gal. 3:26), of the seed of Abraham (v. 29), legitimate heirs to every spiritual promise God made to the fathers, sharing equally in all blessings and the heavenly inheritance. As one people of God throughout time, all covenanters are brothers benefiting equally from God's gracious, saving agreement.

The new covenant described in Hebrews is "better" because temporal animal sacrifices had been replaced by the permanent, sufficient sacrifice of Jesus (see Chapter Three). The temporality of the Levitical arrangement yielded to an endless priesthood after the order of Melchizedek. Further, the covenantal agreement now embraces Gentile God-fearers as part of the worldwide household of God, with Christ as Head and Sustainer, reinforcing every hope and promise revealed to Israel by the ancient prophets and teachers of old.

II Corinthians Three

In this chapter, Paul speaks of Christ's people as servants of a new covenant, one "not of the letter but of the Spirit, for the letter kills but the Spirit gives life" (v.6). Verse 14 mentions the reading of the old covenant, which the next verse explains as the teaching of Moses. In these verses, two-covenant advocates contrast distinct old and new covenants, arguing that even as Paul wrote the covenant through Moses was fading away (vv. 11, 13). They say further that either the law had been fulfilled, or it is still binding (Matt. 5:17-18).

Instead, II Corinthians 3 apparently echoes the Judaizers' first-century legalistic approach toward religion wherein burdensome law had been substituted for spirit (4:6). The letter/spirit dichotomy of II Corinthians 3 seems to address the outward/inward tension between the intent of God's will, often embodied in broad principles as practiced by faithful Jews, and party-centered Judaism's pervasive indexing of the law, which began in the late Jewish period and continued into Paul's day (see Chapter Four). This "letter" approach led the tradition-blinded Pharisees to reject Jesus (John 5:39-40). They burdened the people with rules and regulations of their own, inventing fresh requirements for others to follow, and going beyond the intent of a law that is "spiritual . . . holy, just, and good" (Rom. 7:12, 14).

In any era the letter kills, for life is imparted through the spirit, which is the attitude and disposition engraved upon the tablets of the heart of the inward man (vv. 3,6). Paul's legalistic adversaries had essentially petrified the eternal covenant, making the God-given law that regulated it a text that killed. The apostle called such party-centered religion an "old covenant," a term which adequately expressed an unspiritual state which resulted when Moses was read without Christ in view, and with Moses as the hero of the covenant (Heb. 12:2).

Moses' ministry was one of death (v. 7) and condemnation (v. 9) as long as its admittedly glorious types and shadows and ceremonial aspects had to be followed by everyone, as insisted upon by legalistic Judaizers who saw no Christ fulfillment. The glory of Moses' ministry would have been permanently veiled, with no hope, resulting in spiritual death, because animal blood could not take away sin. As the author of Hebrews teaches, forgiveness is secured for all of the faithful from Abraham until the present, in the eternal covenant, because of the complete and final sacrifice of Christ (9:15-18). See also Chapter Three.

Even more important, a two-covenant proponent is hard pressed to justify treatment of righteous Jewish covenant people as "under a ministry of condemnation" which had "no glory" because of the glory of Christ (vv. 9-10). Were the minds of *all* Jews hardened, possessing no godly spirit (v. 14)? Or, was it rather a smaller group of people, law-dependent Talmudic Judaizers with their misguided belief that a proper relationship with God rested upon meticulously keeping their interpretation of Moses, or else being regarded with no favor? A veiled gospel is possible on either side of the cross, among those who are perishing (4:3, see also 3:14).

Actually, faithful Jews under the prophets (and before) were justified, had the mind of God, looked forward to the promised One, and practiced Moses' moral law and ceremonial duties to the best of their ability. Isaiah, Jeremiah, Hosea, and innumerable other ancient worthies (see Heb. 11), steadfastly depended upon a merciful God, trusting and believing that He had chosen them as members of a body of covenant people equipped in the righteousness of God and enjoying present salvation.

Paul's II Corinthians 3, therefore, is not a blanket declaration that all of Moses' people were condemned, for in one lengthy context Paul clearly confirmed God's enduring love for covenant Israel (Rom. 9:3-11:32). Even after the preaching of Christ's gospel had begun, as recorded in Acts, God never abandoned the Jewish faithful, and they were still fellow-members of God's body, the *ekklesia*, as aptly stated in Romans 9:3-4· "My kinsmen . . . who are Israelites, to whom belongs [present tense] the adoption as sons and the glory of the covenants and the giving of the law and the temple service and the promises . . ." Assuredly, Christ was protecting them also (see v. 5). Paul's teaching blended nicely with God's plan, as embodied in the everlasting agreement spoken by the prophets (see Chapter Six).

Therefore, it was fully acceptable for messianic Jews to

continue to follow all teachings of the prophets, even in observing various aspects of Moses' law, as amply shown in Chapter Eight. In Jerusalem alone, thousands among the Jews who followed Christ staunchly upheld the law (Acts 21:20). It was the Judaizers who appealed solely to Moses and their legalistic additions to his law as a basis of salvation that Paul stingingly rebuked in II Corinthians 3, for they failed to embrace Jesus as the Christ and hope of Israel. Their hardened hearts would not allow the removal of the veil which would come about if they would only accept Jesus.

Galatians Four

In his Galatian letter Paul borrowed from Genesis to illustrate the freedom that God's people enjoy in Christ, climaxing in 4:22-26: " . . . Abraham had two sons, one by the bondwoman and one by the free woman . . . for these two women are two covenants, one proceeding from Mount Sinai, bearing slave children, but the Jerusalem above is free . . ."

It is insisted that Paul, in these verses, teaches two distinct covenants, old (Sinai) and new (Jerusalem), and that the first one is to be "cast out" (v. 30). The old one thus done away, an entirely new covenant was supposedly instituted. But the context of Galatians 4, which reaches back into the previous chapter, suggests that the contrast is between *bondage* and *freedom*, and not between a so-called Mosaic legal system allegedly void of spiritual favor and a new covenant regime which supposedly monopolizes grace and freedom.

As Paul emphatically rebuked entrenched legalism in Galatians 4:21-31, he equated the "covenant" of Sinai/bondage/Hagar/*present* Jerusalem with the Christ-rejecting, first century Judaistic parties whom he and his Master continually encountered. To describe Judaism's pitiful, spiritual condition as a "covenant" was indeed ironic, for their law-based work system was the very antithesis of God's eternal arrangement (see Chapter Eleven). Pollution of it through a defense of legalistic ritualism ultimately resulted in a breaking of God's gracious covenant (see Matt. 23:2-35, Jer. 31:32).

In contrast, the "covenant" corresponding to freedom/Sarah/Jerusalem *from above* allegorically stands for the children of promise, the sons of the free woman, enjoying the God of covenant in an authentic, merciful relationship. Paul concluded this illustration of salvation based upon familiar Jewish figures by saying, "Get rid of the bondwoman and her son, for [he] shall not share in the inheritance with the son of the free woman" (v. 30). Here is a stinging, emphatic rejection of legalistic Judaism, even as verse 20 states, "Tell me, you who desire to be under law . . ."

All of the key words in Galatians 4:21-31 – covenant, promise, bondage, and law – should be interpreted in light of their usage in Galatians 3. Let that chapter function as a Bible dictionary. The emptiness of this "covenant" without God's grace is explained in 3:10; the cursings in the following verses refer back to those in Genesis 3:14-19 – those on people, the earth, animals, etc. – all in view of sin. To offset them, God made promises to Abraham in Genesis 12 and 15.

Galatians 3-4 shows that Christ has redeemed us from these various curses, and that under Christ we are free and not under legal bondage. God had graciously employed a tutor – miracles, the Passover, types and shadows, and sacrifices (Heb. 10:1-10), to lead to Christ (Gal. 3:24). These transitory aspects of Mosaic law are now dismissed (see Chapter Eleven), but not the entire body of Old Testament scriptures, for its moral precepts are timeless.

It is unthinkable to suggest that David, Daniel, Zechariah, and numerous other faithful Jews, were all slaves to a "Mount Sinai covenant," fit to be "cast out" (vv. 24, 30). To the contrary, a just God fully accepted, saved, sanctified, and justified all of these worthies in the eternal covenant by grace through faith. The religion of Moses was by no means a system of carnal law, for God stood ready as the justifier of *all* who diligently sought Him with pure hearts. The people of Moses experienced the reality of sonship to the same intensity as Christians do.

Six times in Galatians 3, Paul left no doubt that his Christ-centered teaching was intimately connected with God's original purposes, first revealed to Abraham (Gen. 12-17). This unbreakable 2000-year-long continuity of the gospel demonstrates that ultimately all nations would experience God's favor through the ancient Patriarch, and that the Gentiles would be justified by faith in Christ (Gal. 3:8). Because of the blessing given to Abraham and fulfilled in Christ (v. 14), the saints in Paul's day could be redeemed – purchased back by God.

Thus, all of God's spiritual promises to Abraham and his descendants were consummated in the person Jesus Christ, "the Seed of Abraham" (v. 16). In the intervening period, the law of Moses had to be added, along with its ceremonies, types and shadows, "until the Seed to whom the promise referred had come" (v. 19). In addition to Christ, *all* the faithful covenanted ones through the ages also are of this family or "seed" of Abraham, and are heirs according to God's promises embodied in His longstanding, gracious agreement (v. 29). As Abraham's spiritual descendants, the people of Christ cherish these ancient promises from God as basic to everything which Christ came to accomplish in redeeming man.

The point in Galatians 3-4 is driven home at 5:1: in Christ God's elect are free, "therefore stand firm in your freedom and do not subject yourself to a yoke of slavery," the bondage of Jewish law-keeping in a works system. Paul wrote the Galatian letter in the first place to show the necessity of covenant union with God and in the folly of relapsing into legalism. Judaism's approach toward law as the means to sustain themselves is the bone of contention, for the foolish Galatians (3:1) had been bewitched into believing that a gulf existed between themselves and Christ, one which had to be constantly bridged by the good works of the Torah.

Consequently, anyone who regarded the Old Testament

scriptures as a structured law (Torah) was indeed enslaved, unable to enjoy the blessing of freedom in Christ, who had once for all removed the bondage with its curses. In verse 21, Paul is exhorting the Galatians not to entangle themselves in any party-centered Judaistic legal system, something thoroughly condemned throughout the Galatian letter (1:9, 4:30, 5:4, etc.). Indeed, all free men live because of faith (3:11), voluntarily enslaved only to Jesus Christ.

Summary

The popular two-covenant doctrine has as its prominent characteristic a new law to govern all who have entered a Christian new covenant, an arrangement believed to be clearly distinguishable and separate from the Jewish phase of the covenant to which was added the law of Moses. The phrase "new covenant" appears seven times in four New Testament books. In 8:8f and 10:16f, the author of Hebrews quoted Jeremiah 31:31f which contains the term, further declaring that in 9:15 and 12:24 that Christ is the mediator of a new covenant. Luke's gospel connects the Lord's Supper cup with the new covenant (22:20, as does Paul I Cor. 11:27), while in II Corinthians 3 Paul speaks of both new and old covenants (vv. 6, 14).

The phrase "new covenant" is further allied with the "second" or the "better" (superior) covenant in one New Testament passage – Hebrews 8:6-7. (The word "first" is used with "covenant" in 8:7, 13; 9:1, 15.) Additionally, in the context of an allegory about two women, Paul in Galatians 4:24 describes two covenants. Of further relevance is the fact that the same writer also refers to the Mosaic order in the plural–"covenants" (Eph. 2:12, Rom. 9:4).

Evidence presented both in Chapter Eleven and earlier in this chapter, specifically explains in context the meanings of these various phrases of covenant. In brief, Paul's use of irony in connection with covenant suggests a special, limited use of the word "new," while the phrase "new covenant" in Luke 22:20 is simply rendered "covenant" in the parallel accounts in the other synoptic gospels (Mark 14:24, Matt. 26:28). Even as the author of Hebrews used the words "new" and "better" as descriptive of covenant, he did *not* present a case for the establishment of a new-in-kind agreement between God and man, one to be *contrasted* with the Mosaic order.

Nevertheless, on the strength of these passages written to a minority of the first century saints, some theorists advance the extremely far-reaching doctrine of distinct old and new covenants, each with its own law and separated by time and place of origin. Significantly, no other authors of New Testament books, among them Matthew, Mark, John, James, Peter and Jude, mentioned these post-apostolic concepts (see Chapter Five) involving twin covenants and laws. Among the nearly thirty earliest non-canonical writings of the church fathers during the years 95 to 180 (see Chapter Five), none expressed anything resembling the two-covenant concept in conjunction with another law, allegedly inaugurated in AD 33 on the first Pentecost after Christ's resurrection (Acts 2).

It should be evident, then, that the two-covenant concept cannot claim an apostolic origin, or else it would surely have been the foundation of the primitive church's system of teaching and the subject of significant written discussion and amplification, not only in the canonical books of the present New Testament, but also in the letters and treatises of the earliest of church fathers. Such developments never took place. Instead, the stalwarts of the faith of the first three centuries regularly wrote about such relevant topics as the nature of God, the mission and person of Christ, the nature of faith, the assembly and its organization and worship (especially the Lord's Supper), as well as the love feast, the resurrection and conversely, opposed heretical views on these same subjects. The nature of covenant was not debated.

Finally, in the writings of Irenaeus (AD 180), Tertullian about thirty years later, and especially later power-conscious church fathers, the two-covenant concept and contrasting laws emerged as devices to solidify an ecclesiastical structure in emerging institutional religion. And it was only much later, in fact well into the fourth century, that any church official assigned the term "new covenant" to a *body* of writings, a canon of New Testament scriptures, the present day common practice.

Therefore, applying the common two-covenant concept to the writings of Paul and the author of Hebrews is surely anachronistic, for such teaching was not promulgated for at least 150 years after the ministry of the One who came not to destroy the law and the prophets (Matt. 5:17), but rather to fulfill them in the eternal covenant (Heb. 13:20), and renew the ancient moral teachings, amplifying them and fleshing them out for the people of God after the time of Christ.

~

The Eternal Covenant of Peace

G OD'S ETERNAL/EVERLASTING covenant is a mutually binding agreement with His people, freely promising them blessings and protection, and calling for submission and trust in response. Not a legal agreement based upon commandments, statutes, or ordinances, the covenant is a gracious, saving *compact* based on Heavenly assurance of a present right-standing before God, accompanied by blessings and cursings.

Contrary to the multi-covenants of dispensationalism, which essentially disregard each other, God's eternal agreement, initiated with the oath and promise to Abraham in Genesis 12:1-3, 15:6-17, elaborates upon a single concept: God's plan for man's redemption through Jesus Christ. Further, each mention of covenant by Moses, David, the Jewish prophets, and the apostles, successively and extensively revealed more about how God gives to sinners present blessings and salvation, assuring them with an oath sworn by Himself. Man only needs to trust in this divine arrangement and constantly uphold it through respecting God and honoring Him through living righteously.

As explained in Chapters Two and Eleven, the terms of God's magnificent everlasting covenant embrace five fundamental concepts:

(1) God promises that He will give us a new heart by developing a wholesome respect for God's moral law and a resolve to apply it in all aspects of living.

(2) The moral law is written on the hearts of covenant people. There is no codified law glaring at us, as fashioned first by Jewish legalists and constantly reinvented by authoritarian church groups over the centuries. Instead, God's mind and will dwell inside us, bubbling up spontaneously as principles of new life.

(3) in this covenant exchange and relationship, God declares that, "I will be your God and you will be my people." In these terms, God gives us His own character, and the fruit of the spirit is exhibited (Gal. 5:22), demonstrating that Christ abides within us. Additionally, we will have a new name, because we have become a new creation in Christ (II Cor. 5:7). In Isaiah 61:8, 62:2, the everlasting covenant is associated with the new name.

(4) Further, He will put a new spirit within us, a magnificent promise to all covenanters who strive to develop the mind and disposition of the One who created the world and continues to bathe it with favor.

(5) In the gracious terms of covenant, sin is forgiven and remembered no more. Surely here is the supreme blessing of the ages, God bestowing upon sinful creatures full pardon of their transgressions. Through this act of grace they are allowed to appear before the throne of heaven spotless and without blemish. Further, through the blood of Christ, God is able to keep clean all good

hearts who respect the covenant and plead it before the world.

As a memorial of His glorious resurrection, the faithful of God enthusiastically partake of the covenant meal – unleavened bread and the fruit of the vine – honoring the blood of the new agreement, in which formerly sin-claimed men now freely enjoy a binding, love-centered union with the living God. Constantly seeking the truth and coming to His light (John 3:21), the people of Christ live a life of faithfulness, and are always protected and enveloped by Yahweh's love and grace. Such overcomers are true winners (Rev. 2-3), who celebrate their victory over sin. Then, at the final return of Christ, they are guaranteed a new body (I Cor. 15:12-57, I Thess. 4:13-17; see also Matt. 25:31-46, II Thess. 1:7-9), so that they may dwell forever in the Lord's heavenly home, ruling with God from the new heaven and the new earth (Rev. 21:1-22:5).

Various Uses of the Word 'Covenant'

Like many other biblical words, such as lust, pride, covetous, deceptive, and jealousy, the word "covenant" may convey different meanings, depending on context. In most occurrences, a covenant is a mutually binding agreement between two parties, in which promises are exchanged; in the case of the God-authored unilateral everlasting covenant with man, it is tempered by grace and mercy. A special meaning of the word "covenant," suggesting a figurative or limited usage, occurs in the following instances:

(a) In Isaiah 42:6 and 49:8 (and possibly in Malachi 2:17), Christ Himself is personified in the word "covenant," the future deliverer and restorer of the people of Judah as they travailed with the messianic hope burning within them.

(b) In Galatians 4, two women personified as covenants are known as "present Jerusalem" and "Jerusalem from above." In this context, the word covenant actually contrasts two different religious systems.

(c) In II Corinthians 3, a covenant is equated with "the reading of Moses" (vv. 14-15). In this context, therefore it is not an agreement. Rather, as explained in Chapters Eleven and Thirteen, the covenant stands for a *perversion* of Moses' law and teaching in its reading.

(d) In Hebrews 8, the covenant is God's gracious agreement, but the word is associated with the adjective "new," a true irony, in that none of the terms of the old covenant were altered in any way to inaugurate in the first century an alleged innovation in the history of God's dealing with man, a new covenant to be contrasted with an old one (see Chapters Eleven and Thirteen). Rather, the argument by the author of Hebrews restates and renews all essentials of an agreement which had been in force since Abraham. The term "new covenant" in Hebrews 8 points to longstanding anticipation of Jewish hope, and messianic fulfillment of God's promises to His people.

The Newness of the New Covenant

In a strict sense, how is the new covenant "new?" How is it "better" than previous arrangements between God and man? (Heb. 8:13). God's eternal covenant is qualified in the Christian era, because a realized Christ is preferred over the anticipated Christ of Jewish prophecy. Dutiful animal sacrifices and other ceremonial arrangements, along with types and shadows, were fulfilled in the covenant victim, Jesus Christ, who forever rendered obsolete the "schoolmaster" Levitical system.

Best of all, with Christ as central figure in the everlasting covenant, first made with Abraham's family, then extended and renewed in the eras of Moses and David, and again at the time of Isaiah, Jeremiah, and other prophets, the ancient agreement reached its ultimate glory and completeness. Thus, in the Christian era, the everlasting covenant is legitimately referred to as "new," in that its scope has been significantly enlarged forever by integrating the Gentiles into God's covenantal family, whose head is now Christ.

The concepts old covenant and new covenant therefore embody *one* gracious, saving relationship for all faithful people with a loving God, who has displayed His mind and will – His plan for man – in a single purposeful program, though there are several aspects or stages to it. Through the ages, there has been but one heavenly agreement whose purposeful objective is to present to the world a unified revelation of the true and living God. Some of His word, His plan and purposes for man, were disclosed to Abraham (and even to others before him), then to Jewish poets and prophets, and finally gloriously realized in the person of Christ, through His teachings and manner of life.

The gracious age-lasting covenant is the one vehicle of this revelation of God's self-disclosure to sinful creatures. Its primary objective is to redeem man from sin, through His instrument Israel, so that through His son in the messianic era the Father may have a relationship with *all* men, including peoples once afar off – the Gentiles. God's eternal plan for man is borne out in the following chart which historically shows various aspects of the one everlasting covenant:

STAGE	DATING POINT	PARTICIPANTS	HIGHLIGHTS	OUTWARD SIGNS
ABRAHAMIC Genesis 15-17 *Everlasting* Gen. 17:7	Anticipated possession of Canaan	Family of righteous Abraham as patriarchal Head of household.	Unconditional promis by God to fulfill a land promise; conditional to Abraham's descendants.	Circumcision (Gen. 17:11-14) (The Sabbath)
MOSAIC Exodus 20 *Everlasting* Psa. 105:10	"When I [God] took you out of Egypt . . ."	Israel, as descendants of Abraham, Isaac and Jacob, redeemed people from bondage to an earthly power, Egypt.	Conditional divine divine pledge to be Israel's Guarantor of its desitny, subject to His people's service and consecration to God.	Circumcision The Sabbath (Ex. 31:13-17, 20:10-12), a perpetual obligation.
DAVIDIC II Samuel 7 *Everlasting* II Sam 23:5	Election of David to the kingship of Israel.	Israel, as faithful subjects of David, in continuity with descendants of Abraham.	Unconditional divine promise to maintain Davidic dynasty, an implicit pledge to Israel. Godly king like David to come as Messiah.	Circumcision The Sabbath Anointing of king David demonstrated his Election by God
PROPHETIC Jeremiah 31-32 Ezekiel 36-37 *Everlasting* Jer. 32:40 Ezek. 37-26	When God took Israel out of Babylon under a renewed covenant (Jer. 16:14-15, 23:7-8).	Israel, as about to be renewed in its return to the promised land from Babylonian captivity, after having rebelled.	Unconditional promise by God to unfaithful Israel to maintain the Davidic dynasty forever, with a Godly king like David.	Circumcision the Sabbath
MESSIANIC Hebrews 8 *Eternal* Heb. 13:20	Life and sacrificial death of Jesus Christ as a "new covenant" (Heb. 9:15-18, 10:9).	All nations and peoples as extension of moral Israel, now internationalized.	The king like unto David realized in the consummate servant, Jesus Christ. Passing of types and shadows and Jewish sacrificial system.	The Lord's Supper Baptism

Each phase of the everlasting (eternal) covenant is "new" in relation to the preceding one, and is a restoration and renewal of the participants in earlier phases, not the establishment of something entirely new through a *different* type of covenant than its predecessor. All phases of covenant have a dating point of inception. The messianic restoration and renewal of covenant has the better promises, priesthood, sacrifices, etc., as taught by the author of the book of Hebrews.

The new covenant in the messianic stage already had passed through distinct phases, as does the eternal moon. But the covenant is *not* new in the sense of never having existed before. In precisely the same way that the "new covenant" Jeremiah promised the people after the Babylonian exile in 536 B.C. was not a fresh agreement, distinct from earlier Davidic or Mosaic stages of covenant.

Therefore, the realization of the new covenant in the messianic era does not set forth an innovation in history, for it has always been part of the eternal covenant, in the same way that the appearance of the new moon about once monthly (after it had passed through its other phases) does not present something new – it is the same eternal moon (see p. 93).

The Goal of the Covenant

In extending to man the eternal covenant, God's intent has been the cementing of a relationship between Himself and the created. To this divine arrangement, God never established any kind of add-on systematized law, consisting of obligatory wooden do's and dont's, in which inflexible compliance to them would be the objective. The state of the heart must be considered.

Nevertheless, in all phases of covenant the same attitude of obedience has been required. Indeed, proper responses to God's instructive commandments are outward expressions of participation in the eternal covenant, as follows:

(i) Abrahamic phase: The people living in the days of the patriarchs obeyed God's charge – His commandments, statutes and law, as shown in Genesis 26:6.

(ii) Mosaic phase: God's laws and instruction revealed through Moses were accompanied by blessings, but also cursings for disobedience explained in Deuteronomy 27-28.

(iii) Davidic phase: Deuteronomy 30:8-10, I Kings 2:2-4, and the teaching of the prophets, point to the necessity of following God's ways and instruction.

(iv) Prophetic phase: As God brought His elect back from Babylonian captivity, under the promise of a "new covenant," God emphasized the necessity of His people to follow the law as a display of spiritual vitality (Dan. 9:10-14; Jer. 7:23, 11:3-8, 26:13; Zech. 6:15).

(v) Christian phase: The unfolding of Christ's teaching shows that God required His covenanted ones to follow the divine will as embodied in statements structured if . . . then, as in Deuteronomy (John 14:15, 15:17; see also I John 5:3, II John 6). Such a response purified the soul (I Pet. 1:22).

The Infinite Covenant

God's unique, everlasting, infinite covenant will never terminate, because that which is eternal has no end. If the covenant should ever cease, whether at the death of each person or at the future time of judgment and the earth's destruction, what would happen to the eternal life possessed individually by each of God's holy ones, all saints throughout time?

Therefore, in the heavenly world to come, where Christians and faithful Jews before the cross will be forever in one heavenly location, all will still be in covenant union with their God. In Revelation 21:1f, where the saints are pictured at home with God, we are assured that the covenantal term "I will be their God and we will His people," will still be in force (v. 3). Evidently, God's everlasting agreement continues on and on, even as God's everlasting love never ends.

A problem for all two-covenant teachers is to determine *which* of five biblical everlasting (eternal) covenants – the Abrahamic (Gen. 17:7) the Davidic (II Sam. 23:5), the prophet (Jer. 32:40), the "old" (Mosaic, to Israel, I Chron. 16:7, Psa. 105:10), or the "new" (Christian, Heb. 13:20) – will be operative forever in heaven. Since there cannot be more than one eternal covenant existing simultaneously, which one of these will prevail in the next life? To choose the "new" (messianic) one will, of necessity, leave out all of the covenant patriarchs and Jews of Old Testament times.

Since the final judgment does not mark the cessation of God's enduring love for His people, nor of Christ's authentic Melchizedek priesthood which is to remain forever, similarly the end of time yet future does not terminate the covenant itself, especially His continuing promise to remain in union with the faithful forever in the consummated, heavenly state. The only defensible conclusion is that there has been – and always will be – only one gracious, everlasting, saving agreement which extends from Genesis through the Jewish and Christian eras to the end of earthly time, past the judgment, and far, far beyond, into endless eternity.

Jeremiah 31:31-34 In Context

The interpretation of any text of scripture must take into consideration its historical, social and literary contexts. Chapter Ten shows that the proclamation of Jeremiah's famous new covenant prophecy, issued in about 593 B.C., had an immediate application to the Jews of the prophet's day and the subsequent generation, to encourage loyalty during the present bleak circumstances.

All who heard Jeremiah's preaching would construe his new covenant terms and blessings of 31:31-34, not so much as a prophecy to be fulfilled hundreds of years into the future, but as comforting, purposeful words for contemporary Judeans who faced impending Babylonian captivity. Therefore, it was the people of Jeremiah's day who would see God's blessings realized in the near future (in fact, within fifty years), wherein their immediate descendants would experience new hearts and spirits and a renewed resolve to follow God after returning to their homeland, as part of the revival of their ancient covenant with God.

And so, it is probable that, in the mid-first century, the author of Hebrews in 8:6-13 (as well as in other parts of his treatise), referred back to familiar circumstances and concepts – angels, priesthood, worship, sacrifice, and covenant – for purposes of comparison with the past, by declaring that now everything is "better," rather than citing Jeremiah 31:31-34 *primarily* as a prophetic fulfillment. Further, the new covenant in the messianic era was not a different type of covenant renewal than what Judah had experienced during the Jerusalem Conference after Babylonian captivity (under a new covenant – Jer. 31:31-34), and even earlier in the days of David and Moses.

Are Christians Superior to Old Testament Jews?

Two-covenant proponents often contend that God's people under Christ and the apostles possess a totally distinct religion from Moses and the prophets – in fact, as different as night and day. They see Christians as head and shoulders above the Israel of old, who are somehow weak, in bondage to a law system, and are generally earthly and carnal (see Chapter Twelve). More than these things, the nation Israel is perceived as placed in God's plan *only* so that there would be a pure lineage to bring forth the Messiah.

But even in Old Testament times God was interested in

THE ETERNAL COVENANT OF PEACE

stabilizing His people Israel spiritually for their *own* sake, in respect of a relationship, promising them blessings and divine favor even apart from messianic anticipation, as embodied in the term *chesed*, covenant favor. God was saving them by grace through faith. In fact, the father of the faithful throughout the ages, Abraham without wavering constantly obeyed his Creator, despite the lack of full understanding and of lengthy explanations of commandments, whether oral or written.

The vital key to Abraham's relationship with God was his faith: "And he believed in God, and it was reckoned to him for righteousness" (Gen. 15:6). Even today, Abraham serves as the high standard of faith, as expressed in the theological expression, "Abrahamic faith." No Christian saint compares with him in respect to quality of faith. Further, no New Testament writings contain a Christian "roll call of faith" similar to the one compiled by the author of Hebrews, consisting of persevering faithful patriarchs, children of Israel, Jews, and Gentiles alike (Heb. 11:5–39). The individuals named are not one whit behind Christians in their quality of faith and commitment to the everlasting covenant.

Any separation of faithful Jews of the prophetic era from Christians, by insisting that each group relates to God through separate old and new covenants, is akin to dispensationalism, unwittingly the first step toward premillennialism. In fact, two-covenant proponents freely talk of three dispensations – Patriarchal, the Mosaic, and the Christian – though neither the Hebrew nor the Greek scriptures hint at such distinctions.

Teaching that God's people this side of the cross have a separate identity and labor under far superior heavenly instruction, two-covenant advocates through such segregation actually display spiritual elitism before God. The New Testament has no dramatic scriptural figure to demonstrate the two-covenant concept, nor is there a type or a shadow of it anywhere in the Old Testament.

On the other hand, the single covenant doctrine is very much at home among all of the biblical "one's" – one promise, one flock, one city of God, one body (Eph. 4:4-5), etc. (see Chapter Five) – and in the two striking figures of covenantal unity in Chapter Six: the celestial woman of Revelation 12 and the olive tree of Romans 11. The woman figure shows that the New Testament people of God, following Christ's commandments (Rev. 12:17), are actually embodied in the longstanding (formerly exclusively) Jewish radiant woman, not the other way around. Therefore, it was Christians who had to be fully integrated with faithful covenant Israel, in the woman figure.

Similarly, in Paul's olive tree illustration in Romans 11, God would not attach faithful Jews of old to the *ekklesia* of Christ; rather, it was just the opposite – saints in Christ were grafted onto the ancient olive tree whose stock (trunk) and roots are Abraham, Isaac and Jacob. For centuries during the time of David and later prophets, the branches of the olive tree were exclusively Jews. In the first century and afterward, Christ's disciples were grafted into the ancient olive tree, together with reformed Jews. Therefore, the corollary of Hebrews 11:40 is also true: apart from *them,* Christians could not be made perfect.

As with Revelation's covenant woman, the olive tree demonstrates continuity of covenant, pointing to one eternal arrangement between God and man throughout time, whose terms have ever remained the same – the promise of a new heart with the law written in it, the comforting interdwelling of God and man, the continual remission of sins, etc., as elaborated upon in Chapters Two and Eleven.

All of God's faithful – Jews before the cross and Christians alike – share in the same heavenly destination and its benefits, the eternal presence of God in the New Jerusalem with its river of life and continual fruit bearing trees. Therefore, there is no worthy spiritual purpose in separating God's people throughout the ages by a two-covenant dispensational process. Rather, a merciful God who has never shown respect of persons have forever unified all of these people by means of one everlasting agreement, the eternal covenant, displayed through one instrument, Israel.

Summary

The God of grace personified in selfless *agape* love, is a covenant-making God. He initiated the everlasting agreement with man because He loved us, even to the giving of His only begotten Son (John 3:16), who took the form of sinful man, so that every person, even the lowliest of men, potentially could make peace with his Creator. Through this special relationship, detailed in prophetic and apostolic revelation, and because of the universal revelation of natural law, there are, in Heaven's arrangement, God-fearers as numerous as the sands of the sea, originating from "every tongue and tribe, people and nation" (Rev. 5:9, 7:9; see also Gen. 17:1-7).

For mere men to be able to enter into a covenant relationship with the one true spirit God in lovingkindness (*chesed*), through the gospel of Christ, is indeed good news. God's grace allows us to be His covenant children, through the One who died for our sins. He loves us and saves us for who He is, not through any kind of human effort, good deeds performed in response to law. What a comfort! The alternative means that covenanters are lost, saved, dead, alive, cast off, reaccepted – all on the basis of man's performance, successes and failures, in keeping law.

Serving God in a covenantal relationship, as opposed to any type of law-works system, is indeed a vital choice between two vastly different thought systems, approaches toward religion. Simple covenant theology is consistently applicable to how to live a godly live and make proper decisions, day-in and day-out. It answers questions instead of raising them. It exalts Christ and authentic righteousness, for worship of God is cold and lifeless without the truth that God loves His people, and that He is mindful of man in a covenantal relationship.

Therefore, a proper understanding of the eternal (everlasting) covenant lies at the root of authentic faith. It is filled with positive "shalls" and "wills," long-lasting purposes, pledges and oaths, made sure by the blood of the covenant (see Chapter Three). Salvation is emphatically by grace only, and recipients of the covenant live by faith. A sovereign God calls us to trust and honor him, through sanctified living and in leading a Christ-centered life.

The binding truth of the ages is that our compassionate God will never let us go – no, never! Hebrews 13:5 reminds us magnificently that God has said, "I will not in any way fail you nor give you up nor leave you without support. [I will] not, [I will] not, [I will] not in any degree leave you helpless, nor forsake nor let [you] down – assuredly not!" (Amplified translation). God has always stood by everyone who trusts in Him (Josh. 1:5, I Sam. 12:22, Gen. 28:15, Isa. 41:17).

The great message of the Jewish prophets is that God will not abandon His people anymore than a woman would ever forget the baby at her breast (Isa. 49:15). In contrast with a mother who might abandon her child, God shall not forget His people, for they are engraven upon the palms of His hands (v. 16).

Isaiah further expressed the length and breadth of God's steadfastness toward His people by saying, "For the mountains be shaken and the hills may totter, but my faithful love will never leave you, my covenant of peace will never totter, says the Lord who takes pity on you" (54:10).

Because of His lovingkindness (*chesed*), God will assuredly not fail us nor leave us without life-giving support. He will not let His covenanted ones down. He will not relax His hold on us. Instead, He saves us by cleansing us. For He is the God of covenant, who fulfills every promise which He has ever made to man, in abounding eternal love. May God's *chesed* be with us always. Shalom. Amen and amen!

Scripture Index

Index

Subject Index

Abraham, 14, 27, 100, 103-5, 108-9, 120, 130, 142, 182, 183, 186, 202, 212, 213, 260, 265, 269
  blessings of, 112, 215
  call of, 15-6, 122
  gospel to, 104
  standard of faith, 208, 275
Appointed, 63
Assembly, the one, 101, 239
Apollos, 170

Blessings, continuity of, 224
  see also Love, new and old
Blood, 55-73, 232
Body, the one, 101, 126, 152, 239
Book of Consolation, 197, 206

Campbell, K. M., quoted, 68
Ceremonial law, 116, 131, 208, 220, 233-6, 253, 259
  see also Tutor
Chesed, 13, 14, 17, 19, 20, 22, 52, 105, 107, 111, 122, 140, 141, 149, 246, 275, 277, 278,
Christians (the people of God),
  body, 101, 126, 152
  city of God, 183
  disciple, 134, 159, 170
  family, 100-1, 130
  flock of God, 137
  group, 101
  in 2nd-3rd centuries, 86
  Israel of God, 158, 183, 184
  Jerusalem, 183, 184
  Jewish roots, 180-6
  living stones, 110
  New Jerusalem, 136, 184
  remnant, 136
  sect of the way, 161, 173, 180, 186
  spiritual temple, 136

Christians (the people of God), *cont'd*
  temple of God, 183
  twelve tribes, 183
Church fathers, cited, 86, 113-7, 151, 163, 185, 233, 254, 255, 263
"City of truth", 204
COVENANT, everlasting (eternal),
  author of, 32-5, 72, 146
  benefits, 22
  blessings of, 42, 199, 213
  blood of, 14, 55-73, 232
  breaking of, 19, 59, 199, 250
  broken agreement, 218, 222, 254
  ceremony to initiate, 14, 16, 20-1, 59, 60-1, 63, 64, 198
  coexistence of two, 179-80
  conditional - unconditional, 236-7
  confirmed, 96
  continuity of, concepts showing, 119, 137
  contrast of old and new, 156-7, 192, 209, 232-3, 238, 251-3, 258-9, 261, 274-6
  curses, 21, 67-70, 255
  dating of, 199, 209, 253-254, 271
  of death, old, allegedly a system of, 218-20, 246, 256-258
  defined, 13, 22, 87, 96, 203, 265, 269
  entering into, 20
  and faith, 89
  "faulty", old, 252
  goal of, 271-2
  God in, 32-5, 40, 105
  and gospel, 28-9
  and grace, 27
  heart in, 200
  and heaven, 272-3
  history of, 15
  holy, 96
  the infinite, 272-3

Acknowledgments

There is probably no more sublime thought than to realize that mere mortals can enter into a gracious peace agreement with the One who created heaven and earth and can simultaneously hear the prayers of all who are in covenant with Him.

Appreciation of this great biblical theme, as well as an understanding that the great promises and comforting statements of the Jewish prophets find fulfillment not only in the messianic era but also in the Jewish period, was gained in the early 1980s through studies with James Puterbaugh. Other individuals made specific suggestions which greatly strengthened doctrines and concepts in connection with covenant theology. In particular, Gene Peacock generously devoted time to clarifying much of the material in this book, and also aided in sentence structure.

Substantive contributions to the text also came from Guthrie Dean, Wanda Shirk, and Ron McRay. Richard Akins carefully read the manuscript, and made corrections. Others who assisted the general development of the work include Ray Seidel, Gary Cage, and Edward Fudge. Captain Ken McFelia, Dr. Ray Lobb, Olan Hicks, Ben Copeland, Michael Hall, and Charles Goodall all read most of the manuscript prior to publication. Indeed, one of the most rewarding aspects of writing this book was the confidence displayed by friends and acquaintances, who encouraged publication of material on the subject of covenant for the benefit of general readers.

Throughout this project, technical assistance also came from many people. The skilled hand and creativity of Roy Purcell resulted in the splendid cover illustration, which depicts the ancient covenantal ceremony with obvious modifications; Roy's artwork also appears throughout the chapters. K. C. Den Dooven coordinated the color work on the front cover; color separations were made by Dan Weeden at Imperial Color in Reno. Through many generations of computer input and manuscript revision, Kathye Thornton often went beyond the call of duty. Final page layouts were generated by Paul Cirac of White Sage Studios, and by Paul David Morrison, who also assisted with the cover design and display typography.

To one and all, my sincere thanks.

— S. W. P.

BOOKS BY NEVADA PUBLICATIONS

Write to address below for prices and a complete catalog.

THAT YOU MAY BELIEVE by Homer Hailey. Subtitled "Studies in the Gospel of John," this book is designed to lay a firm foundation of faith for a consistent Christian life. John's gospel was written to help dispel doubt about the deity of Christ. This topical study is packed with helpful material adequate for individual or group study. 200 pages.

FROM CREATION TO THE DAY OF ETERNITY God's Great Plan to the Day of Eternity by Homer Hailey. This book builds faith in God's system of redemption. God is seen in nature, in providence and in His Christ. Next is a simple retelling of the story of creation, the introduction of man, the home and the fall. Lofty Old Testament themes are evident in the historical section which shows God's hope-inspiring promise, the purpose of law, and Israel's apostasy, captivity and restoration. Later chapters relate Christ's birth, ministry, death, and His resurrection, and also studies on godly character, the church, the "second coming," the resurrection and judgment. A well-written book, easily understood by readers of all ages. Indexed, 226 pages.

HAILEY'S COMMENTS by Homer Hailey, This study touches upon the Exodus, Genesis, the Passover, and the giving of the law. Following a significant article on "Studying the Prophets" are extensive commentaries on Amos, Hosea, Isaiah, Daniel, Ezekiel, and Jeremiah. Next comes Jesus and the virgin birth, His baptism, temptation, transfiguration, the last supper and His prayers. "Comments on Evangelism" furnishes information for both the church and individuals. The author details the nature of the rule of elders. Other chapters involve stewardship, the need for a savior, and the saints amid a secular world, the soul, heaven and hell, suffering, II Peter 3, etc. Vol. I, 347 pages, Vol. II, 384 pages, a matching set with scripture and general indices, color covers.

Upcoming Titles

Manuscripts are completed. Call 702-747-0800 for information.
Advance print-outs of the texts now available for $6 each, postpaid.

◆ Natural Law: Universal in Scope, Moral in Design
◆ The Kingdom of God: A Relationship Not an Institution
◆ The Identity of Babylon as Rome and the Dating of the Book of Revelation — with supplemental material on the "AD 70 Doctrine"
◆ The Nature of Inspiration and the Development of the New Testament Canon ($7.50)
◆ Coping with Church Sharks (A Twelve-Step Guide for Recovery)

NEVADA PUBLICATIONS Box 15444 ◆ Las Vegas, Nev. 89114

MATTHEW 24:

First Century Fulfillment or End-time Expectation?

by Stanley W. Paher

192 pages, color cover

Wars and rumors of wars! Famines and earthquakes in diverse places ... tribulation and apostasy and the gospel to all the world in this generation ... false teachers ... and finally the portentous abomination of desolation!

These utterances by Jesus on the Mount of Olives, recorded in Matthew Chapter 24, have been sensationalized by modern evangelists who apply all of them to a future time in prelude to the end of the world. They say that these "signs of the times" will tell us when the "latter days" will be, so that we can expect the yet future return of Jesus "on the clouds of heaven."

Using the Old Testament as precedent, the author reviews each idea and symbol of Matthew 24 and shows unmistakably that the entire chapter describes the destruction of Jerusalem in AD 70: the setting at a time of unrest and war, the great tribulation, and finally the siege and capture of the city.

This book studies all texts referring to the "latter days" and the "end time," showing that they refer directly to ancient societies, especially the Jewish nation which fell to the Romans in AD 70. Any effort to extend these prophecies to the present and future encounters immense difficulties.

Here is a valuable compendium of scriptures that describes every aspect of the tragic end of the Jewish nation — the setting at a time of unrest and war, and the tribulation, siege and capture of Jerusalem in AD 70. This book will surely edify students of the Bible and ancient history.

There is also information on how to recognize figurative language, and a valuable index to scriptures used, as well as a general index. This book was originally titled *If Thou Hadst Known,* but the new edition is greatly expanded and extensively rewritten.